The Grace and Task
of Preaching

DEDICATED TO THE MEMORY OF

Damian Byrne OP

Master of the Order of Preachers

1983 – 1992

The Grace and Task
of Preaching

Edited by

Michael Monshau OP

DOMINICAN PUBLICATIONS

First published (2006) by
Dominican Publications
42 Parnell Square
Dublin 1

ISBN 1-871552-95-8

British Library Cataloguing in Publications Data.
A catalogue record for this book is available
from the British Library.

Cover design by David Cooke
Cover photographs: IndexOpen

Printed in Ireland by
Betaprint, Dublin 12

CONTENTS

DEDICATION:
DAMIAN BYRNE, OP, 1929—1996

One of the strongest memories treasured by those who knew Fr Damian Byrne was his remarkable commitment to preaching. Throughout his years as a member of the Order of Preachers he proved willing to take every opportunity presented to him to reflect with others on the Word of God and to explore the challenges it presents for life today. This enthusiasm was in no way diminished by his holding positions of leadership in the Order, culminating in his election as Master in September 1983. Indeed, in this post he found the perfect platform from which to encourage all the members of the Dominican Family in their commitment to the grace and task of preaching.

A native of Galway city, Louis Byrne received the name Damian when he entered in September 1949. Solemn profession in 1953 was followed by ordination to the priesthood in 1955. After completing his studies, his first appointment was to teach mathematics and Irish at Newbridge College, then a boys' boarding school, now a much larger co-educational day school, and still under the trusteeship of the Irish province. There followed a term as bursar at St Mary's, Tallaght, then the house of studies of the province. His next appointment, as prior of St Mary's, The Claddagh, in his native city of Galway, was interrupted by his volunteering to be one of a small group from the Irish province setting up a new mission in Argentina and by his being named superior of this group.

This mission, or rather, the preparatory course for it which he attended in Cuernavaca, Mexico, proved a major turning point in Damian's life. Others on the same course remember him arguing, day after day, with Ivan Illich, leader of the course. These discussions led Damian to re-assess many of his pastoral and missionary assumptions. His mind and heart were opened to the

reality of oppression and dispossession so that the man who, up
to then, had been rigidly clerical in outlook, was converted. From
then on, he was enthusiastically committed to the Vatican II
teaching on the Church as the People of God, and the insights of
Lumen Gentium and of *Gaudium et Spes* coloured all his thinking,
his actions and the policies he espoused.

In 1969 Damian was elected Vicar Provincial of his province's
mission in Trinidad and Tobago. At a time of great ferment in
the West Indies, he was able, with confidence, to encourage new
ministries and to co-operate with the local Church as it assumed
responsibility for pastoral tasks that had, up to that point, been in
the hands of expatriate priests. From 1969 onwards, Damian was
constantly in positions of leadership: a second term as Vicar
Provincial in Trinidad was interrupted in 1975 by his appointment by Fr Vincent de Couesnongle to be Provincial of Mexico
with a mandate to bring about unity between the local province
and those brothers from the Spanish vicariate working in that
country. In 1977 there came election as Provincial of Ireland,
followed, during a second provincial term, by election as Master
of the Order in September 1983. His nine years in Santa Sabina
were marked by the opening up of new missions, and by the
setting up of new vice-provinces in the Order. The aspect of his
mastership which, perhaps, meant most to him was the opportunity it gave to encourage all within the Dominican Family in the
task of sharing the word of God. He would insist, simply: 'A love
of preaching should mark every Dominican – priest, brother,
sister, lay Dominican'.

On completing his term as Master, Damian's first choice
would have been to return to Latin America as a missionary. But
the need to spend some time close to his mother, then frail and in
her nineties, suggested that he remain in Ireland. When he was
invited to accept the post of secretary-general of the Conference

of Religious of Ireland (CORI), he asked to be assigned to the small community at Leeson Park in Dublin, and this was the house where he spent his final years.

The Ireland to which Damian returned was remarkably different from the country he had known before he set out on his missionary ministry in Latin America, different also from the situations he had known as Provincial of Ireland. In the face of rapid social change and of unprecedented challenges, Church leadership seemed to be floundering, not least in regard to revelations of child sexual abuse by clergy and religious. Believing that the credibility of the proclamation of the Gospel was at stake in how the Church responded to the problem, Damian set himself, with characteristic vigour, to contribute to a solution.

One of his most effective initiatives was in the seminars he organised in partnership with another Dominican and a dear friend, Fr Míceál O'Regan, founder and director of the Eckhart House Institute of Psychosynthesis in Dublin. At their invitation Fr Steve Rosetti, of St Luke's Institute, Maryland, came to Dublin and alerted, first, religious superiors and, later, bishops, to the full dimensions of the problem. It has been acknowledged that these seminars and Damian's own membership of the Catholic Bishops' Advisory Committee on Child Sexual Abuse by Priests and Religious were vital to the success of the committee's work. This committee brought out its report, *Child Sexual Abuse: Framework for a Church Response*, just days before Damian died.

The years of working in the Conference of Religious and on the Church response to the abuse crisis took their toll. Damian experienced moments of acute self-doubt, and an inner sadness could darken his spirits. But such moments did not impede his commitment to persevering in the tasks he had undertaken.

On the morning of Sunday, 18 February 1996, Damian said that he felt somewhat unwell and that, rather than have lunch, he would lie down and relax while reading the sports sections of the newspapers. When one of the brethren went to him in mid-afternoon with a cup of tea, Damian was found to have died in the interval. At the Requiem Mass on Thursday 22 February, before Damian's burial in the community cemetery at St Mary's, Tallaght, the celebrant and preacher was Damian's successor as Master, Fr Timothy Radcliffe.

As Timothy Radcliffe mentioned in his homily, 'for a man who could be quite shy and silent, Damian had an enormous number of friends.' He was remarkably ascetic in his personal life, sparing in what he would eat (missing a meal never worried him) and neither drinking nor smoking. He was able to set out for visitation journeys that would last months with only carry-on baggage. Resolute in supporting theological freedom and decidedly of a Vatican II cast of mind, he was, at the same time, greatly uneasy in the presence of closed minds, whatever their placing on the liberal / conservative spectrum. In encouraging collaboration, his enthusiasm was for the story of the 1511 Advent sermon condemning injustice in Hispaniola. He loved to repeat the response given by the prior, Peter de Cordoba, to those who objected to what had been said: although Antonio de Montesino spoke the words, it was the community that preached.

Damian Byrne had a deep respect for truth wherever it was to be found, and this quality was always visible. The day after his death one journalist commented: 'He was the only public person I ever dealt with who never put a spin on things: he just wanted to help you understand.'

INTRODUCTION

At Vatican II, the Church recalled its rich heritage of the Word and mandated a restoration of preaching throughout its liturgical praxis. That same Council also charged religious institutes with returning to the charisms of their founders in their pursuit of authentic renewal. For Dominicans, members of the Order of Preachers, that charge, which was understood to mean that Saint Dominic's dynamic vision of the Holy Preaching was to be re-examined and applied anew to the contemporary situation, was taken up with a passion. It was no coincidence, but rather the prompting of the Holy Spirit, that called the Church to renew its preaching mission at precisely the same time the Dominican Order was called upon to renew its commitment to that mission which is known as 'The Holy Preaching' in the Order's parlance.

Father Damian Byrne's mandate as Master of the Dominican Order commenced less than twenty years after the conclusion of Vatican II and, throughout his term, he passionately promoted the Holy Preaching. At the same time, he urged the collaboration of all the branches of the Dominican Family in the pursuit of its shared mission. His faithful attentiveness to the cloistered nuns of the Order revealed his belief that their prayers, study, sacrifices and hidden witness provided a constitutive ingredient of the Order's preaching mission. In *The Challenge of Evangelization Today*, Father Damian's letter to the Order of October, 1988,[1] he recalled that an earlier Master of the Order, Father Aniceto Fernandez, referred to the Sisters of the Order as equals to the friars and invited them to search with the brothers for the best way of carrying out their mission. Father Damian then contin-

---

1. See A. Fernandez, Vincent de Couesnongle, D. Byrne, T. Radcliffe, *To Praise, to Bless, to Preach: Words of Grace and Truth*, 2004, Dublin, Dominican Publications, pp, 205-16.

ued: 'Much has been achieved in the intervening years – collaboration in formation, pastoral ministry, teaching at the University level, preaching, jointly run conference and retreat centres … Wherever such collaboration has been realized, despite initial difficulties, there has been mutual enrichment. And we are only beginning.' Likewise, concerning the lay members of the Order, Father Damian wrote in the same document: 'I urge on you the need for collaboration with the laity in the work of evangelization…' and 'Let me repeat once again what was stated at [the General Chapter of the Order in] Quezon City: "What lies before us at this time is a challenge to become what Saint Dominic had begun: a family joined in unity of life and complementarity of service to the Church and the world".'

Clearly, then, the best way for the Order of Preachers to pay tribute to its beloved former Master is to be obedient to Saint Dominic in his promotion of the Holy Preaching, and to do so in a collaborative family manner. These pages, then, the work of scholars of the English-speaking segment of the Order, attempt to comprise a fitting tribute to Father Damian Byrne, O.P, (1929-1996), the much-loved Irish friar who served as Master of the Order from 1984 through 1993.

The essays in this volume are grouped according to content. Logically enough, the conversation of the book begins with a consideration of preaching and its liturgical content. Father Michael Monshau, O.P., has contributed an historical essay on the Catholic preaching renewal which followed from Vatican II. Using the image of worship as a 'Double-Feast', he demonstrates that the contemporary preaching renewal in Catholicism is a direct result of the Second Vatican Council's restoration of the Church's ancient word/rite structure for all liturgical worship.

The second section, which treats theological reflection on preaching, includes four essays. Choosing the title, 'Boring God:

Theology and Preaching,' Father Vivian Boland explains that 'theology' and 'preaching' are ways of talking with people about God. This chapter seeks to outline the most radical possible theological understanding of preaching, relating it to God's self-revealing utterance of the 'word that breathes love'. The preacher is taken into the Trinitarian missions of Word and Spirit so that the human language of proclamation, praise and teaching carries the eternal Word to birth in every time and place. Theology is not just something the preacher ought to do for the sake of content – the methodologies and challenges of these two kinds of discourse, and the spirituality they presuppose, are intimately related.

Next, Father Donald Goergen engages his study of 'Jesus: Itinerant Preacher'. He explains: Jesus returned to Galilee anointed with the Spirit as a preacher, saying 'Let us go to neighbouring towns so that I might preach there also, for that is why I have come' (Mark 1:38). Today we might ask: Who is Jesus as a preacher of the reign of God? What is the gospel of God that Jesus preached? How did Jesus understand his preaching mission? What does Jesus the preacher and Jesus' preaching teach us about preaching today?

Sister Mary Catherine Hilkert's essay 'Preachers of Grace, Witnesses to the Resurrection' follows. She explains: Faith in the risen Christ is at the core of all Christian preaching. As Paul's Letter to the Corinthians reminds us, 'If Christ is not risen, your faith is in vain.' This essay explores the significance of recent theological explorations into the meaning of that basic Christian claim for preachers.

This section is completed with Father Timothy Radcliffe's contribution on the sacramentality of the Word: 'He Taught Them as One Who Had Authority'. Father Timothy explains that he looked at the claim that preaching is called to be not just the communication of information but a powerful and sacramental event as well. While sadly acknowledging that much preaching is in fact boring and ineffective, he assures his readers that preaching can be transformative of lives and hearts if it shares in the dynamic of the event of the Last Supper, reaching out to people in their silence and puzzlement, gathering them into communion, and pointing them beyond the present to the Kingdom.

The third section of essays is grouped under the heading 'The Homiletic Dynamic,' and concerns itself with issues pertinent to people actually involved in homiletic preaching. Father Rolando de la Rosa promises that his essay, entitled 'The Reception of Preaching: an Instance in History', is not about preaching in the abstract. It is not about general principles on preaching derived from speculative, theological, spiritual, or mystical reflection. Rather, it is about preaching as shaped by concrete historical processes. It deals with preaching as generally understood by missionaries who came to Latin America during the sixteenth century, the prevailing theological doctrines that influenced their understanding of it, the political and cultural exigencies that help shape their practice of preaching, and the natives' reception of it. In particular, he focuses on the missionaries' use of indigenous children as a means of catechizing, and their *tabula rasa* model for imparting instruction. He proceeds to examine how relations with the Latin American cultures disintegrated, and why an indigenous clergy was not established. The conclusion offers insights that suggest catechesis modelled after modes of reception that attempt to integrate as far as may be possible, rather than discard, indigenous cultures and values are worth further attention and investigation.

Father Rolando's work is followed by an essay contributed by Father James P. Donleavy entitled 'This Glorious and Transcendent Place'. In these pages Father Donleavy draws upon his own experience of forty-plus years of preaching to offer homiletic advice to others.

Next comes Sister Cathleen M. Going's essay entitled 'The Role of the Question in Preaching: Adult Educational Models'. Sister writes: 'this essay supports an affirmation of the primacy of questions – in human development generally, and specifically in education and in the preaching effort. The introduction sketches some congruencies and divergences among the contexts and goals of educators and of preachers. The QUESTION will be presented as operator of development and correlate of Mystery. Advertence to the dialectic "questions/convictions," a dialectic important in religion, in learning, and in preaching, will lead to reflection on the variegated character of human consciousness, and on the authenticity of educator and of preacher.' The reflections presented in the article seem confirmed by an important teacher of preaching, F. Craddock, and have been prompted by insights from B. Lonergan, E. Voegelin, P. Ricoeur, and from the experience available in two specific educational settings: university-level studies for older adults, and studies in a monastic community. Sister's conclusion suggests the images of 'the Singer' and of 'saving the Tale that saves us' as evoking comprehensibly the challenges their roles offer to educator and to preacher.

'Preaching and Scripture' is the common thread for the next section of essays. Sister Barbara Green entitled her work, '"But Why Do We Have to Know That?" Preaching and Critical Biblical Study'. She explores briefly the topic of why preaching is enhanced by critical biblical study in its various facets, arguing against those who would dismiss such information for various reasons. Utilizing the book of Jeremiah as an example, since it is relatively well-represented in the lectionary, the chapter addresses what preachers need to know, what use can be made of relevant information, and what is not necessary to provide from the pulpit. It concludes by naming the challenges Scripture poses, whether in preaching, in prayer, or in the education of preachers.

Also appearing in this section is Father Mark O'Brien's essay, 'Prophetic Stories as a Preaching Resource: The Elisha Collection'. He wrote: the preaching ministry is often associated with prophecy, the proclaiming of God's word. Understandably, interest tends to focus on the great prophetic books of the Old Testament. This essay, using the stories of Elisha the prophet in 2 Kings 2-8, with particular attention being paid to the story of Elisha and the woman of Shunem in 2 Kings 4:8-37, shows readers the potential for preaching in the prophetic stories of the Old Testament, and indeed Old Testament narrative in general.

Three authors have contributed on the subject of Dominican preaching, which can be of service to Dominican preachers of the Gospel as well as to preachers who are not members of the Dominican Order. Father Paul Murray inaugurates this section with 'A Wine of Encouragement: Preaching in a Time of Disillusion'. Father Paul explains, when talking about their work as preachers and about the impact of the Gospel on their lives, the early Dominicans loved to use the image of drinking or of being made drunk on the Word. Accordingly, in this essay, the author addresses two tasks: first, he tries to understand why the early Dominicans were instinctively drawn to this image, and then he indicates the possible usefulness and relevance of this image at a time of crisis in the Irish Church and in the Irish Dominican Province.

Placing himself in dialogue with the motto of the Dominican Order, Father Albert Nolan's essay, 'Preaching and Contemplation' explores the meaning of Dominican preaching as the giving to others of the fruits or results of our contemplation. In the words of the 2001 General Chapter in Providence, 'Our preaching is more than a repetition of doctrines and moral exhortations. It is the sharing of our contemplative insights.' The author argues that a serious return to the contemplative dimension of our lives as Dominicans would bring about a radical transformation of both what we preach and the impact our preaching might have on our postmodern world. Finally, Father Thomas O'Meara has contributed 'Preaching and Ministry in a Time of Expansion'. He wrote that preaching and ministry since Vatican II have had similar expansive histories. This is not surprising since each involves the other. In the Churches of the New Testament there is a variety of ministries, and preaching is connected to ministry. We can surmise that each important ministry holds some form of preaching. Damian Byrne followed that expansion of preaching and ministry and he linked preaching to culture, to the milieu and context of the people hearing the Word, and to inculturation. His own ministry as Master involved travelling around the world, affirming preaching in the Dominican family, and pointing out the characteristics of preaching and ministries today, especially inculturation. His realization of being Master involved a new form of that ministry which made his message on preaching global.

The final section of this volume treats the subject of preaching and praxis. Five rich articles complement one another in this section. Father Charles Bouchard writes 'Text or Topic? Doing or Being? The Challenge of Preaching on Morality'. He explains: Few of us have heard preaching on a moral issue, and if we have, it was probably not very edifying or helpful. Preachers avoid moral topics for fear of causing division, neglecting the biblical text, or being 'moralistic'. Uncovering the distinctive character of the Catholic approach to morality will help shape a distinctively Catholic understanding of 'moral preaching'. This essay describes how the author's own understanding of moral preaching has changed. It will help the preacher develop an approach to preaching on moral issues that avoids the usual pitfalls and addresses real concerns.

Father Richard Finn's 'Preaching Generosity: Lessons from the Fathers' reveals that the later Roman empire saw the sustained and highly distinctive promotion of almsgiving by Christian preachers and writers, who incorporated this practice within the virtues of justice and generosity to fashion an ethic without parallel among pagan priests or philosophers. The essay examines how this was accomplished as well as its significance for bishops, monks and lay people; it concludes by drawing lessons from this history for contemporary preachers. Next, in 'Preaching on the Wider World', Father John Orme Mills explains his topic by writing that nearly half a century ago R.E.C. Browne said that one of the major tasks of preachers was 'making an atmosphere in which men and women may be aware of the manifold calls of God to creative activity.' Whether preachers are talking intelligently about the need to work for justice and peace or about the need to deepen one's prayer life, they must start from here, i.e. 'making an atmosphere in which men and women may be aware of the manifold calls of God to creative activity.'

In 'Preaching Biblical Justice,' Sister Barbara Reid offers an essay that first explores the biblical terms for 'justice' and their various nuances, and then looks to the Gospel parables for a model of preaching biblical justice. In 'A Homiletic of Mercy,' the volume's final chapter, Brother Edward van Merrienboer explores the meaning and application of mercy to interpersonal and societal relations in the context of preaching. The purpose of this exploration is to demonstrate that for humans to reach for the divine in their historical journey they must move beyond justice and enter into the mystery of divine mercy. Brother Edward concludes that through the 'lens' of mercy, the Christian community is challenged to take on a new worldview beyond that which is strictly human.

The creation of this volume on preaching, published in memory of the late Father Damian Byrne, O.P., was a labour of love for the score of Dominicans engaged in its production. In particular, thanks for this volume are due to the three Dominican friars who administer the impressive publishing effort at Dominican Publications, Dublin: Fathers Austin Flannery, Bernard Treacy and Tom Jordan. Without their enthusiasm, support, communication efforts, and editorial precision, this work would be nothing more than a notepad of ideas in a friar's file drawer.

Also significant to the production of this work are the five Dominicans who agreed to serve on its editorial board and whose suggestions, comments and critiques ensured its credibility. They are Father Donald Goergen, Sister Barbara Green, Sister Mary O'Driscoll, Father Thomas O'Meara, and Brother Edward van Merrienboer. In addition to producing their scholarly efforts which grace the pages of this volume, the authors of the essays contained herein were consistently dependable, agreeable and adaptable as deadlines arrived and passed; it was a pleasure to work with each of them.

Of course, the greatest appreciation is due Father Damian himself, whose ministry of leadership among us challenged us all to immerse ourselves in the grace and task of preaching. May these pages inspire others to do the same.

Father Michael Monshau, O.P.
Berkeley, California U.S.A.

PART 1

Preaching and Its Liturgical Context

THE SECOND VATICAN COUNCIL'S RESTORATION OF LITURGICAL PREACHING

MICHAEL MONSHAU, O.P.

With the promulgation of its liturgy constitution, *Sacrosanctum Concilium*, Vatican II restored the historical, two-fold structure of word and sacrament to Catholic worship. In doing so, the Church acknowledged the integral role of the word of God at liturgy, which in turn launched a preaching renewal throughout the Church that continues to unfold today. Although the reclamation of this liturgical structure actually heralded Catholicism's return to its own ancient traditions, it called for a dynamic so radically different from the common practice of the time that it seemed as if this directive were breaking new ground rather than reclaiming authentic tradition.

Indeed, the role of the word of God had suffered ignominy in pre-conciliar life, piety and worship. Catholics of that era were not noted for their biblical literacy, nor were they often to be found praying with Scripture, although they prayed their rosaries, novenas, and other devotions with remarkable fidelity, and often at Mass. The reading of the Scriptures, let alone preaching at most of these various devotions, was virtually non-existent and at Mass, the Scripture readings were not necessarily proclaimed in the vernacular. The Sunday Mass obligation could be fulfilled even if one had arrived after the conclusion of the entire liturgy of the word! It is not surprising that a result, the value of preaching was recognized minimally if at all in the pre-conciliar liturgy. This unfortunate practice constituted a betrayal of the Church's ancient heritage of the word.

Vatican II decreed a dramatic shift in this liturgical praxis by introducing far more than a simple adjustment of the rubrics. As a result of assiduous study of the ancient biblical, patristic and liturgical sources, the Council identified certain normative liturgical principles, applied unevenly over the centuries and only minimally in the recent past, upon which the contemporary preaching renewal is based. If the preaching renewal is to endure, it must be understood that it is not simply a result of the Church's response to the modern era of communications and the media (which had dawned by the middle of the twentieth century), but is based upon Christianity's ancient heritage of word and worship. Accordingly, this paper will identify the Council's recognition and promulgation of those normative liturgical values that resulted in what can be called today's Catholic renewal of preaching.

CONGREGATIONAL PARTICIPATION IN THE LITURGY

Foundational to the Council's recognition of the constitutive role of preaching at liturgy was the recognition of the participative nature of the congregation's role at worship. Theodor Klauser describes lay involvement in the liturgy during the pre-conciliar period:

> …while the celebrant 'read' the mass at the altar with his back to the people, the faithful were busy with other devotional exercises … They sang hymns in the vernacular, whose content had little or even nothing at all to do with the liturgy; they read, wrapped up in themselves, a 'mass devotion' or prayed the Rosary silently to themselves. Only at the three main parts of the eucharist: the offertory, the consecration, and the communion did the faithful, raised by the server's bell, turn their attention briefly to the sacred action that was being performed at the altar.… [1]

1. Theodor Klauser, *A Short History of the Western Liturgy: An Account and Some Reflections*, 2d ed., trans. John Halliburton (Oxford: Oxford University Press, 1979), 120.

In his 1947 encyclical, *Mediator Dei*, Pius XII called for greater lay participation, but his description of what greater lay participation at liturgy should look like was astonishingly passive by later conciliar standards. Pius wrote:

> It is ... desirable ... that all ... should be aware that to participate in the Eucharistic Sacrifice is their chief duty and supreme dignity, and that not in an inert and negligent fashion, giving way to distractions and day-dreaming, but with ... earnestness and concentration .... [T]hey are to be praised who with the idea of getting the Christian people to take part more easily and more fruitfully in the Mass, strive to make them familiar with the 'Roman Missal,' so that the faithful, united with the priest, may pray together in the very words and sentiments of the Church. They are also to be commended who strive to make the Liturgy even in an external way a sacred act in which all who are present may share. This can be done ... when, for instance, the whole congregation in accordance with the rules of the Liturgy, either answer the priest in an orderly and fitting manner, or sing hymns suitable to the different parts of the Mass, or do both, or finally in High Masses when they answer the prayers of the minister of Jesus Christ and also sing the liturgical chant.[2]

As praiseworthy as this directive sounds, today's reader will be surprised to learn that later in the same document, the Pope clarified that the desired lay participation of a more active nature was only significant for pastoral purposes and was not necessary for the valid celebration of the Mass:

> [Those] methods of participation in the Mass are to be approved

2. Claudia Carlen, ed., *Mediator Dei*, in *The Papal Encyclicals 1939-1958,* vol. 4. *The Papal Encyclicals*, Consortium Books, (n.p. McGrath Publishing Co., 1981), 133-137.

and commended when they are in complete agreement with the precepts of the Church and the rubrics of the Liturgy. Their chief aim is to foster and promote the people's piety and intimate union with Christ and His visible minister and to arouse those internal sentiments and dispositions which should make our hearts become like [Christ's]. However, ... they are by no means necessary to constitute it a public act or to give it a social character.[3]

Less than two decades later, Vatican II dismantled all structures distancing the congregation from its active role at worship. In fact, commenting upon this shift, H. Schmidt wrote: 'participation in the liturgy on the part of the faithful is mentioned so many times in the Constitution that it resembles a chorus. It is like the "Pray for us" or the "spare us, O Lord" that we repeat in the litanies.' [4]

Sacrosanctum Concilium, the first document promulgated by Vatican II, announced the reformed role of the laity at worship. Article 2 provides a theological articulation of how the liturgy functions in the lives of the faithful. The article reads:

For the liturgy, making the work of our redemption a present actuality, most of all in the divine sacrifice of the eucharist, is the outstanding means whereby the faithful may express in their lives and manifest to others the mystery of Christ and the real nature of the true Church.

Article 6 recalls the liturgical expression of the primitive Christians and recalls also that by their baptism, all the faithful

3. Ibid., 106.
4. H. Schmidt, 'Il popolo cristiano al centro del rinnovamento liturgico,' *La Civilta Cattolica* 115, Vol. I (1964): 123, quoted in William Baraúna, *The Liturgy of Vatican II: A Symposium in Two Volumes*, English ed. Jovian Lang (Chicago: Franciscan Herald Press, 1966), 132.

were called to participation in those events of praise and witness. Article 7 identifies the various ways in which Christ becomes present to the Church, particularly, in the Church's worship, and included among the various manifestations named is the presence of Christ that is effected by the praying, singing and gathering of the community itself. Article 8 further clarifies that the congregation is active at worship by the use of active verbs in its description of what the Church does at liturgy. These verbs show that at worship, the Church 'takes part,' 'journeys,' 'sings,' 'venerates,' 'hopes,' 'awaits,' and 'appears.' Article 10 appropriates the active verbs 'praise,' 'take part,' and 'eat,' to the liturgical congregation and also makes quite clear that the community's role at worship is an active one.

The Brazilian theologian William Baraúna pointed out that the verbs used to describe the activity of the faithful at liturgy were changed completely. Prior to Vatican II, a lay person 'heard' Mass, 'assisted' at Mass, or perhaps 'went' to Mass, but the Council is employing the verb 'participate' to describe the laity's role at worship, and furthermore, that verb is more fully described by the modifiers 'full,' 'active' and 'conscious'.[5] Not only do the faithful participate in the sacred rites, but article 11 exacts of them careful preparation for their participation in the liturgy. This shift is profound for the Church. The clarion call for the full, active participation of the laity at worship as a duty and not merely as a privilege is contained in article 14, which reads:

> The Church earnestly desires that all the faithful be led to that full, conscious, and active participation in the liturgical celebrations called for by the very nature of the liturgy. Such participation by the Christian people as 'a chosen race, a royal priesthood, a holy nation, God's own people' … is their right

5. Ibid., 134.

and duty by reason of their baptism.

Thereafter, with consistency throughout the liturgy constitution, the correct nature of active lay participation at liturgy is identified and strategies are formulated to facilitate that participation. Speaking with great enthusiasm to a general audience in 1969 about the new order of the Mass that was about to be introduced, Pope Paul VI promised his listeners that 'You will also notice a fresh appeal for the assistance of the faithful at the eucharistic sacrifice; at Mass they are 'the Church' and they have a sense that this is so.' [6]

Accordingly, it is clear that Vatican II did more than simply replace a custom whereby the sanctuary was the exclusive reserve of the clergy with new norms that allowed for greater lay participation. Rather, the Council inaugurated a fresh liturgical theology, one that recognized the priesthood of the baptized and noted their necessary and active role in the official worship of the Church.

THE INTEGRITY OF THE COMMUNICATIVE VALUE
OF THE HUMAN WORD AT LITURGICAL WORSHIP

The consequent step of the conciliar recognition of the integral role of the laity at liturgy is the recognition that, if the laity are to be actively present and participating in the liturgy, the proceedings of the liturgical event must be made intelligible to them. The Council made this step by acknowledging that not only are the ritualized words and liturgical formulae essential to the liturgy, but the human component of the communicative value of those words is also constitutive. Hence, the Council restored the use of the vernacular at worship, while further insisting upon the integrity of the human word itself through intelligibility and

6. Paul VI, Address to a general audience, ICEL, 1759.

audibility.

For most Catholics of that era, the audibility of any of the words pronounced by the celebrant throughout the entire Mass was not to be taken for granted and, for many, the very reading of the Scriptural texts in the vernacular was revolutionary, to say nothing of the preached word!

The starting point for the shift was discussion over the ancient formula '*ex opere operato*.' This position expresses Roman Catholic belief that in sacramental worship, the sacrament is validly affected when the duly authorized minister, with the right intention, performs the correct actions with the correct materials and the correct formulaic wording. Upon the eve of Vatican II, there was no sense that in addition to the valid articulation of the correct words it was necessary for the congregation to hear or understand those words. The sacraments were regarded as being so efficacious that no human words could add to their value, and human conversation would only serve to compromise the solemnity of the sacramental moment. Thus, the post-Tridentine liturgy had effectively dismantled the communicative value inherent in the ritual words used at worship.

Sacrosanctum Concilium reversed this. Article 11 contains the first such teaching and it also includes another new idea, namely, that the faithful have a role in the effectiveness of the liturgy:

> [W]hen the liturgy is celebrated something more is required than the mere observance of the laws governing valid and lawful celebration; it is also [necessary] to insure that the faithful take part fully aware of what they are doing, actively engaged in the rite, and enriched by its effects.[7]

Article 14 notes that the fuller lay participation sought by the

7. ICEL, 7.

Council is nothing less than the spiritual heritage of the Church, and Article 21 calls again for clarity in ritual words to facilitate understanding among the faithful:

> In this reform both texts and rites should be so drawn up that they express more clearly the holy things they signify and that the Christian people, as far as possible, are able to understand them with ease and to take part in the rites fully, actively, as befits a community.[8]

Article 48 also notes the value of the ritual words as it directs that 'through a good understanding of the rites and prayers … [the faithful] should take part in the sacred service conscious of what they are doing, with devotion and full involvement.'[9]

Even before the Council was concluded, Paul VI drew attention to the communicative value of the ritual words by identifying the responsibility incumbent upon the renewed liturgy to speak clearly to the people. Excerpts follow:

> You must have the conviction that the formularies of public prayer cannot be worthy of God unless they faithfully express Catholic teaching … The prayers should breathe with the religious spirit of devotion; they should evince a splendor in their brevity and clear simplicity that will assure right understanding and the ready perception of their truth and beauty.[10]

In the following paragraph, the pope called even more explicitly upon the clarity of the rites to engage the congregation in their sacred movement in the spirit of the ancient principle of *lex orandi, lex credendi*:

8. Ibid., 9.
9. Ibid., 14.
10. Paul VI, Address to the members and *periti* of the Consilium, ICEL, 220.

[One's] outlook on the liturgical reform ... [must] take into account the effectiveness of the sacred rites to teach ... [T]he conciliar Fathers ... had ... the pastoral objective of a more intense liturgical participation on the part of the faithful.... As the Constitution ... counsels ... the liturgy ... contains much instruction for the faithful. God in the liturgy is speaking to his own people; Christ continues there to proclaim his Gospel. Yours, therefore, should be a special care that liturgical worship really turns out to be a school for the Christian people. Liturgy should be a schooling in devotion that teaches the faithful to cultivate an intimate exchange with God; a schooling in truth in which visible symbols lead the spirit to the understanding and love of things invisible; a schooling in Christian charity ... [11]

Two years later, Paul insisted:

The Council has taken the fundamental position that the faithful have to understand what the priest is saying and to share in the liturgy; to be not just passive spectators at Mass but souls alive ... Look at the altar, now placed for dialogue with the assembly; consider the remarkable sacrifice of the Latin, the priceless repository of the Church's treasure. The repository has been opened up, as the peoples' own spoken language becomes part of their prayer. Lips that have often been still, sealed as it were, now at last begin to move, as the whole assembly can speak its colloquy with the priest. [12]

The pope's statement here is remarkable, not only for the corrected status of liturgical worship that it rehearses, but also in its implication that past practice had been faulty. Paul's statement

11. Ibid.
12. Pope Paul VI, Homily at Parish of Mary Immaculate, March 27, 1966, Rome, ICEL, 125.

notes that in the past, the laity functioned merely as 'passive spectators' whose lips had been unfortunately sealed.

Those days of canonical minimalism that insisted only upon the priest's personal pronunciation of the ritual words, inaudibly and in Latin, were a thing of the past! Naturally, a Council that would take such great pains to acknowledge the communicative value of the human words at liturgy would also be a Council that would make noteworthy recognition of the Scriptural word within worship, the next step in this structural reclamation.

A RECLAMATION: THE ROLE OF SCRIPTURE
IN THE ROMAN CATHOLIC CONTEXT

Prior to Vatican II, although the Roman Catholic attitude toward the use of the Bible was inconsistent, all too often it was regarded with suspicion. Neither in liturgical practice, private devotion nor personal study could pre-conciliar Catholics be called a people of the Word. Bernard Botte wrote, 'The Bible was regarded as a venerable but somewhat bothersome document. It often came under attack; you did well to protect it by speaking about it as little as possible.' [13] Hans Küng wrote that in the post-Tridentine Church ' ... scripture had become neglected to a frightening degree both in theology and preaching.' [14] This statement could well have referred to the private use of Scripture as well. Vatican II called for a total reassessment of the Roman Catholic attitude toward Scripture and the preaching of the Gospel.

The evangelical responsibility of every baptized member of the Church is identified in *Lumen Gentium*, article 17, which places familiarity with Scripture and the promulgation of the

---

13. Botte, 5.
14. Hans Küng, *The Church* (Garden City: Doubleday and Company, Inc., Image Books, 1976), 260.

Scriptural message not only at the heart of the Church's mission, but at the heart of every individual Christian's personal agenda as well.

Dei Verbum provides a profoundly wholesome description of the Church's attitude toward the word of God. Although previous Church legislation did not necessarily run contrary to its contents, the lived experience of the past centuries was so different that it sounded new when the Church stated:

> The Church has always revered sacred Scripture even as it has revered the Body of the Lord, because, above all in the liturgy, it never ceases to receive the bread of life from the table both of God's word and of Christ's body and to offer it to the faithful. The Church has always held and continues to hold that the Scriptures along with sacred tradition are the supreme rule of its own faith, because being inspired by God and consigned once and for all to writing, the Scriptures impart without change the word of God himself and the cause of the voice of the Holy Spirit to be heard in the words of the apostles and prophets.[15]

Dei Verbum identifies Scripture as 'the speech of God as it is put down in writing under the breath of the Holy Spirit' in Article 9. Article 22 insists that the people of God must have ready access to Scripture. Article 23 encourages deeper familiarity with Scripture.[16] Article 24 calls for 'the study of the sacred page' to inform the on-going theological enterprise of the Church. Article 25 places the expectation of responsible Scripture study upon priests, deacons and others who participate in the ministry of the word.[17] Article 26 again invites the laity to grow in their

15. Vatican Council II, *Dei Verbum*, ICEL, 61.
16. ICEL, 61.
17. ICEL, 60-61.

relationship with the Scriptures. This final article in this section reads:

> Through the reading and study of the Bible, then, 'may the word of the Lord speed on and triumph' (2 Thess 3:1); may the treasure of revelation entrusted to the Church more and more fill up the hearts of all. Even as the life of the Church receives increase from constantly turning to the mystery of the eucharist, so too there is reason to hope for a new awakening of the spiritual life deriving from an increased dedication to God's word, which 'abides forever' (Is 40:8; 1 Pet 1:23-25).[18]

As they call for greater attentiveness to the word of God, the words 'increased dedication' in the preceding quotation also contain a conciliar admission that the Catholic relationship to Scripture in the past had been lacking, the phraseology in the Council documents claiming that the Church has 'always and everywhere' loved Scripture notwithstanding.

The conciliar reforms clearly called for a reversal of the recent Catholic unfamiliarity with the pages of the Bible. Having identified statements which serve to evidence the Church's desire that the faithful attitudinally and practically strengthen the role of Scripture in their personal lives and in their communal church experiences, the Church logically also called for a substantially increased role for Scripture at worship.

RECOGNISING THE INTEGRITY OF THE LITURGY OF THE WORD AT WORSHIP

Given the minimal emphasis upon Scripture in pre-Conciliar Catholic life, it is no wonder that the value of the celebration of the word at liturgy was similarly minimized. Louis Bouyer

18. ICEL, 62.

described the role of the word at liturgy before the Council. 'The priest certainly read the Epistle and the Gospel, but to himself, turning his back on everyone else, in a language that nobody understood, and without taking any pains to be heard by anyone.'[19] The importance attached to the liturgy of the word was so minimal in the pre-Vatican II Church that Catholics, bound by the obligation to participate at Mass every Sunday, fulfilled their obligation even if they had arrived after the conclusion of the entire liturgy of the word! Furthermore, outside of specially scheduled preaching events such as parish missions or retreats, on Sundays the preaching could be dispensed with at the discretion of the priest; preaching occurred only rarely at Eucharistic liturgies on weekdays. In effect, the sermon was not considered to be an integral ingredient of worship, but rather was regarded as a dispensable pastoral excursus from the movement of the liturgy itself.

Annibale Bugnini described the pervasiveness inattentiveness to Scripture before the Council and the conciliar corrective to that situation:

> After centuries of neglect, the word of God is regaining its place as alive and life-giving in all the liturgical rites. First the word, then the sacrament or blessing. This pedagogical approach, used even by God, changed over the centuries and reached us in a defective, distorted and skeletal form. We have returned to the principle: no liturgical action without the word as part of it.[20]

Bugnini describes here the position of the Council on the role of

---

19. Louis Bouyer, 'The Word of God Lives in the Liturgy,' in *The Liturgy and the Word of God,* Third National Congress of the Centre de Pastoral Liturgique, Strasbourg (Collegeville, Minn ., The Liturgical Press, 1959), 54.
20. Bugnini, 46.

the Word at liturgy. Given the Council's enthusiasm for reclaiming Scripture as an integral ingredient of Christian life, it is not surprising that this enthusiasm should spill over into the Church's liturgical life as well, demonstrated by the promulgated rubric that no sacrament should be celebrated without a hearing of the word. Hence, Vatican II reinvigorated a long dormant piece of Christian tradition, namely, the word and rite structure for Christian liturgy.[21]

As sound as this reclaimed structure proves to be when tested by historical, theological and pastoral wisdom, it was so significantly at variance with immediate past practice that its promulgation represented a profound victory for its proponents. In reclaiming the central role of the word of God for Catholic life and worship, Vatican II reclaimed the authentic worship structure of the ancient Church for it was the uncovered liturgical praxis located in Scripture itself and in primitive Church documents that dictated this profound change.

Foundationally, the liturgical structure of word and sacrament is evident in first century Jewish worship, the precursor to apostolic Christian worship. Later, the Pauline Letters provide evidence that the primitive Church had indeed appropriated this structure as its own, as did later evidence found in Justin Martyr's mid-second century letter and other ancient Church orders. Clearly, the prototypical Christian Eucharistic gathering consisted

---

21. In a paper delivered to the Third National Congress of the Centre de Pastorale Liturgique at Strasbourg in 1958, A. M. Roguet explained: 'A perfectly legitimate kind of liturgical casuistry in resolving the problem posed by accidental lateness in getting to Mass has been unduly generalized in the minds of the faithful, to the point of their thinking that only the Eucharistic liturgy is important, for it alone 'counts' for obeying the precept of assistance at Sunday Mass. This … casuistic solution has been crystallized and, as it were, institutionalized in certain places by the sound of the bell rung by the server at the moment when the celebrant unveils the chalice.' A. M. Roguet, 'The Whole Man Proclaims the Word of God,' *The Liturgy and the Word of God*, 68.

of a service of the word followed by the table sharing. Thus, Vatican II's structural reclamation of the liturgy was the fruit of scriptural, historical and liturgical scholarship in which scholars had been engaged for many years. Given the complexity of the issue, it is interesting to note the manner in which the Council established the reclamation of this structure.

Sacrosanctum Concilium contains an interesting collection of theological statements on the importance of Scripture, the dignity of the word at worship, rubrical directives on the resultant place of the homily at Mass, and a startling assertion that the homily constitutes an essential element of the liturgy itself. Article 56 of *Sacrosanctum Concilium* announces that Scripture itself comprises the liturgy of the word that is of itself a constitutive element of the liturgy. Given the popular understanding of the role of the liturgy of the word at the Mass before the Council, it should not be difficult to imagine the surprise of many when the Council announced:

> The two parts that, in a certain sense, go to make up the Mass, namely, the liturgy of the word and the liturgy of the eucharist, are so closely connected with each other that they form but one single act of worship. Accordingly this Council strongly urges pastors that in their catechesis they insistently teach the faithful to take part in the entire Mass, especially on Sundays and holydays of obligation.[22]

The liturgy constitution contains numerous other citations relative to this issue. Article 24 is quite clear in defining the rediscovered importance of Scripture at worship:

> Sacred Scripture is of the greatest importance in the celebration of the liturgy. For it is from Scripture that the readings are

22. ICEL, 15.

given and explained in the homily and that psalms are sung; the prayers, collects and liturgical songs are scriptural in their inspiration; it is from the Scriptures that actions and signs derive their meaning. Thus to achieve the reform, progress, and adaptation of the liturgy, it is essential to promote that warm and living love for Scripture to which ... venerable tradition ... gives testimony.[23]

Article 7 asserts that the presence of Christ, so commonly believed by Catholics to be present in the Eucharistic elements, is also present in the gathered community as well as in the proclaimed Word, for 'He is present in his word, since it is he himself who speaks when the holy scriptures are read in the church.' Article 9 identifies preaching to the faithful as well as to those outside the Church as an ecclesial responsibility. Article 33 advances that 'although the liturgy is above all things the worship of the divine majesty, it likewise contains rich instruction for the faithful. For in the liturgy God is speaking to his people and Christ is still proclaiming his Gospel.' Article 35 states so 'that the intimate connection between rite and words may be apparent in the liturgy ... in sacred celebrations there is to be more reading from holy Scripture and it is to be more varied and apposite.' Article 48 dictates that, when the faithful are gathered for the Eucharistic liturgy, ' ... they should be instructed by God's word and be nourished at the table of the Lord's body ... ' Article 51 is rather explicit in its call for a richer Scriptural role at Eucharistic liturgy. 'The treasures of the Bible are to be opened up more lavishly, so that a richer share in God's word may be provided for the faithful. In this way a more representative portion of holy Scripture will be read to the people in the course of a prescribed number of years.'

23. Ibid., 9-10.

On April 3, 1969, the Apostolic Constitution approving the new Roman Missal, explained:

> All this has been planned to arouse among the faithful a greater hunger for the word of God. Under the guidance of the Holy Spirit, this hunger is meant, so to speak, to impel the people of the New Covenant toward the perfect unity of the Church. We are fully confident that under this arrangement both priest and faithful will prepare their minds and hearts more devoutly for the Lord's Supper and that, meditating on the Scriptures, they will be nourished more each day by the words of the Lord. In accord with the teachings of the Second Vatican Council, all will thus regard sacred Scripture as the abiding source of spiritual life, the foundation for Christian instruction, and the core of all theological study.[24]

Eucharisticum Mysterium, the Sacred Congregation for Rites' 1967 instruction, noted: 'In order to achieve a deeper understanding of the eucharistic mystery, the faithful should be instructed in the principal modes by which the Lord is present to his Church in liturgical celebrations.'[25] The text then enumerated those modes by asserting that at liturgy, Christ is present: in the community itself, in the word, in the person of the minister, and in the Eucharistic elements. Relative to the word, the text reads: 'He is also present in his word, for it is he who is speaking as the sacred Scriptures are read in the church.'[26] Elsewhere, *Eucharisticum Mysterium* identifies the liturgy of the word and the Eucharist so closely that together they comprise one unified worship event.[27] Paul VI's 1972 address entitled 'Eucharistic

---

24. Paul VI, *Missale Romanum*, ICEL, pp. 459-60.
25. ICEL, 400.
26. Ibid.
27. Ibid., 401.

Worship in the Church's Life', delivered to selected members of the Permanent Council on International Eucharistic Congresses, reiterates the same.[28] The Sacred Congregation for Divine Worship's directives for Holy Communion and Worship of the Eucharist outside Mass also rehearses its recognition of the various modes of Christ's presence, not failing to include the presence in the word.

These remarkable statements reveal the Council's development of a theology of the word. Up to this time, many Catholics would have been very suspicious of any rhetoric employing the word 'presence' if its intent were to describe any presence other than the 'Real Presence' in the Eucharistic Species. An understanding of the partnership of word and sacrament in effecting Christ's presence is clearly articulated as the Council commenced with the promulgation of its documents.

The wording of several other official sources lends evidence to the Church's recognition than its encouragement for frequent use of the Scriptures simultaneously serves to countermand former custom. The introduction to the *Lectionary for Mass*, published May 25, 1969, is of paramount value in assessing Vatican II's attitude toward the word at worship. With this publication, official legislation was promulgated which would cause Catholic people to hear a much more extensive part of the Scriptural canon over time. This significant shift was all the more dramatic when one recalls that prior to Vatican II, liturgical legislation required only that the Scriptural texts be read in Latin. Now, not only were the Scriptures to be read in the vernacular, but also much emphasis was now to be placed upon the value of the congregants' hearing as much of the Bible as possible at worship. The first article of the Lectionary's Introduction

28. Paul VI, Address of 1 March 1972, ICEL, 424.

enumerates the general principles that were followed in its construction:

> The Church loves ... Scripture and is anxious ... to nourish its own life by studying these sacred writings. Vatican Council II ... directed that in the revision of liturgical celebrations there should be 'more reading from Holy Scripture and it should be more varied and apposite' (*Sacrosanctum Concilium*, art. 35). The Council further directed that at Mass " ... a more representative portion of holy Scripture will be read to the people over a prescribed number of years" (*Sacrosanctum Concilium*, art. 51).
>
> ... By means of sacred Scripture, read during the liturgy of the Word and explained during the homily, 'God is speaking to his people, opening up to them the mystery of redemption and salvation and nourishing their spirit; Christ is present to the faithful through his own word' (*General Instruction on the Roman Missal*, no. 33). Thus the Church at Mass 'never ceases to receive from the altar and to offer to the faithful as the bread of life both the word of God and the body of Christ' (*Dei Verbum*, no. 21).[29]

Following these opening remarks, the Introduction proceeds to outline the pattern of scriptural readings for liturgy and to explain the choices described. Principles enacted by the Council relative to the Liturgy of the Word include: 1) so as to expose the faithful to as much of Scripture as possible, readings for Sunday liturgies will be on a three-year cycle, so that a particular text is never repeated within a period of three years; 2) for weekday liturgies, the Gospel readings are arranged on a one-year cycle, but the first reading has a two-year cycle; 3) each Sunday Mass (or

29. Sacred Congregation for Divine Worship, *Lectionary for Mass*, ICEL, 573-574.

Mass of obligation) will feature three readings, the first will be from the Hebrew Bible, the second will be taken from the writings of the apostles, and the third will be a Gospel reading; 4) weekday Masses will feature two readings with the second reading always being a Gospel text; 5) all Masses will feature a canticle or psalm response before the Gospel acclamation; 6) seasons and feasts will feature their own assigned cycles of readings as will certain ritual, votive or occasional events. In creating the lectionary with these features, the Church intended to conform to all that the Council had legislated.

Great care to provide greater breadth in Scriptural offerings is also noted in the guidelines provided for the celebration of the various sacraments and rites of the Church, as well as for the liturgy of the hours. Too, great care was taken by Church leadership to communicate that sacraments were not to be celebrated without the proper and constitutive role given to the word-event. The necessity of the word-event is typically included in the directives for all of the rites, including those outside of Mass.

Paul VI described this restored word and rite structure when he addressed the topic of the new rite of Mass at a general audience on November 19, 1969, just weeks before the new rite would be promulgated. The pope promised: 'You will find set into the new rite with greater clarity the relationship between the liturgy of the word and the liturgy of the Eucharist, so that the second corresponds to the first as its actualization.'[30]

In 1971, Cardinal Villot, Vatican Secretary of State, indicated that the pope asked that several issues receive careful consideration at Italy's twenty-second National Liturgical Week Conference, among them 'the close relationship between the liturgy of the

30. Paul VI, Address of 19 November 1969, ICEL, 540.

word and the liturgy of the Eucharist as two components of the one act of worship' and that 'the liturgy of the word ... is still an indispensable and requisite part of the celebration.' [31]

The Church committed itself at Vatican II to a renewed immersion in sacred Scripture, particularly at worship. The immersion has occurred successfully. There is nothing meager about the Scriptural diet the Church is serving itself in this new program, nor has the Church lacked fervor in reclaiming the role of the word at worship. Even non-liturgical devotions have typically experienced new life as a result of careful Scriptural application to their meaning. It can be said positively that the Church has reclaimed for its own liturgical life the word and rite structure that Vatican II identified as the Church's historically and theologically correct heritage. One might ask next to what extent this reclamation of the constitutive role of the word at worship has included liturgical preaching.

THE ROLE OF THE HOMILY
WITHIN THE LITURGY OF THE WORD

Strictly speaking, the reclamation of the word-event as a constitutive element of Catholic liturgical worship, as has been described here, would not necessarily be understood as constituting the reclamation of liturgical preaching. In a certain sense, the mere restoration of the correct emphasis upon the scriptural word at the liturgy was itself a Herculean accomplishment. The teachings of the Council, however, go further in decreeing that preaching is also to be regarded as a constitutive element of the liturgy of the word. Therefore, Vatican II's reclamation of the word and rite structure for liturgical worship was simultaneously an affirmation of the critical role of preaching at such worship.

31. Secretariat of State, Letter to Bishop Rossi of 30 August 1971, ICEL, 547-548.

The Dominican liturgist Frank Quinn has written,

> [L]iturgical preaching is integral to, and part of, the liturgy of
> the word: God's word proclaimed in the assembly, is brought
> into contemporary life, continued in corporate prayer, and
> lives in daily life. From the beginning … liturgical preaching
> has been a constitutive part of the liturgy, an element of what
> we today speak of as the liturgy of the word, itself most often
> part of a larger sacramental action such as the eucharist.[32]

One senses, however, from the context of Quinn's article that
he is writing apologetically, with the expectation that at least
some of his readers might find this concept surprising, even if not
debatable.[32] Quinn does not stand alone among liturgical experts
in experiencing the need to insist upon essential role of preaching
at worship.

More than twenty years ago, the Roman Catholic liturgical
scholar Lucien Deiss wrote: 'We may formulate a principle:
Every time the word is proclaimed to a community, it should be
actualized. In practice this means that there should be a homily
at every Mass and at every celebration of the word.'[34] It is
noteworthy that Deiss, writing a decade after the conclusion of
Vatican II, began his assertion with the words 'We may formulate
a principle.' Deiss bases his thesis upon the directives of Vatican
II, yet his wording betrays the problem: although the principle is
rooted in Vatican II, Deiss feels that he must 'formulate the
principle' as late as the 1970s! Had Vatican II not already

---

32. Frank Quinn, 'Liturgy: Foundation and Context for Preaching,' in *In the Company
    of Preachers*, Faculty of the Aquinas Institute of Theology (Collegeville, Minn.:
    Liturgical Press, 1993), 7.
33. Quinn, telephone conversation; in this conversation, Father Quinn agreed that
    these comments accurately reflect his own thought on the matter.
34. Lucien Deiss, *God's Word and God's People*, trans. Matthew J. O'Connell (Collegeville,
    Minn.: The Liturgical Press, 1976), 292.

formulated the principle? Why is this apologetic tone discernable in the writings of Quinn, Deiss and many of their peers?

Undoubtedly, this is so because liturgical preaching is one of those specific areas of the liturgical reform in which enthusiasm is sometimes wanting. Theologians, liturgists and homileticians frequently find themselves employing sources like Quinn and Deiss in establishing the recognition of the critical role of preaching at liturgical worship, precisely because they are convinced that there is a need to do so. Is this the product of inconsistency on this issue in the documents of Vatican II? Yes, and no. Vatican II clearly asserts, consistently and frequently, that preaching is a feature of the reclamation of the word and rite structure for liturgical worship. Unfortunately, the same conciliar documents also introduce ambiguities that may have lent strength to those who see little value in promoting an exceptionless norm for preaching at liturgy.

The conciliar documents consistently clarify that preaching is appropriate for all liturgical events, not just the Mass. All of the rites provide for preaching in the introductory comments to their respective ritual books. In principle, the same applies to the Eucharistic liturgy, although with some inconsistency. The references to the constitutive role of the homily at the Mass are extensive.

Lumen Gentium emphasizes the responsibility incumbent upon the Church to preach the Gospel (article 17); the importance of the hierarchical role of the bishop is seeing that the Gospel is preached (article 25); and the primary responsibility of the ordained is to assist the bishops in the preaching of the Gospel; additionally, it situates this priestly preaching within its liturgical context. This is reiterated in *Christus Dominus*, the conciliar decree on the pastoral office of bishops, where the preaching of the Gospel is described as 'pre-eminent' among all of a bishop's duties.[35] The same document reminds pastors of their responsibility to assist the bishops in that important responsibility.[36] *Presbyterorum Ordinis*, the decree treating the ministry and life of priests, legislated in article 4 the requirement that all sacramental ministry must include preaching because the sacraments find their very origin and nourishment in the word.

Predictably, the most significant references are found in *Sacrosanctum Concilium*. Article 35 enjoys the distinction of conveying the first conciliar identification of the constitutive role the homily plays at liturgy:

> Because the spoken word is part of the liturgical service, the best place for it, consistent with the nature of the rite, is to be indicated even in the rubrics; the ministry of preaching is to be filled with exactitude and fidelity. Preaching should draw its content mainly from scriptural and liturgical sources, being a proclamation of God's wonderful works in the history of salvation, the mystery of Christ, ever present and active within us, especially in the celebration of the liturgy.[37]

Article 52 becomes even more explicit in asserting the obligation of the Church to provide preaching at Mass. It reads: 'The homily, therefore, is to be highly esteemed as part of the liturgy itself. In fact, at those Masses which are celebrated on Sundays and holy days of obligation, with the people assisting, it should not be omitted except for a serious reason.'[38]

Thus, the liturgy of the word, including the homily, was officially recognized as an essential ingredient of liturgical

35. Vatican Council II, *Christus Dominus*, ICEL, 50.
36. Ibid., 51.
37. ICEL, 11.
38. Ibid., 14.

structure in this early conciliar document. In January, 1964, Paul
VI promulgated some of the prescriptions called for in
Sacrosanctum Concilium, which included a clarification of the
requirement of a homily at public Masses on Sundays and holy
days of obligation.[39] Several months later the Sacred Congregation
for Rites issued its instruction further implementing *Sacrosanctum
Concilium*, which repeated the new norm requiring a homily as
a constitutive element of all Masses of obligation, and added, 'On
days other than Sundays and holydays a homily is recommended,
especially on some of the weekdays of Advent and Lent or on
other occasions, when the faithful come to church in large
numbers.' [40]

Mysterium Fidei, issued on September 3, 1965, on the doctrine
and worship of the Eucharist, had similarly attested to the role of
liturgical preaching: 'In yet a different but most real way, [Christ]
is present in the Church as it preaches.' [41] On May 27, 1967, the
Sacred Congregation for Rites published an instruction on the
worship of the Eucharist,[42] in which it also acknowledges the
modes of Christ's presence at the Mass include his presence in the
word (articles 9, 55); article 10 reiterates the intrinsic connection
between the word and the Eucharist at the Mass, and article 20
states, 'The people have the right to be nourished by the word of
God proclaimed and explained. Accordingly, priests are to give
a homily whenever it is prescribed or seems advisable … '

The *Lectionary for Mass* (May, 1969), explained the dynamic
operative in the Council's reinstatement of the dignity of the
homily. After noting the Council's directive that more varied and
extensive selections from Scripture be introduced into the Mass

39. Paul VI, *Sacram Liturgiam*, ICEL, 85.
40. ICEL, 100.
41. ICEL, 385.
42. Sacred Congregation for Rites. *Eucharisticum Mysterium*, May 27, 1967.

on a cyclical basis, the document explains:

> By means of sacred Scripture, read during the liturgy of the
> word and explained during the homily, 'God is speaking to his
> people....' Thus the Church at Mass 'never ceases to receive
> from the altar and to offer to the faithful as the bread of life
> both the word of God and the body of Christ.' [43]

The third instruction on the correct implementation of
Sacrosanctum Concilium, under the title *Liturgiae Instaurationes*
(1970) stressed a familiar concept, that the homily is part of the
liturgy of the word and that 'the liturgy of the word prepares and
leads up to the liturgy of the Eucharist, forming with it the one
act of worship.' [44] The same point was repeated in 1973 in the
Sacred Congregation for Divine Worship's circular letter on
Eucharistic prayers, *Eucharistiae Participationem*, issued to the
presidents of the conferences of bishops throughout the world.

In the *General Instruction on the Roman Missal*, the constitutive
role of the liturgy of the word is presumed. The instruction states:
'In the readings, explained by the homily, God is speaking to his
people; opening up to them the mystery of redemption and
salvation, and nourishing their spirit; Christ is present to the
faithful through his own word.'[45] The value here invested in the
homily as a human function emphasizes once again the Council's
sense that the revelation of God's word to the Church is a
dialogical and a relational dynamic shared between God and the
Church.

The *General Instruction on the Roman Missal* is also explicit in
its treatment of the liturgy of the word, and its reference to the
homily as an ingredient of the Mass. The text is interesting in that

43. ICEL, 574.
44. Sacred Congregation for Divine Worship, *Liturgicae Instaurationes*, ICEL, 161.
45. ICEL, 477.

it shows the advancement made by the discussions surrounding the homily. The text reads:

> There must be a homily on Sundays and holydays of obligation at all Masses that are celebrated with a congregation. It is recommended on other days, especially on the weekdays of Advent, Lent, and the Easter season, as well as on other feasts and occasions when the people come to church in large numbers.

One notes in this 1975 document, that *Sacrosanctum Concilium's* (1963) allowance for the omission of the homily on Sundays and holydays of obligation 'for serious reason' is now itself omitted. Too, the recommendation for a daily homily, first encountered in *Inter Oecumenici* (1964), is not only included, but is expanded to include the weekdays of the Easter season and other feasts. Obviously Church leadership developed slowly but consistently in its understanding that the homily is not merely an effective tool for catechetics or pastoral care, but that its role at liturgy is integral.

Ten years after the conclusion of Vatican II, Pope Paul VI, ever faithful to his task of implementing the conciliar spirit and directives, wrote a landmark encyclical letter on evangelization entitled *Evangelii Nuntiandi*. This encyclical guaranteed that the word and table structure of liturgy, reclaimed at the Council, would not be lost.

In article 43, Paul had accentuated the dignity of the homily:

> [A]t a time when the liturgy renewed by the Council has given greatly increased value to the Liturgy of the Word, it would be a mistake not to see in the homily an important and very adaptable instrument of evangelization ... the eucharistic celebration is not the only appropriate moment for the homily. The homily has a place and must not be neglected in the

celebration of all the Sacraments, at paraliturgies, and in assemblies of the faithful. It will always be a privileged occasion for communicating the Word of the Lord.

Paul VI proclaimed in article 47: 'Evangelization [which he had identified as the primary work of the Church earlier in the document] thus exercises its full capacity when it achieves the most intimate relationship, or better still a permanent and unbroken intercommunication, between the Word and the Sacraments.' Thus, Paul VI assured the Church that its most important function, evangelization, reaches its fullest potential when it comprises the word and the Eucharist as two equal parts of one united act of worship. *Evangelii Nuntiandi* evidences that Paul VI and, in general, the Church under his leadership, came to embrace the principle that the authentic structure for Christian Eucharistic liturgy, as bequeathed to Christians of all times by the apostolic Church, is that of word and table, and constitutive of the word dimension is the preaching event.

Vatican II clearly legislated for a total reclamation of the word and sacrament structure for every liturgical rite, and this reclamation specifically includes a renewal of preaching, now generally regarded as obligatory at the Eucharistic liturgy.

As a result of this reclamation, Catholics are once again fully a people of the word. All of the Church's prayer today, liturgical or private, is biblically based. Even non-liturgical devotions derive value today from the degree to which they lead participants to reflection upon the Gospel. The renewal in preaching has extended to lay preaching, and Church journals and periodicals today are filled with advertisements for summer institutes, workshops, conventions and the like, all designed toward the preaching ministry. As Church members today explore new constructs for ministry, the proclamation of the word stands as a wonderful opportunity for ritually making Christ present through the ministries and charisms of a variety of persons. Although Catholicism is not yet known in a popular sense for outstanding preaching, clergy and laity alike are well aware that at liturgy, both components, word and sacrament, are gifts that come in tandem for making Christ present in the midst of those who are gathered in his name. Although the task of implementing the word and table structure at Eucharistic liturgy (as well as at all sacramental events) is challenging and sometimes slow, the Church's important journey toward this goal now has nearly four successful decades to its credit after a recess of several hundred years.

PART 2

Theological Reflection on Preaching

BORING GOD:
THEOLOGY AND PREACHING

VIVIAN BOLAND, O.P.

In a technical sense, to which I shall turn presently, preaching has to be boring. For the moment there is comfort in knowing that all who have ever been bored, tired, irritated or distracted during preaching have a patron saint in the New Testament, Eutychus, who was put to sleep by Saint Paul's preaching. We read about it in the Acts of the Apostles:

> On the first day of the week, when we met to break bread, Paul was holding a discussion with them; since he intended to leave the next day, he continued speaking until midnight. There were many lamps in the room upstairs where we were meeting. A young man named Eutychus, who was sitting in the window, began to sink off into a deep sleep while Paul talked still longer. Overcome by sleep, he fell to the ground three floors below and was picked up dead. But Paul went down, and bending over him took him in his arms, and said, 'Do not be alarmed, for his life is in him.' Then Paul went upstairs, and after he had broken bread and eaten, he continued to converse with them until dawn; then he left. Meanwhile they had taken the boy away alive and were not a little comforted (Acts 20:7-12).

It is encouraging to recall that Saint Paul, preacher of the gospel to the pagans and founder of Churches across the Roman Empire, may not have been always at his scintillating best. If in fact he had a scintillating best. His preaching on the Areopagus broke down and he retreated in some confusion (Acts 17:32-34). From there he went to Corinth, but 'in fear and trembling' as he says himself (1 Cor 2:1-5). 'His letters are strong but his bodily presence is weak and his speech contemptible,' according to some of his critics (2 Cor 10:10). All of this, along with the fact that he seems to have bored Eutychus to death, might be taken as evidence that Paul, arguably the greatest of the preachers of the gospel, was diffident and not necessarily inspiring in the actual task of speaking the Word.

THOUGHTS ABOUT THE WORD 'BORING'

The term 'boring' is actually more interesting than it ought to be. Normally it refers to what is tedious, tiresome and irritating as opposed to what is exciting, stimulating and interesting. We use it as an adjective in this sense – 'boring God' would then mean that God is boring or that the God we manage to present to ourselves and to others is boring: unexciting, uninteresting, not stimulating. The original meaning of the word is connected with excavation. One bores in order to find some valuable resource like water, gold or oil. In that sense, 'boring God' can refer either to God getting into us, penetrating us in some way or it can refer to us seeking to penetrate God, trying to 'get into God'. Finbar Ryan, O.P., Archbishop of Port of Spain, neatly combined both meanings of the term in his advice to apprentice preachers: 'if you don't strike oil, stop boring'.

So what about 'boredom' in the technical sense referred to? Dictionaries of Jungian and Kleinian thought do not have anything to say about it but the psychoanalytic tradition, as one would expect, comes up trumps and recognises boredom as an aspect of human experience worth thinking about. One of Freud's wisest and most humane followers in England, Charles Rycroft, describes boredom as

… the emotion that ensues when an individual fails to find interests and activities which fully engage him. It may arise

either as a result of external limitations, e.g. solitary
confinement, sensory deprivation, or monotonous work, or as
a result of internal inhibition. According to Fenichel (*Collected
Papers*, 1954), neurotic boredom is a state of instinctual tension
in which the instinctual aim is missing. As a result, the bored
person seeks an object 'not in order to act upon it with his
instinctual impulses, but rather to be helped by it to find an
instinctual aim which he lacks'. He knows he wants something,
but doesn't know what it is. As a consequence, irritability and
restlessness are present, and inseparable from boredom. [1]

It is worth noting that what stimulates boredom – if one might
be allowed such a paradoxical expression – is as likely to be
internal as external. The bored person wants something but does
not know what it is he wants. What he does know is that what he
is currently being offered is not it. A sweater for 3 year-olds sold
in London shops contains the legend 'I don't know what I want
but I want it now!' In certain ways human beings never grow
beyond this particular need for something that remains unknown.

Augustine famously speaks of the human heart as restless until
it rests in God: 'you have made us for yourself and our heart is
restless until it rests in you' (*Confessions* I.1). Thomas Aquinas
says that in this life we are united with God 'as with something
unknown' (*quasi ignoto coniungamur*, *Summa Theologiae* I 12, 13
ad 1). Putting these two thoughts together means that the human
being is condemned, so to speak, to be a creature who wants
without knowing what it is he or she wants. It follows also that
boredom in the technical, Freudian, sense is always on the point
of breaking out in regard to this deepest of our desires. In fact it

1. Charles Rycroft, *A Critical Dictionary of Psychoanalysis*, Second Edition, 1995,
    London, Penguin Books, page 16. The reference within the quote from Rycroft is
    to O. Fenichel, *Collected Papers* (First Series), 1954, London, Routledge and Kegan
    Paul. I have left it as it appears in Rycroft where no page number is given.

seems more likely the more intensely we experience this need and seek its fulfilment. The more deeply we enter into the unknown in which our happiness lies, the more sharply we will feel the gap between wanting and knowing. For Augustine, desire increases the closer we approach our goal. For Aquinas, and the Christian Neoplatonist tradition generally, knowledge darkens and language fails the closer we approach our goal.

For philosophers of all generations knowing and speaking belong together. For some, language articulates and gives voice to things already known within the mind. For others, it is through language that human beings come to realise what it is they know. Either way, knowing and speaking are intimately related. So – if Augustine and Aquinas are right – all our efforts at discourse in relation to God, our attempts to establish a satisfactory conversation whether in theology, preaching or prayer, seem doomed to fail for very good reasons. Theology is an attempt to speak about God, preaching an attempt to speak of God and prayer an attempt to speak with God. All of them, as human efforts, are subject to the same limitations of distance and difference, of inadequate language and boredom. We are quite familiar with this point in relation to 'negative theology', which has been enjoying something of a resurgence in recent times. But it applies also to preaching and to prayer, related human efforts at discourse appropriate to the subject of God. If Augustine and Aquinas are right, then these too, as human speakings, are bound to fall short of that which we most desire and the potential for boredom is correspondingly enormous.

CONVERSATION AND COMMUNITY

But it is not just human conversations in some way related to God that are subject to this kind of difficulty. Adolescents who are bored by celebrations of the Eucharist, for example, are usually bored by many other aspects of family life, of school life and of life in general. In a short but pregnant book about conversation, Theodore Zeldin (better known perhaps for his *Intimate History of Humanity*) examines the problems which beset any conversation between human beings, not just attempts at conversations involving God. Conversation, he contends, is a key concern for contemporary culture, which can change not only the way the world is seen, but can change the world itself. Why make such huge claims for an ordinary thing like conversation? Of course you will not regard conversation as making much difference, he says,

> ... if you believe that the world is ruled by over-powering economic and political forces, that conflict is the essence of life, that humans are basically animals and that history is just a long struggle for survival and domination. If that's true, you can't change much. All you can do is have conversations that distract or amuse you. But I see the world differently, as made of individuals searching for a partner, for a lover, for a guru, for God. The most important, life-changing events are the meetings of these individuals. Some people get disappointed, give up searching and become cynics. But some keep on searching for new meetings.[2]

Where the effort required for poetry, love, and philosophy (or for prayer, preaching and theology) is not valued, then conversation becomes problematic and people make do with what distracts and amuses. But there have been 'conversational revolutions' in the past, says Zeldin, just as important as wars and riots and famines:

2. Theodore Zeldin, *Conversation: How Talk Can Change Our Lives*, 1998, London, The Harvill Press, page 4. See also *An Intimate History of Humanity*, 1994, London, Sinclair-Stevenson.

When problems have appeared insoluble, when life has seemed to be meaningless, when governments have been powerless, people have sometimes found a way out by changing the subject of their conversation, or the way they talked, or the persons they talked to. ... Now it's time for the New Conversation.[3]

Zeldin's ideas echo thoughts of Thomas Aquinas in his commentary on Aristotle's *Politics*. Aristotle argued that human beings differ from the other animals in having speech. Thomas is very keen on this, believing that *communicatio facit civitatem* a phrase we can translate with 'conversation builds the city' or even with 'no community without communication'. There is no human society or community that is not built on conversation, exchange and communication. Talking to one another (with its essential counterpart, we might even say its essential environment, of listening to one another) is the way to establish and sustain life together. Thomas writes:

There is a difference between language (*sermo*) and simple voice (*vox simplex*). Voice is a sign of sadness and delight, and so of other emotions like anger and fear which are all related to delight and sadness, as is said in the second book of the *Ethics*. And so various animals have voice so that they might sense delight and sadness and signify this to each other by various natural sounds, as the lion by roaring and the dog by barking. For this purpose human beings have exclamations. But human speech signifies what is useful and what is harmful, which means it signifies what is just and unjust. Justice and injustice arise when useful and harmful matters are balanced or unbalanced. So speech is proper to human beings, because

3. Theodore Zeldin, *Conversation: How Talk Can Change Our Lives*, page 5.

it is also proper to them to have knowledge of good and evil, justice and injustice, and other things, which can be signified by speech. The human being, by his nature, has speech, and speech makes possible that human beings communicate with one another as regards usefulness and harm, justice and injustice, etc. It follows – since 'nature works nothing in vain' – that human beings naturally communicate with one another in these matters. But because relating in this way leads to the home and the state being set up, it follows that the human being is naturally a domestic and political animal.[4]

The Bible contains the same teaching about the connection between conversation and community. The story of the tower of Babel in Genesis 11 comes to a climax with the confusion of human languages and the consequent fragmentation of the human community. Salvation involves the rectification of this situation, a time when the Lord, the God of Israel, will 'change the speech of the peoples to a pure speech, that all of them may call on the name of the Lord' (Zeph 3:8-9). This prophecy Christians believe to have been fulfilled in the events of Pentecost when 'the crowd was bewildered because each one heard the disciples speaking in the native language of each' (Acts 2:6). The disaster of Babel with its confusion of tongues and destruction of solidarity is undone by Pentecost with its gift of tongues and establishment of a new community (new conversation = new community).

The Scriptural story of Pentecost makes it explicit that successful (that is truthful) human conversation depends on the gift of the Holy Spirit. Speaking a word that counts is only done under the influence of the Spirit. There are hints of this in Zeldin's work already mentioned with his reference to those who

4. Thomas Aquinas, *In Libros Politicorum Aristotelis Expositio*, 1951, Turin and Rome, Marietti, page 11, paragraphs 36-37 (translation by Vivian Boland).

seek a conversation that goes deeper than what is simply amusing and distracting. In a wonderful analysis of human sensuality in relation to God, Timothy Gorringe speaks about the priority of the oral over the visual in human cultures. This is connected, he says, not just with the fact that writing is a late invention but because a person's word marks their interiority. The spoken word moves from interior to interior, and encounters between human beings are achieved largely through voice. The film *Last Tango in Paris*, where the protagonists mostly grunt at one another, ends in death and alienation.[5]

For Christians, these difficulties are of greater significance for we live a faith that comes through hearing (Rom 10:17). The Spirit is received by believing what is heard (Gal 3:1-5) and faith, born of the Word, is nourished by the Word (Vatican II, *Decree on the Life and Ministry of Priests*, paragraph 4). Suffice for the moment to note this additional dimension to which we shall return presently.

In developing his thoughts about the importance of hearing in human experience, Gorringe uses some ideas of George Steiner that are most fully developed in his 1989 book *Real Presences: Is There Anything* in *What We Say?*[6] There, Steiner argued that in the many billions of words that are now processed every day little of any ultimate consequence is said. There is little or no depth of meaning in this ocean of words. Although they may amuse or distract, there is little or no satisfying truth in most of our words. Steiner is concerned particularly with art, music and literature, which he says have lost depth and point to the extent that their practitioners have given up wrestling with the transcendent. The

5. See Timothy J. Gorringe, *The Education of Desire: Towards a Theology of the Senses*, 2001, London, SCM Press, pages 13-14.
6. George Steiner, *Real Presences: Is There Anything* in *What We Say?* 1989, London, Faber and Faber.

sharp anger of atheism and the passionate disappointment of apostasy at least continued to fight with the transcendent or with its absence. In one of his final interviews Samuel Beckett, asked about his thoughts on God, replied 'he does not exist, the bastard'.[7] Even that hint of disappointment vanishes in a culture that is theologically indifferent.

The 'hints of transcendence' whispered by Zeldin are proclaimed unambiguously by Steiner. The fact that language has its frontiers in light, music and silence

> ... gives proof of a transcendent presence in the fabric of the world. It is just because we can go no further, because speech so marvellously fails us, that we experience the certitude of a divine meaning surpassing and enfolding ours. What lies beyond man's word is eloquent of God.[8]

The argument so far may be gathered as follows. It is not only human efforts to speak of God that are difficult, all human conversation is marked by difficulty, some of it inherent to the kind of being we are, some of it to do with the cultural environment in which we live. But it is only where people continue to try to talk about God, or with God, or of God – in other words where people continue their efforts at theology, preaching and prayer – that conversation with each other worthy of human dignity remains a possibility. Ordinary human conversation is worthy only when it is set within attempts – albeit doomed to failure – to talk about God, of God and with God. What Zeldin, Gorringe and Steiner suggest may be given a more explicitly Christian form in the claim that without the Word, words cannot bear the weight of

7. Samuel Beckett's comment I quote from memory: it was in a newspaper interview he gave shortly before his death and I have not kept the reference.
8. George Steiner, 'Silence and the Poet', in *Language and Silence*, 1967, London, Faber and Faber, page 58, quoted in Timothy J. Gorringe, *The Education of Desire: Towards a Theology of the Senses*, 2001, London, SCM Press, page 15.

meaning we need them to bear; that without the Spirit who searches the depths of everything, we cannot understand the gifts bestowed on us by God (1 Cor 1:12).

'GOD SPOKE BEFORE THEM ALL'

According to a traditional Irish saying, which might well be taken as a fair translation of the first verse of Saint John's Gospel, 'God spoke before them all'. It means that any subsequent speaking is always echo and response. In the beginning, we believe, was the Word who was with God and was God. This same Word became flesh in Jesus Christ, the image of the invisible God and the only Son from the Father. It is this same Word that we declare, proclaim and expound in theology, preaching and prayer (1 Jn 1:1-4). All things have been created in the Word, through the Word and for the Word, and all things hold together in the Word (Jn 1:2-4; Col 1:15-17). The original 'text' then is this Word, first known to us perhaps through the translation of it that we call creation, the same creation that forms the first chapter in the history of salvation. Within this view all human conversation, discourse or talk may be understood as an echo of an earlier, radically fundamental conversation, discourse or expression. The Wisdom literature of the Bible speaks marvellously about this, of how all the achievements of science and knowledge, all the wisdom of politics and law, every gain in understanding and technology, is an unfolding or expression of wisdom. This wisdom, that orders all things well (Wisdom 8:1), was 'beside' the Creator, like a master worker, at play and taking delight in everything about the world and about humanity (Prov 8:30-31). All human conversation or speaking, insofar as it attains something of meaning and truth, is an echo of this primordial discourse. Where our conversation is directly concerned with

God it is not only an echo but has also the character of response, a reply to something already spoken.

George Steiner, as noted already, says that silence and music are at the frontiers of language. I am not aware that this triad of silence, language and music has ever been used as a way of thinking about the Trinity but it would not be surprising if it has been. To the best of my knowledge, Marius Victorinus, one of Augustine's heroes and helpers on the way to conversion, comes closest. He refers to the Father as *vox in silentio* (voice in silence), to the Son as *vox* (voice) and to the Spirit as *vox vocis* (voice of the voice).[9] The God revealed in Jesus Christ is a kind of conversation, then, a set of relationships of knowing and loving that are the persons of the Trinity. If we think of the Father as silence, of the Word as voice and of the Spirit as music we are clearly proposing a metaphor but one, which illuminates the argument being developed here, and which is not entirely fanciful as the comments of Marius Victorinus show.

We can look also to Thomas Aquinas for support. In *Prima Pars* question 43 of the *Summa Theologiae* he speaks about the missions of the persons of the Trinity. The Father is not sent. The mission of the Word in creation and its history reflects the procession of the Son in the eternity of God's life. He is the Word, the perfect expression of the Father's glory. He is Wisdom, the intelligibility, meaning and truth that is found in all things. The mission of the Spirit in creation and its history reflects the procession of the Third Person in the eternity of God's life. He is Love, the bond that seals the relationship of Father and Son. He is Gift, the inexhaustible and gratuitous source of all the gifts

9. Marius Victorinus, *Adversus Arium* I 13, lines 30-31 [*Traités Théologiques sur la Trinité I* Texte établi par Paul Henry. Introduction, traduction et notes par Pierre Hadot. Sources Chrétiennes 68, 1960, Paris, Les Éditions du Cerf, p. 216]

with which God glorifies his people and God's people glorify God.

We have become accustomed to the impressive attempts by contemporary theologians to place the Trinity once again at the centre of Christian theology and spirituality. One need refer only to the works of Gilles Emery[11] and David Coffey[11] in support of this. The biblical Trinity leads us to thinking about the economic Trinity, which must in turn be related to the immanent Trinity. God who is Father, Word and Spirit for us is eternally Father, Word and Spirit. The Son has made God known and on his return to the Father has sent the Spirit to seal the relationship into which human beings are called, their participation in the life of the Blessed Trinity.

This question on the missions of the Persons of the Trinity is also one of the first places in the *Summa* where Thomas talks about grace. The human creature, made in the image and likeness of God, is therefore 'apt' to receive God so as to be in relationship with God through understanding and love (*Summa Theologiae* I 43, 3). The Word, Aquinas says, is not just any Word but is always *Verbum spirans amorem*, 'the love-breathing Word' (43, 5 ad 2). To hear this Word is to understand not simply in an intellectual way. We cannot truly hear this Word without 'receiving' Him, allowing the Word to dwell within us and to plant in our hearts the gift of the Spirit. This Word must always breathe this Love so that those who do receive the Word become doers of the Word and not just hearers, they become lovers in their turn and not just people who are loved. 'To all who received him, who believed in his name, he gave power to become children of God, who were

10. Gilles Emery, O.P., *La Trinité Créatrice*, Bibliothêque Thomiste XLVII, 1995, Paris, Librairie Philosophique J. Vrin.
11. David Coffey, *Deus Trinitas: The Doctrine of the Triune God*, 1999, Oxford and New York, Oxford University Press.

born, not of blood or of the will of the flesh or of the will of man, but of God' (Jn 1:12-13).

Now what does all this mean for our subject matter? It means that wherever there is truth and goodness, wherever there is justice and wisdom in our relationships and in the conversations that sustain those relationships, we are echoing something that is true about the universe itself and about its origin in a source that is wise and loving. Human conversation, exchange and communication that are worthy of human beings echo that conversation, exchange and communication which Christians believe God to be. Thomas Aquinas once again encourages us in thinking along these lines, this time with his endorsement of a comment attributed to Saint Ambrose, that 'any truth, no matter by whom it is said, is from the Holy Spirit' (*Summa Theologiae* I.II 109,1).

PREACHING AS LITURGICAL ACTION

When our conversation seeks to include God explicitly, whether in theology, preaching or prayer, it necessarily has the character of a reply, a response to an earlier expression. It is no longer just an echo of the eternal conversation but is a response to it, or better, a response within it. All our preaching, then, insofar as it is a preaching of the Word of God is within the conversation that Father and Son carry on in the Spirit. We live in Trinity.

This point is illustrated by the liturgical sense that the term *praedicare* seems to have in the earliest Dominican traditions. We know that the thirteenth century masters in theology at the University of Paris were obliged to read or lecture (*legere*), to dispute or argue (*disputare*) and to 'preach' or proclaim (*praedicare*). This may seem to suggest that preaching is an extension of teaching, that it belongs with the lecture and seminar, with the catechetical exposition and Scripture commentary, as a kind of pedagogical exercise, a moment of instruction. While it is true that preaching is so related, good teaching is never simply the communication of information to hearers who have not known it before. It is a much richer task involving not only material or doctrines to be taught but the relationship between the teacher and the ones taught. Any good teaching is a conversation with a view to wisdom and appreciation, and will have something of the mysterious about it. None of this is to be denied.

But what needs emphasis here is the fundamentally liturgical sense that is to be given to *'praedicare'*. If the masters did preach after their lectures and disputations, then it was at the liturgy that they preached and not in the classroom or in the lecture-hall. This is obvious.

Preaching for the Dominicans always began in this liturgical service of the Word of God, in the hours of choral office and in the daily celebration of the Eucharist. One of the prefaces of the Dominican liturgy identifies the responsibilities of the Order as praising, blessing and preaching (*laudare, benedicere, praedicare*). The first two are liturgical terms and it seems reasonable that the third be taken in that sense also. The *berakah* blessing of the Jewish liturgies is the essential background to Christian liturgies of the Word in which the wonderful works of God are proclaimed and acknowledged and in which their author is thanked and praised. The canon of the Mass itself was at one time referred to as *praedicatio*. Vatican II's Constitution on Divine Revelation echoes this tradition in its opening paragraphs (*Dei Verbum*, paragraphs 1-3). They speak about the eternal life which was with the Father, which has appeared to us in the Word of God whom we have seen and heard and touched, and which is proclaimed in the Church as it announces the *praeconium*, the glory and praise, of salvation.

If the argument being developed here points to any programme for action, it is in the direction of trying to recover a sense of *praedicare* as primarily a liturgical and sacramental action rather than simply a catechetical or pedagogical one. This is not to deny the importance of these ways of serving the Word of God. Understanding preaching as primarily a liturgical and sacramental action, helps us to see that it must have the character of a response, it must concern itself with praise and thanks, and it must, in some sense, include God in its audience. Saint John Chrysostom, who is the patron of preachers in the Church, confirms this understanding of it. In his work *On the Priesthood* he says that 'the sole object of the preacher must be to please God rather than men'.[12] (In a dusty file I find a quote attributed to John Chrysostom to the effect that 'the preacher ought to preach, whether people listen to him or not' but I cannot now trace the source of it. It is certainly a plausible sentiment in view of the reaction to his own preaching and it states even more strongly the idea that preaching is to be understood as liturgical action: something that must simply continue to be done.) Of course if God is the addressee and not just the subject of our preaching then a final sense of the phrase 'boring God' becomes possible!

As we recall and remember – in the strong biblical sense of 'remember' – the wonderful deeds of God, we echo his Word and seek to name, in faltering human terms, the refractions of that Word in human experience. In preaching we seek, as Catherine Hilkert puts it, 'to name grace'. Our attempt to do so is itself a grace, the 'grace of preaching', by which we are given a place within the missions of the Son and the Spirit, called to speak at various times and in various different ways the one Love-breathing

---

12. John Chrysostom, *Six Books on the Priesthood* V.7, translated with an Introduction by Graham Neville, 1964, London, SPCK, page 133.

and saving Word. This is the wonder of this grace, that the human language of proclamation, praise and teaching carries the eternal Word to birth in every time and place.

A SPIRITUALITY OF PREACHING

If we turn, finally, to consider the spirituality demanded by this understanding of preaching, it will be a way of living for which silence, conversation and music are central. In this too it will be a 'theological life', an image among human beings of a God who may be thought about as Silence, Word and Music.

Without silence there is no hope of contemplation or prayer. One of the first pieces of advice handed on to Dominican novices is that 'silence is the father of preachers'. The school of silence is an essential place of learning for the preacher. As we struggle to find something worthwhile to say it is good to recall that it was 'while gentle silence enveloped all things ... (that) your all-powerful word leaped from heaven ... into the midst of the land that was doomed' (Wisdom 18:14-15).

Without talking, of course, there is no preaching. This is not just the actual speaking of the preaching when the time comes to do it, but the entire engagement and involvement of the preacher with the community in which the preaching is to be done. Just as a teacher must adapt to the language and circumstances of those listening, so the preacher must be conversant with what is happening in the world and in the lives of those who listen.

In the 'Life of Jesus' which we find in the *Tertia Pars* of the *Summa Theologiae*, Thomas Aquinas speaks of Christ's 'mode of conversation' among us (*De modo conversationis Christi – Summa Theologiae*, III 40). It is a question about what we would now call a person's 'lifestyle' or 'form of life'. To readers who are not Dominicans, it may have a slightly chauvinistic feel as Thomas paints a portrait of Christ's way of life which is remarkably close to that which Saint Dominic envisaged for the members of his Order. The best possible form of life, Thomas says, is the one whereby a person is called to share with others, through preaching and teaching, what has been contemplated. Christ's mission was to bear witness to the truth and this required a public life of preaching. He lived as he did, Thomas says, in order to give an example to preachers (*ut daret exemplum praedicatoribus – Summa Theologiae*, III 40,1). He lived a balanced life of prayer and preaching. To facilitate his work among them Christ did not live in solitude but shared the living conditions of the people and conformed to their circumstances (40,2). He lived among them in poverty, Thomas continues, because this is appropriate to the task of preaching. Christ taught the apostles that they must live in simplicity and detachment if they were to carry through effectively the mission he was entrusting to them and he gave them an example of this in how he spent his days (40,3).

So what then about music? If language is bordered on one side by silence, on the other it becomes music. At the end of Brian Friel's play *Dancing at Lughnasa*, the narrator, Michael, speaks of his memories of the summer in which the events of the play take place, a memory nostalgic with music, he says,

> ... a dream music that is both heard and imagined; that seems to be both itself and its own echo. ... When I remember it, I think of it as dancing. ... Dancing as if language has surrendered to movement. ... Dancing as if language no longer existed, because words were no longer necessary ... [13]

Preaching unsupported by silence and music is likely to be boring. Sometimes the music of the words themselves will be

---

13. Brian Friel, *Dancing at Lughnasa*, 1990, London and Boston, Faber and Faber, page 71.

sufficient, for good preaching is a kind of poetry. More often, though, it is an actual liturgical celebration of the Word of God that supports preaching. It will involve silence and music and perhaps even dancing (if only the highly formalised dancing of bowing, genuflecting and processing).

In a report prepared for the 1980 general chapter of the Dominicans, Yves (later Cardinal) Congar identifies the prior, the lector or librarian, and the cantor as the three essential offices within a Dominican community (or a 'preaching' as it was called in the early days). He says that 'these three functions correspond to the form of our life': a common life overseen by the prior, a life of study encouraged by the lector or librarian, and a liturgical or 'doxological' life led by the cantor.[14]

This can be applied more generally within the Church. Effective preaching presupposes a community, that the preacher is conversant (day by day) with fellow Christians. The network of relationships in which the preacher is involved helps to shape the preaching and there can be no effective preaching where the one who speaks and the ones who listen are, in a strict sense, strangers to each other. Effective preaching is theologically informed, nourished and strengthened by constant study. Study means a kind of anxiety for the truth, a concern that what is said be true. Such a zeal or love sets challenges that are never-ending. Aquinas says that the moral life can never be completely free from anxiety (*Summa Theologiae* II.II 49,4; 49,8) and preaching is, of course, a practice within such a life.

Effective preaching, finally, is always within the liturgical and doxological life of the Church. There has been a return to this theme in recent times, largely through the influence of Hans Urs

14. The report by Yves Congar to the Dominican General Chapter of 1980 has never been published as far as I know. It is not given as an appendix to the acts of that chapter and I have used the copy circulated at the time to members of the Order.

von Balthasar. But it is important to remember that it is a recovery, part of the *ressourcement* in which Balthasar, de Lubac and others of their generation were involved. In particular the writings of Pseudo-Dionysius, central for Christian theology and liturgy in the Middle Ages, provide Balthasar and others with a classical exemplar of a theology which is always also a doxology, a 'hymning' of the truth and goodness of God, to use Pseudo-Dionysius' own term (*On the Divine Names* I.7).[15]

CONCLUDING COMMENT

One of the Advent prefaces tells us that the Virgin Mother bore Christ in her womb 'with love beyond all telling'. Alan Paton begins *Cry The Beloved Country*, his wonderful novel about South Africa, with the description of hills that are 'lovely beyond any singing of it'.[16] Ultimately, the preacher of the Word of God is engaged with a matter that is beautiful beyond any singing of it. If silence is in some way the source of preaching, silence is also its destination. Even our music, dancing and singing, come to an end that is not yet the end we seek. God is the Father who has sent the Love-breathing Word to us so that we already have the mind of Christ (1 Cor 2:16) and we are already the children of God (1 Jn 3:2). We speak already of these things in words not taught by human wisdom (1 Cor 2:13). Where it happens that someone hears, through our preaching, the silent music of eternal love – *la musica callada* of John of the Cross [17] – then, of course, it is not we who speak (in spite of all our talking) but the Spirit of our Father speaking through us (Mt 10:20).

15. Pseudo-Dionysius, *The Complete Works* The Classics of Western Spirituality, 1987, London, SPCK, page 56.

16 Alan Paton, *Cry the Beloved Country*, 2002, London, Vintage, page 7.

17. John of the Cross, *Cantico Espiritual: Canciones entre el alma y el Esposo*, in San Juan de la Cruz, *Obras Completas*, 1988, Madrid, Editorial de Espiritualidad, page 577.

JESUS OF NAZARETH, ITINERANT PREACHER

DONALD J. GOERGEN, O.P.

'Who do you say that I am?' (Mk 8: 29) is one of the more significant and most asked questions in Christian theology. The first five centuries struggled deeply and philosophically with the question. Today we struggle with it just as deeply but more historically. It is a biblical, patristic, medieval and modern question. There is no one answer. Varied responses give us insights into the mystery – the *mysterium Christi*. The question has been posed in modern times in a different form, given our modern emphasis on the centrality of the subject. Who did Jesus say that he was? This phrasing has manifested an effort, impossible in the long run, to get at Jesus' own self-understanding or consciousness. I say impossible in the long run since it is such a modern question, since our sources did not seek to answer it in any direct fashion, since consciousness itself is a very fluid reality, and since Jesus was a very un-self-preoccupied person.[1] Nevertheless there are in the biblical texts intimations of how Jesus perceived his mission, how he saw his relationship with God, and how profoundly Jewish his faith was.

There is one text in which Jesus just comes out and says how he saw himself. The text comes early in the Gospel of Mark. Jesus had been baptized, driven into the wilderness, and then returned to Galilee after the arrest of John 'preaching the gospel of God' (Mk 1: 14, RSV). Later in that same chapter, after Jesus' ministry had begun, after he had sought a place apart in order to pray, Simon and those who were with him found Jesus and informed him that people were looking for him. Jesus replied, 'Let us go on

---

1. Cf. Donald J. Goergen, *The Mission and Ministry of Jesus*, 1986, Collegeville, MN, The Liturgical Press, pp. 146-76, especially pp. 157-60.

to the nearby villages that I may preach there also. For this purpose have I come' (Mk 1:38, NAB). Whatever else can be said, Jesus saw his mission as one of preaching, as proclaiming God's reign. There is ample evidence in the Gospels of Jesus' preaching, healings, exorcisms, as well as symbolic actions including table fellowship with poor and rich alike. We may be inclined to think of these as distinct ministries in the life of Jesus. They rather form an integrated whole. Jesus would hardly have thought of them as distinct. They are all preaching, proclamation, and manifestations of God's reign. Jesus' preaching reflects the influence of both the prophetic and sapiential traditions in Israel.[2] Jesus preached in word and deed. The symbolic actions were as much preaching as was the ministry of the word, and often may have been the more effective preaching. Which was more likely to have had the greater impact, washing the feet of the disciples (Jn 13: 1-16) or instructing them: ' The Son of Humanity has not come to be served but to serve' (Mk 10: 45)? Jesus' preaching flowed into praxis and his praxis, the praxis of the reign of God, was preaching. He lived what he proclaimed.

The healings and exorcisms, abundantly attested, were among the many symbolic actions Jesus performed and all were preaching. When Jesus said, 'Let us go on to the nearby villages that I may preach there also,' he was not excluding going there to heal the sick, drive our demons, or share table fellowship with the people. There was no need to enumerate the many ways in which the reign of God could be proclaimed. They were all proclamation; they were all preaching. Sometimes the preaching was a saying, sometimes a story, sometimes a discourse, sometimes an act of mercy, sometimes the healing of a leper, sometimes the cure of a demoniac, sometimes a festive meal, sometimes summoning

2. Ibid., pp. 146-76 on Jesus as prophet, pp. 207-77 on Jesus as teacher of wisdom.

children to come to him. People saw him as a prophet (Mk 8: 28; Mt 16: 14; Lk 9: 19), and prophecy and preaching were practically synonymous. The Greek word *prophetes* suggests someone who speaks on behalf of someone else. R. B. Y. Scott writes, 'The prophets were primarily *preachers* in the highest sense of that term.'[3] Jesus was known as a prophetic and itinerant preacher and that is how he saw himself as well. He felt entrusted with the message of God's reign.

WHAT JESUS PREACHED

Jesus saw himself, in terms of his mission, primarily as a preacher, but what did Jesus preach? We can answer that question with two phrases which end up being practically synonymous: 'the reign of God,' and 'the gospel of God.'

Now after Jesus was arrested, Jesus came into Galilee, preaching the gospel of God, and saying, 'The time is fulfilled, and the kingdom of God is at hand; repent and believe in the gospel.' (Mk 1:14-15, RSV)

Let us take a closer look at these two expressions.

Jesus' preaching and teaching comprised a prayer he taught (Lk 11: 2-4); various proverbial wisdom sayings (e.g. Mk 3:24-26, 27; 7:15; 8:35; 10:15, 23, 25, 31; Lk 9: 60a, 62; 11:20; 14:11; 17:20-21; Mt 5:39b-41; 5:44-48; 7: 13-14; 11:12); and parables.[4] All speak of the reign of God. Most parables ask, 'To what shall we compare the reign of God?' or indicate 'The reign of God is like ... ' The parables are not about Jesus but about God. Although much has been written about the expression 'reign of God,' it is best understood as a Jewish targumic circumlocutional way of speak-

3. R.B.Y. Scott, *The Relevance of the Prophets*, 1971, New York, Macmillan Co., p. 14. Emphasis in the original.
4. Donald Goergen, op. cit., p. 209.

ing – as Jesus' way of speaking about God, rooted in the metaphor
of God as king. Our king is God. God's rule is the primary
concern. This 'reign of God' is a way of speaking about God, a
reverent way of speaking connoting God as near, present, or
coming. The sense of the expression is better gained by simply
using the word God. The reign of God is God. The usage is not
peculiar to Jesus but is nevertheless characteristic of Jesus.[5]

Let us now take the word 'gospel.' The word is predominantly
Pauline (60 of the 76 occurrences in the New Testament). James
D. G. Dunn suggests that Paul himself coined the word.[6] Six
times Paul speaks simply of 'the gospel of God' (Rom 1:1; 15:16;
2 Cor 11:7; 1 Thes 2:2, 8, 9). '*Euangelizomai*' is to proclaim good
news from God and about God. The expression 'gospel of God'
is also found in Mark (1:14) as we saw above. When people hear
the word 'gospel,' however, they ordinarily think of the four
Gospels. These four Gospels came to be so called, however,
because they contain 'the gospel of Jesus Christ.' However, we
can distinguish between the gospel about Jesus Christ (Jesus as
the object of the preaching, the good news of the life, death and
resurrection of Jesus) and the gospel that Jesus preached. This
latter, what Jesus himself preached, is the gospel of God. In this
latter use, Jesus is the subject, the Preacher. The object of the
preaching is God: Jesus' experience and understanding of God.
There are thus three levels at which we can understand the word
'gospel': a literary form (the four Gospels); the story of Jesus as the
Christ of God (the gospel about Jesus); and the God whom Jesus
proclaimed. Ultimately again, the gospel is God.

Jesus preached God. It is in this that a parallel with St Dominic

---

5. Ibid., pp. 225-26. Also see Bruce David Chilton, 'Regnum Dei Deus Est,' *Scottish
    Journal of Theology* 31,1978, pp. 261-70.
6. James D. G. Dunn, *The Theology of Paul the Apostle*, 1998, Grand Rapids, MI,
    William B. Eerdmans Pub. Co., pp. 164-69.

is so strong. Dominic saw his mission as well as that of his friars
as preaching. He wanted his order to be an order of preachers.
Preaching required itinerancy – the freedom to go where called
or where sent. As Jesus said, 'Let us go to the neighbouring
villages so that I can preach there also' (Mk 1:38). Dominic not
only followed after Jesus by being an itinerant preacher, but also
by realizing that preaching is all about God, proclaiming the
truth about God. As was remembered by his friars and recorded
in their primitive constitutions (LCO 1/II), Dominic was known
to speak only to God or about God (*cum Deo vel de Deo*).
Preaching for Dominic, as well as for Jesus, was *de Deo*.

God was the content of Jesus' preaching. Thus the question for
our preaching is who is the God we preach? There is the axiom
in post-Bultmannian biblical studies that Jesus preached the
kingdom and the Church preached Jesus. But this dichotomy is
not what it seems. To say that Jesus preached the kingdom, if
properly understood, is to say that Jesus preached God, who the
God of Israel truly is, that Jesus preached Someone, not something. The question is not what Jesus preached but whom Jesus
preached. And to say that the Church preached Jesus is to say that
the Church found in Jesus, his life, mission, death and resurrection the story of God, the embodiment of who God is. Christology
is theology. Jesus reveals the truth about God.

The Gospels state the gospel quite succinctly: God is power
(Paul); God is near (Mark); God is compassion (Luke); God is
demanding (Matthew); God is love (John). God is love, and love
is a power that is compassionate, demanding, and close at hand.
God is like a forgiving father, a woman in search of a lost coin, a
pearl of great price, a mustard seed. Jesus wanted the people of
Israel and Judah to know, especially the outcasts of the house of
Israel, that they were of concern to God, that God cared for them
and was not indifferent toward them, that indeed God belongs to

them just as they belong to God. 'Blessed are you poor, for God is yours' (Lk 6: 20).

We can picture the crowds composed of the poor, the hungry, the sad, the sick, the lame, the outcasts, the uneducated, and the unclean. What could Jesus say to them that might have been a word of consolation? Nothing would have taken away their poverty, their sadness; no words were going to clothe or feed them. Yet the heart of the compassionate Jesus reached out to them. What could he have said? He knew his heavenly Father's love reached out to them as well. And so he said all that he could say: God is yours. The message did not remove the poverty or hunger or pain. And yet it was a word of consolation. And it expressed one of the fundamental religious insights in the teaching of Jesus: GOD BELONGS TO THE PEOPLE.[7] Nothing can separate them from God's love. They may fall outside the realm of the Law or social acceptability but they do not fall outside the realm of God. God belongs to them.

All preaching is searching for God,[8] revealing God, and letting God speak. It's all about God. And therefore the preacher is first and foremost a man or woman of God. One cannot preach what one does not know. Nor is it a question of knowing a lot about God but rather of knowing God. The preacher, as was Jesus, is God-intoxicated.

HOW JESUS PREACHED

Noteworthy in what Jesus preached is the fact that his preaching manifested the power of the Spirit. Jesus spoke about God in terms of the reign of God which was near, here, at hand, coming, to be anticipated, and Jesus proclaimed the gospel of God, that

7. Donald Goergen, op. cit., p. 227.
8. Donald Goergen, 'Preaching as Searching for God,' *Dominican Ashram*, 19, March, 2000, pp. 12-17.

God's love is compassionate and challenging, merciful and just. Yet Jesus the preacher was under the influence of the Spirit. He preached through the power of the Spirit. This is most apparent in his inaugural preaching in Nazareth upon his return there after his baptism. 'Then Jesus, filled with the power of the Spirit, returned to Galilee ... ' (Lk 4: 14). When he came to Nazareth he went to the synagogue on the Sabbath day, as was his custom. As he stood up to read, the scroll of the prophet Isaiah was given to him. He unrolled the scroll until he came to the text at Isaiah 61: 1-2 and then read:

> The Spirit of the Lord is upon me, because he has anointed me to bring good news to the poor. He has sent me to proclaim release to the captives and recovery of sight to the blind, to let the oppressed go free, to proclaim the year of the Lord's favour.

The Gospel of Luke emphasizes clearly the role and presence of the Holy Spirit in the mission and preaching of Jesus. In Luke's infancy narrative the Holy Spirit is mentioned in reference to John the Baptizer who would be filled with the Holy Spirit (1: 15), to Elizabeth who was filled with the Holy Spirit (1: 41), to Zechariah who was also filled with the Holy Spirit (1:67), to Mary who would conceive through the power of the Spirit (1:35), and to Simeon in the temple who was inspired by the Spirit to prophesy (2: 25-27). Clearly the Holy Spirit is the ambience within which the Jesus story takes place.

Following this infancy narrative, John indicates that someday Jesus would baptize with the Holy Spirit: 'I baptize you with water ... he will baptize you with the Holy Spirit' (3: 16). Jesus' mission is associated with the Spirit. It is what Jesus will give or bring or unleash. Jesus himself is baptized, following which the Holy Spirit descended upon him (3: 21-22). Jesus is then described by Luke as 'full of the Holy Spirit' (4:1) and Jesus is then 'led by the Spirit' (4:1) into the wilderness where the Spirit attends to him during this ordeal. It is following this wilderness experience that Jesus returns to Galilee in the power of the Spirit (4:14) where Jesus preaches, heals, and drives out demons – all through the power of the Spirit. If anything can be said about Jesus, he was a man of the Spirit. The Spirit was the source of his power and his preaching. In one sense one could say it is not Jesus but the Spirit who preaches.

In terms of Jesus' enigmatic self-understanding, we can say that he was aware of the Spirit as was indicated in his first preaching in Nazareth. Jesus saw himself as belonging to the Spirit. He was aware of both the source of his strength and message as well as its content. 'The Spirit of the Lord is upon me, because he has anointed me to bring good news to the poor.' At this point Jesus identified his mission in Isaian terms. He was to bring a gospel to those for whom the preaching or teaching of the Pharisees and Sadducees had not been good news. Even though in so many ways those to whom Jesus preached stood outside the Law, they were not outside the pale of salvation. Indeed salvation, the reign of God, was theirs. Jesus' courageous message could be proclaimed because the Spirit was with him. It was not through his own power, but through that of the Spirit that he preached with an authority that amazed people as well as captivated them. They recognized in him the Spirit. In him they met the Holy Spirit. It is not that he spoke about the Spirit but did not seem to know that of which he spoke. He was speaking out of the context of his own experience. If Jesus' preaching was prophetic, it was because he was first a mystic. He knew God and knew the God he preached. His own experience was his testimony, and his experience was confirmed by the Hebrew Scriptures which played a formative role in his life.

What role, however, did the Scriptures play in Jesus' preaching? How did he relate to them? Although more needs to be done in this area, Bruce Chilton has explored Jesus' style of preaching.[9] We will try to come to some understanding of it here, for it is not only the fact that Jesus preached but also how he preached that is of importance. Jesus seems to have been familiar with the interpretative tradition preserved in the targums. The Hebrew of the Bible would have been unfamiliar to the majority of the Jewish people in Jesus' time and thus required translation and interpretation. Nevertheless, the reading from the Bible in Hebrew constituted the core of synagogue worship. It was thus necessarily followed by an interpretative translation in Aramaic, the language of the people. These interpretative Aramaic translations were the targums. Jesus did not necessarily know the text of the targums as we have them today (e.g., the Isaiah Targum) but was familiar with the traditions preserved in the targums. He seems in fact to have used material we now find in the Isaiah Targum. (Compare Mk 4: 11-12 and Is 6: 9-10 and Is Targum 6: 9-10; Mk 4: 24, Mt 7: 2 and Is 27:8 and Is Targum 27:8; Mt 26: 52 and Is 50:11 and Is Targum 50:11.)

Jesus was aware, as we are, that the Bible does not speak to us, our situation and our questions directly. It is preaching that makes that connection. But how is that connection made? In Jesus' preaching, the starting point was not the text of the Bible itself, but rather the human experience which one was addressing. It is this that leads Bruce Chilton to describe Jesus' preaching as experiential. It was not exegetical but homiletic. Naturally one brings to the Bible the conviction that it is an expression of one's own faith, that it brings to expression one's faith, that it illumi-

---

9. Bruce Chilton, *A Galilean Rabbi and His Bible*, 1987, Wilmington DE, Michael Glazier.

nates or has the capacity to illuminate one's own experience of
God. Yet Jesus' preaching is not an interpretation of a text as such,
neither the Bible nor its targumic translations. For Jesus 'the
reign of God' was not a targumic expression, which it was, but
rather God experienced. It had an experiential referent. However, Jesus' God-experience was something illuminated by the
Bible. The Bible helped Jesus to understand and interpret the
experience; it was not the experience that helped him to understand or interpret the Bible. Jesus had no particular method for
interpreting Scripture but his faith in Scripture allowed him to
believe that it would help to interpret experience.

In other words, the categories, images, language and stories in
the biblical and targumic traditions helped the interpretation of
experience. They were not the starting point but a point of
illumination. The language of the kingdom, for Jesus, referred to
God's action and presence here and now, not to something that
took place in the past. Scripture helps us to understand what God
is doing in the present, not what God did in the past.

We might immediately ask how Jesus moved from his Bible,
the Hebrew Bible, our Old Testament, to its relevance to a
contemporary situation. But that is to ask the wrong question, for
the starting point for Jesus' preaching was not the text of the Bible
but the situation or experience to be interpreted or understood. In
other words, the 'text' for Jesus' preaching was God's activity in
the present and the Scriptures or targumic tradition the vehicle
for articulating it. As Chilton puts it:

> Jesus seems to have broken new ground ... in making God's
> present activity, not the text, his point of departure. The
> wealth and variety of biblical language and imagery in Jesus'
> sayings indicate that he did not use the circumstances of the
> present to explain the meaning of Scripture; he rather used the

Scripture to assert God's meaning for the present.[10]

Chilton calls Jesus' style of preaching not only experiential but also analogical in that the biblical references provided analogies to contemporary experiences or events. Again the Scriptures are a vehicle for interpreting an event and not the other way around.

Jesus' preaching in that sense was not primarily interpretative. Understanding Scripture was not for him the goal of preaching.[11] It was not a question of what a text meant and interpreting it. Jesus used texts to reveal continuity with God's actions and thus enable people to see or experience God acting now. God's action in the present was Jesus' concern and the biblical tradition provided ample analogies to facilitate one's awareness of that. Jesus enabled people to move beyond their faith in God to an experience of God by recognizing God as present with them now. Jesus' analogical and experiential approach to preaching fulfilled the Scriptures in the sense that what the Scriptures were describing was still being experienced by the people.

Our approach to Scripture often manifests the attitude that the past is more holy than the present, that God acted more in the past than God does now. Jesus rather saw God acting in his own time as in every time and used the Scriptures to confirm that. But it was God now, not then, that was the core of Jesus' preaching about God. Jesus' preaching brought people into an experience of God now in their lives, in their current circumstances, an experience of God as present, near, compassionate, demanding and loving. As a man of the Spirit, he saw the Spirit's presence now and its continuity with that same Spirit's presence to God's people throughout history. Jesus was not concerned primarily with whether they understood the Bible but with whether they real-

10. Op. cit., p. 187.
11. Op. cit., p. 188.

ized God was with them. Jesus preached out of his own solidarity
with God and invited his hearers into that same intimacy.

JESUS' SOLIDARITY WITH GOD

Pre-eminent in the biblical texts upon which we rely as our
sources for interpreting Jesus is the depiction of Jesus as a man of
prayer. The starting point for Jesus is God, Jesus' Abba. Within
this frame of reference are the Scriptures which mediated the
God-experiences of the Hebrew people for Jesus as well as his
own personal experience of God in prayer. The significant
Marcan text to which we have already referred begins with our
finding Jesus at prayer.

In the morning, while it was still very dark, he got up and went
out to a deserted place, and there he prayed. And Simon and his
companions hunted for him. When they found him, they said to
him, 'Everyone is searching for you.' He answered, 'Let us go on
to the neighbouring towns, so that I may proclaim the message
there also; for that is what I came out to do.' And he went
throughout Galilee, proclaiming the message in their synagogue
and casting out demons. (Mk: 1: 35-39, NRV; also see Mk 6:46)

The Gospel of Luke in particular gives emphasis to Jesus'
prayer (Lk 3:21; 5:16; 6:12; 9:18, 28). Jesus observed the Sabbath
(Lk 4:16). He participated in the annual festive religious celebrations of the Jewish people, such as the traditional Pesach or
Passover. The Gospel of Mark presents Jesus in his personal
prayer as addressing God in Aramaic as Abba (Mk 14:36; also Gal
4: 6; Rom 8: 15). Like other Jewish men, he would have prayed his
prayers thrice daily. The daily prayer involved the recitation of
the *Shema* (Deut 6:4-5) twice a day, at the morning and evening
hours.

The *Shema* itself gives insight into Jesus. Jesus would have
prayed it regularly throughout his life. The Lucan and Matthean

interpretations of Jesus' ordeal in the wilderness suggest that it was a source of strength for Jesus there where his battle with the Evil One was won by his recourse to chapters six to eight from the Book of Deuteronomy, the story of the wilderness experience of his people following their exodus from Egypt. It is no accident that Jesus recited the *Shema* when asked which commandment was the great commandment of the Law. 'Hear, O Israel: The Lord is our God, the Lord alone. You shall love the Lord your God with all your heart, and with all your soul, and with all your might.' (Deut 6: 4-5)

This text which Jesus recites, which every devout Jew would have known and prayed more than any other in their lives, which manifests the heart and soul of Judaism, is the foundation stone of Jesus' own life and ministry. He knew it to be the great commandment because it was the guiding principle in his own life and prayer. As a man of prayer, one could say that Jesus was someone who loved the Lord, his God, with all his heart, all his soul, and all his strength. This perhaps better than anything else answers the question of who Jesus was.

Jesus' baptism was for him an experience of God, the first publicly available religious experience in the life of Jesus. Jesus' experience in the wilderness was another experience of the Spirit. God was with him. The desert/wilderness motif itself reveals Jesus as God's, as someone in solidarity with God, someone put to the test and coming through the test as faithful to God. This northern Moses-exodus-wilderness-prophet-servant spirituality helps us to understand Jesus more than the southern David-Jerusalem-Zion-messiah-king tradition. Jesus learned in the wilderness, if he had not learned it before, that God was king. Jesus was recognized by his disciples as a man of prayer, they asked him to teach them to pray, and he gave them a prayer that put first things first. It began: 'Abba, may your name be held holy, let your reign begin' (Lk 11:2).

Prayer sustained Jesus' awareness of his mission and who he was. It was his fidelity to God, his darling Abba. It enabled him to forgive (Lk 22:31f). He prayed before significant decisions such as choosing disciples (Lk 6: 12). In prayer he entered into union with God returning to share what he received (Lk 9: 29). One could say that he exemplified Thomas Aquinas' later understanding of the vocation of Dominic: *'contemplari et contemplata aliis tradere,'* to contemplate and to hand on the fruits of one's contemplation (*Summa Theologiae* II-II, q 188, a 6). The *'contemplari'* is as essential to the preaching mission as is the *'tradere.'* It determines whether what is handed on is 'of God' or not. Jesus did not preach himself but God, the reign of God, the gospel of God. That means that his preaching was grounded in a deeper source than his own musings or even the tradition as others may have taught it to him. It came out of his own experience of God, his personal experience of who the God of the Hebrew Scriptures was. Jesus could identify his experience in the Scriptures. He could see himself there.

The prophetic preacher was first a wholehearted mystic. His contemplation or prayer overflowed into his love of neighbour. Dominic was described as a man who spoke only with God (in prayer) and about God (in preaching). As in the life of Jesus, the *cum Deo* and *de Deo* are intrinsically interconnected and give each other life. Jesus' solidarity with God was the starting point for his authoritative and holy preaching.

JESUS' SOLIDARITY WITH THE PEOPLE

The twofold solidarity is essential to Jesus the preacher. Although the starting point for understanding Jesus, and indeed for Jesus' own self-understanding, is God, Jesus' love of God with his whole heart and soul, his surrender to God as God's servant, nevertheless equally significant in the life of Jesus is the status which he gave to a law from the book of Leviticus, chapter nineteen, verse eighteen: 'You shall not take vengeance or bear a grudge against any of your people, but you shall love your neighbour as yourself: I am the Lord.' When asked which commandment was the first, Jesus' reply according to Mark was: 'The first is, "Hear, O Israel: the Lord our God, the Lord is one; you shall love the Lord your God with all your heart, and with all your soul, and with all your mind, and with all your strength." The second is this, "You shall love your neighbour as yourself." There is no other commandment greater than these.' (Mk 12: 29-31)

Matthew's Jesus says, 'This is the great and first command-ment. And a second is like it ... On these two commandments depend the whole law and the prophets' (Mt 22: 38-40). What is radical in the teaching and preaching of Jesus is not the primacy and emphasis he gave to 'the great commandment,' but that there was a second equivalent to it. Jesus gave love of neighbour an emphasis equal to love of God. Although radical, this too simply went to the heart of the Israelite and Judean prophetic traditions where concern for the stranger, the widow and the orphan were paramount. There is no true love of God that does not include a concern for the other, the outcast, the vulnerable, the one without status in society.

Numerous texts from the prophets as well as the psalms and wisdom literature attest to this social awareness. In the New Testament it gets translated as 'Whatever you did to the least of my brothers or sisters you did it to me' (Mt 25: 40); and 'Those who do not love a brother or sister whom they have seen cannot love God whom they have not seen' (1 Jn 4:20). This all recapitu-lates Abraham's experience of hospitality to the three strangers who turned out to be a visitation from God (Gen 18). Love of God

and love of neighbour are not two but one. Solidarity with God
is solidarity with God's people and vice-versa. Jesus' experience
of God as One-Who-Is-With-Us (Imanu-El), as well as the
Isaian attestation to that awareness (Is 7: 14), as well as the
prophet's witness to a God-consciousness as being always a social
consciousness put Jesus in the mainstream of what true religion
is. Preaching is always in the end praxis and vice-versa. Jesus
preached the praxis of God for his disciples and the praxis of God
comprised loving as God loves. Even St Paul, for whom faith is
the principle of salvation and who expounds that so clearly in his
letters to the Romans and the Galatians, nevertheless realizes that
'the whole law is summed up in a single commandment, "You
shall love your neighbour as yourself"' (Gal 5: 14). Or as Jesus had
said, 'Blessed are you poor, for God is yours' (Lk 6:20). God
belongs with the people. Solidarity with God is solidarity with
God's people.

IN CONCLUSION

Jesus of Nazareth understood himself as a preacher whose
mission was to proclaim God's reign, the news that God is good
news. Jesus' preaching was not limited to a ministry of the word.
His symbolic actions, table fellowship, healings and exorcisms
said as much about God and the presence of God as did his stories
and memorable metaphors. Preaching and praxis were inextri-
cably intertwined for Jesus. Indeed praxis was preaching. Jesus
lived what he proclaimed — the nearness, the power, and the
compassion of God.

The starting point in Jesus' life was always God, the God of
Israel, the God of love, the God of the covenant, the God of the
Hebrew Scriptures, the great commandment, the holy Shema.
The starting points for his preaching then were the concerns of
God, namely people, humanity, creation, the suffering, the lowly,

the outcast. Jesus' preaching began where true knowledge of God leads us — with compassion for people. A second commandment is equivalent to the first. Preaching elucidates the lives and experiences of people by placing them in the context of their relationship to God. Their stories, their needs, their experiences are the text and the Scriptures the context — the context that helps to elucidate their texts, the narratives of peoples' lives.

What God was doing in history, God is doing today. In Jesus' preaching we find the awareness that God is present and active here and now. This is what God does. God forgives, God heals, God loves, God accompanies, God challenges. God is grace, but not cheap grace. Jesus' praxis-grounded preaching brought God to people. He gave them hope. Jesus' message called for joy, expectation, trust, faith and confidence in God. Jesus experienced God breaking into the lives of the people, the ordinary, the poor, and the sinner. Love of neighbour is the supreme manifestation of love of God. To be in solidarity with God is to be in solidarity with God's people.

Jesus, itinerant preacher of the good news that God is with us and for us, preaches as he does through the power of the Spirit. As a Spirit-filled preacher, he preaches with authority. It is the Spirit who speaks through him. He is at home with the Spirit and it is the Spirit in the long run whom he imparts through his preaching, his praxis, and his passion. Jesus longed for us to get God right, and to get us right with God. Jesus, passionate preacher of God, compassionate lover of people, knew himself as nothing other than belonging to God. The *contemplari* could not help but overflow into *tradere*. One demands the other in order to be true to itself. Jesus was both mystic and prophet. Aligned with God and with the truth about God through the power of the Spirit, Jesus was aligned with God's people from whom he received the cues as to what needed to be heard in order that they might know God's word for them at this point in their lives and history. That word was often an enfleshed word, an action, but an action that took place from within contemplation. Jesus the preacher was not contemplative in the midst of action, but active in the midst of contemplation.

PREACHERS OF GRACE, WITNESSES TO THE RESURRECTION

MARY CATHERINE HILKERT, O.P.

Gerhard Ebeling, who shared the dual vocation of theologian and preacher, once wrote that 'theology is necessary to make preaching as hard for the preacher as it has to be.' Nowhere is this more true than in our attempts to search for meaning and truth when speaking of the central conviction at the heart of Christian faith: 'If Christ is not risen, your faith is in vain' (1 Cor 15:17). All Christian preaching is, in the end, preaching of the good news of resurrection. Hence Paul's further reminder, 'if Christ has not been raised, *our preaching is void of content* and your faith is empty too' (1 Cor 15:14). The content of all preaching is the good news of the resurrection – God's final word of saving grace. To announce that word in today's world preachers need to attend to complex philosophical, psychological and scientific debates in addition to biblical and theological disputes – all of which 'make preaching as hard … as it has to be.' We need to grapple with theories of what, if anything, happened to Jesus in the Easter event; whether the resurrection was a subjective experience of the first disciples; what resurrection of the body or language of a 'spiritual body' can possibly mean; and whether there is a future for all of creation. But, in the end, the word of grace we are called to announce is the power of God at work bringing life out of death, first in the Crucified One, and through him and in the power of his Spirit, throughout the world. Preachers of the resurrection proclaim that evil will not have the final word, and death is not the end. In the words of the poet Emily Dickinson, 'this world is not conclusion.'

Christian hope was born in the life and ministry of Jesus, fundamentally called into question by his execution, and definitively sealed in the event we call resurrection. For that reason, theological reflection on the mystery of resurrection cannot be separated from the concrete life, ministry, and death of Jesus. As Jon Sobrino wrote not long after the death of his brother Jesuits and their housekeeper and her daughter in El Salvador, until we are clear about who was raised, why he was raised, and how we gain access to the risen one, the resurrection does not lead to the true Christ. Or, we might add, to authentic Christian preaching.

At the same time, we are called to preach the resurrection in the concrete context of our own time and place. For Christians in Western cultures at the beginning of the third millennium the kinds of historical questions about 'what really happened?' and whether it is credible in a postmodern scientific age to proclaim belief in 'the resurrection of the body,' are not only questions that preachers need to wrestle with, but questions of pastoral concern as well. But the most fundamental stumbling block for the Christian claim, that in the death and resurrection of Jesus the power of sin and death has been broken, is all the evidence to the contrary.

RESURRECTION OF THE CRUCIFIED ONE

It is precisely because we preach good news of resurrection in a world of suffering and injustice that liberation theologians, among others, remind us that the Resurrected One is also the One who was crucified. The claim that God raised Jesus from the dead has implications not only for how we interpret the life, ministry, and death of Jesus, but for our understanding of who God is and how God acts as well. Some theologians, such as Karl Rahner, interpret the resurrection as in fundamental continuity with the life and death of Jesus. In a theology that echoes John's gospel, Rahner views the death and resurrection of Jesus as two aspects of a single event in which Jesus hands over his life's history of freedom to God and God accepts and seals forever the totality of that offering of love.

Others, such as Edward Schillebeeckx, Jon Sobrino, and Elizabeth Johnson, read the relationship between Jesus' life and death differently. They stress that the death of Jesus of Nazareth was an execution. It was no coincidence that Jesus did not die in bed. Rather, he died as a result of capital punishment, executed by the Romans with the complicity of religious leaders from his own tradition as a consequence of the 'dangerous preaching' of his words and liberating lifestyle. His ministry of healing, his prophetic preaching and provocative parables, and his inclusive table companionship threatened the established boundaries that distinguished insiders from outsiders in both religious and political realms. He acted as if he had the authority to forgive sins, and to offer definitive interpretations of Torah. He included women and tax-collectors who collaborated with the Romans among his closest disciples. He touched lepers, spoke with Samaritans, and transgressed strict interpretations of Sabbath observance and ritual purity. He gathered friends, disciples, and enemies at a common table. But in the end the one who created feasts, proclaimed unconditional forgiveness, and announced a God of universal compassion, was betrayed by an intimate disciple, abandoned by many his closest followers, handed over to the Roman empire by religious leaders, sentenced by one who knew him to be innocent, tortured by the government soldiers, and executed as a criminal. This man whose whole life was dedicated to announcing the compassion of God was left to die while God remained silent.

The execution of Jesus as a political rebel by means of crucifixion, which was also the fate of false prophets and blasphemers, called into question the trustworthiness of his proclamation, the success of his mission, and his implicit claim to a unique relationship with Abba. From this perspective, the crucifixion is not a mutual exchange of gifts between the Father and the Son, but rather the result of human evil and injustice. For that reason, political and liberation theologians underline the scandal of the cross. Schillebeeckx, for one, has suggested that in that sense we are saved in spite of the cross of Jesus, rather than because of it.

Nevertheless, in the end Jesus faced the cross as the final consequence of fidelity to his preaching mission with a radical hope in the compassionate God he knew as Abba. He filled an experience that was in itself meaningless and absurd with meaning, love, and a sense of solidarity with all the innocent who suffer. What Christians celebrate is not the cross, nor the sufferings of Jesus, but the power of a love that is faithful even unto death. The triumph of the cross is the triumph of God's mercy bursting the bonds of sin and death – the triumph of resurrection.

Christians preach neither cross, nor resurrection, but the entire paschal mystery of the life, death and resurrection of Jesus. Throughout his ministry Jesus proclaimed and enfleshed the very mystery that the resurrection confirms definitively: death and evil do not have final victory; the power of God does. In and through Jesus' love and fidelity God has taken on the evil and suffering of this world and broken their hold once and for all with the stronger power of love. Placing the resurrection in the context of the life, ministry, and death of Jesus highlights the social and political significance of that love.

Further, the resurrection of Jesus has significance for the entire cosmos. As Rahner proclaimed in one of his Easter sermons:

[Christ] rose not to show that he was leaving the tomb of the earth once and for all, but in order to demonstrate that precisely that tomb of the dead – the body and the earth – has finally changed into the glorious, immeasurable house of the living God and of the God-filled soul of the Son. He did not go forth from the dwelling place of earth by rising from the dead. For he still possesses, of course, definitively and transfigured, his body, which is a piece of the earth, a piece which still belongs to it as a part of its reality and destiny ... His resurrection is like the first eruption of a volcano which shows that in the interior of the world God's fire is already burning, and this will bring everything to blessed ardour in his light. He has risen to show that has already begun. Already from the heart of the world into which he descended in death, the new forces of a transfigured earth are at work (Rahner, *The Great Church Year*, p. 195).

The Christian hope remains that God can and will bring life out of death, and that like Jesus, not only human persons, but all of creation, will be taken into God and transformed. But is that hope credible in a postmodern scientific and suffering world?

RESURRECTION OF THE BODY

Recently a colleague told me of an experience she had after preaching a homily during the Easter season. A woman came up to her and told her that she sounded as if she really believed in the resurrection. She said she was surprised and responded, 'I know it with every ounce of my being.' The parishioner, who seemed equally surprised, replied, 'Well all the other preachers I've heard have never been too sure about it.'

Preachers and teachers know well that what we think we are communicating is not always what is heard. I was reminded of that recently when one of the undergraduate students in a Christology course penned the following message when I asked if there were any questions: 'No matter what you say, I still think it happened.' I had begun the class by reminding the students that the resurrection of Jesus is the hinge on which Christian faith turns. The texts for the course stressed that the resurrection serves as the linchpin for the transition from the first disciples' experience of the life, ministry, and death of Jesus of Nazareth to their faith proclamation that Jesus is the Christ. I attempted to draw on Pauline metaphors of seeds, plants, and waking from sleep and comparable parables in the natural world such as the caterpillar and the butterfly to highlight the transformation that resurrected life involves. I stressed the element of surprise and unexpected disclosure in each of the appearance narratives where even Jesus' closest disciples fail to recognize him. I turned to Matthew 25 for clues to where we encounter the risen Christ in our midst today. In spite of those efforts to point to what remains beyond all imagination, I wondered if the student was hoping to hear something more like John Updike's claim in his 'Seven Stanzas at Easter':

> Make no mistake: if He rose at all
> it was as His body;
> if the cells' dissolution did not reverse, the molecules reknit,
> the amino acids rekindle,
> the Church will fall.
>
> It was not as the flowers,
> each soft spring recurrent;
> it was not as his Spirit in the mouths and fuddled eyes of the
> eleven apostles;
> it was as His flesh: ours.
>
> ...
>
> Let us not mock God with metaphor,
> analogy, sidestepping, transcendence;
> making of the event a parable, a sign painted in the faded

credulity of earlier ages ...
(Updike, *Collected Poems 1953-1993*, pp. 20-21).

The difficulty is that while poets and preachers share the Gospel writers' vocation of evoking faith with richly symbolic language, the theologian's task is to 'seek understanding,' to help to translate and interpret the classic symbols and fundamental claims of the Christian tradition in the context of one's own time and culture. Modern and postmodern scientific thinkers do indeed ask questions that the texts weren't asking - but they are our questions. We bring them with us to our assemblies of faith - at least many believers do.

The theological task of the preacher would be impossible if we, or our hearers, thought that we could grasp or explain the very mystery of God. Christian faith turns on the belief that the Creator God raised the crucified Jesus to new life in and through the power of the Spirit. If that event is what we proclaim—the definitive inauguration of the final reign of God—it should come as no surprise that so many unanswerable questions surround it and have defied the imaginations and language of Christians from the beginning. No theological attempt to explain what happened to Jesus or the first Christian witnesses to the resurrection can prove adequate to an event that is a totally unique act of God's Spirit in our history and cosmos.

Rudolf Bultmann and others have argued that it is not important, much less necessary, to probe the unanswerable question of 'what happened?' We can't get behind the Gospel testimonies to the Easter experience of the first Christians, but neither do we need to, because our faith is mediated by their witness. What the preacher should be concerned about is evoking hope. Like the nature miracles, the resurrection narratives are rich tapestries of literary and theological symbolism. Regardless of their historicity, the narratives carry the power to engender hope and to empower action on behalf of justice, peace, and the integrity of creation. As John Dominic Crossan once declared, 'Emmaus never happened. Emmaus always happens.'

The specific narrative of the Emmaus event may indeed be a Lukan theological creation, but the question of whether and how God responded to the crucifixion of Jesus – and whether God is active in the face of evil, suffering, and death today – is of crucial significance to our communities of faith. This is true especially of those facing death or grappling with grief over the loss of those they love.

Rahner has suggested that the task of the theologian is to locate the mystery, not to try to answer the unanswerable. But theology can help to clear away the stumbling blocks which come from misinterpretations of Christian faith so that a crisis of culture and language does not become identified with a genuine crisis of faith. As Paul Tillich observed in the middle of the last century, 'Many of those who reject the Word of God reject it because the way we say it is utterly meaningless to them' (Tillich, *The New Being*, p 121).

In the context of modern science and the new cosmology, what can we hope for when we proclaim 'I believe in the resurrection of the body'? As with any real mystery of faith, it is easier to say what we don't mean. We have no official Christian anthropology, but Christian hope goes beyond a Hellenistic notion that an immortal soul lives on beyond death. Neither do Christians hope for the resuscitation of a corpse, whether we are speaking of the resurrection appearances of Jesus in the gospel narratives or of our own hope to be reunited with those we love beyond death. Even contemporary believers who easily dismiss the notion of resurrection as resuscitation often find themselves wondering, 'but then, what *do* we believe?' As a student remarked at the end of the class on the resurrection: 'I'm still thinking about my father. I want to know I'm going to see him again, – and that I am going to know that he is my father.' A survey in *Time* magazine a number of years ago showed that people are far more interested in being reunited with those they loved than 'seeing God face to face.' Is that a naive hope projected from our desperate sense of loss or is it part of the promise of resurrection? And what of Updike's charge: 'if the cells' dissolution did not reverse, the molecules reknit, the amino acids rekindle, the Church will fall'? Where are we to locate the mystery?

In a scientific era when we know that matter is recycled and that we are quite literally 'made of stardust,' it has become difficult, if not impossible, to believe that life beyond death means that 'the molecules knit and the amino acids rekindle.' But does that fundamental scientific doubt mean that we mock God's transcendence or that we are pushed to an even more radical hope in the Creator God who creates from nothing?

In her award winning book, *Friends of God and Prophets: A Feminist Reading of the Communion of Saints,* Elizabeth Johnson includes this challenge in her confrontation of the darkness of death:

> The molecules that once belonged to a certain living body are recycled after that body's death, passing as nutrients into the bodies of others. Even during life the body is constantly replenishing itself, daily taking in and giving off materials and replacing its cells with a regular rhythm. What then would constitute the resurrection of a person's body, let alone all the bodies of the world? The impossibility of simultaneously existing bodies with shared molecules would seem to make the demise of literalism complete (Johnson, *Friends of God and Prophets*, p. 185).

But what then becomes the content of our hope, not only for resurrection of the body, but for a future in God for the person who has died? It is precisely here that the mystery of resurrection lies. Christian faith is bold. Our funeral liturgies proclaim, 'life is changed, not ended.' Biblical passages exhort us not to grieve 'as those who have no hope.' Paul's Letter to the Corinthians promises that what 'is sown a physical body' will be 'raised a spiritual body' (1 Cor 1:44) and offers images from nature of seeds that die to give life to plants. John's gospel reminds us that 'unless a grain of wheat dies, it remains only a grain of wheat, but if it dies, it produces much fruit' (Jn 12:24). But what of the theological mediation of this faith in an era of modern scientific awareness? What is the meaning of the Christian claim that Jesus, the first fruits of all of creation, lives at the right hand of God? What is the significance of our hope that the crucified one with his wounds, now lives in God, as a transformed human person, whole and entire, and that that same future awaits us all?

Some have argued that hope for personal immortality is a fundamental denial of mortality and specifically of the limitations of material and embodied existence. Death calls for a final abandonment not only of life as we have known it and our most profound relationships, but quite literally of our very selves. The matter of our bodies is recycled into life for other living beings, and with that goes any possibility of spiritual consciousness or personal identity. What is called for is a radical act of faith as we trust that the lives we have lived will nourish a larger community of life. Johnson refers to this as 'the recycling scenario.' Others propose that resurrection faith promises a future for all persons, and for the rest of creation, precisely in our uniqueness. Transformation involves radical change, but a change that takes place within a larger framework of continuity and identity.

For Karl Rahner, death is the moment when persons – whether consciously or not – sum up the fundamental option they have made with all the core decisions of their lives and become who they will be for all eternity. Death seals our lives as it did that of Jesus. Who we have become in our personal history is who we shall be for all eternity. In her ground-breaking work *God For Us*, Catherine LaCugna describes persons as radically relational, created to live as persons in communion with God and with every other creature. Contrary to the modern emphasis on the individual autonomous self, she proposes a relational ontology which views persons as 'being-toward-the-other'. To put on Christ in baptism is to be drawn into the communion of persons that constitutes the very life of God. From that perspective, death, rather than destroying the basis of personal existence, becomes the passage through which we share fully in the communion of persons that is the very life of the Trinity.

Johnson's own view of the 'darkness of death' is starker. With Bartholomew Collopy she wrestles with the threat of nothingness which death presents to us. In Collopy's words, 'From beginning to end, a dark model would present death as relentless and implacable, a breaking of the whole human person, an unacceptable and repugnant event, disintegration rather than achievement, a final fall into the weakness of being human' (cited by Johnson, p. 200). From that perspective, resurrection becomes not the revelation of the mystery of death, but its overthrow and defeat. Whether one holds to a view of death as paschal passage into mystery or as devastating dissolution of the basis for personal life and relationship, Christian hope rests not in our view of the human condition, but in our trust that there is a power and presence at work in the world and in human life that is the absolute saving presence of the Creator God. Our hope rests in the one who from the beginning has spoken a word of life over the void and created out of nothing. As Johnson concludes her chapter on the darkness of death, 'everything turns on the character of God.'

PREACHING RESURRECTION IN A WORLD OF CRUCIFIXION

The experience of death as the end and of the dissolution of hope was the context in which the kind of Christian faith that is best described as 'hoping against hope' was born. As we reflect on preaching the mystery of resurrection, the challenge of a scientific worldview is not the only - or even the most difficult challenge we face. In a world of radical and global suffering with terrorism and violence on the rise, what does it mean to proclaim that God has broken the bonds of sin and death in the life, death, and resurrection of Jesus? How do we announce the hope of resurrection in situations like the one that confronted a New York priest, on September 11, 2001? He wrote:

> When the planes struck the Twin Towers last year I was literally on my way into a church to preside at a funeral for a woman of 52 years of age who had committed suicide a few days before. Waiting for the funeral procession to arrive I could see the first tower burning quite clearly; it was a bright and clear day here in New York. That tragedy was bad enough and while all hell was breaking loose outside the walls of that parish church, I had to remind myself that my job right now is to name the grace of the moment ... This has been incredibly tough grace to identify, let alone to name for myself and an assembly of people gathered for prayer.

How do we preach resurrection hope in the face of tragedy and terrorism, in the face of devastated hopes and lives? Where and how is hope born?

Again, we have no answers. What we have is the testimony of

the lives of those who have gone before us in faith – both the first disciples and the courageous lives of women, men, and communities of faith through the ages who have lived and died 'hoping against hope.' In each of the gospel narratives, the disciples' experience of the risen Christ occurred in the midst of loss and the devastation of hopes. Whether we are speaking of a woman weeping beside a tomb (Jn 20), two disciples walking away from a place of pain speaking of their loss of hope (Lk 24), frightened disciples in a locked room (Jn 20), a man confronting wounds (Jn 20), or fishers putting down their nets one more time after repeated failures (Jn 21), the basic dynamic in the resurrection stories is the same: God makes a way where there is no way.

But what enables us to see that way forward and to help others to see in the dark? Both the biblical accounts and our human experience suggest that first, we must attend to the darkness and keep vigil with one another there. The gospel narratives suggest that hope begins to stir when we share our stories of pain, speak our doubts and disappointments, when we welcome a stranger to walk with us, when we reach out with whatever limited resources and hopes we have, when we gather together even in fear, when we let down the nets one more time. In the most unlikely of places and persons and times – out of nothing – the power of God opens up a future, rolls away the stone.

We cannot explain how or why the power of God breaks through in the most desperate of circumstances - we can only testify to the experience. Resurrection hope is not something we can cause, control, bring about, or explain. The Spirit of God brings life out of death, creates from nothing. That is the mystery we herald. We testify with words handed down to us, but words born of experience. Magdalene's tears helped form her passionate declaration: 'I have seen the Lord.' Peter's proclamation of redemption was shaped by his own experience of forgiveness beyond betrayal.

But according to the Gospel narratives, those very experiences of conversion and commitment were also formed by words. Amid grief and failed hopes, Mary heard her name and a commission. The women running from the tomb in Matthew encounter Jesus who proclaims a word of peace. The disciples locked in fear in the upper room are greeted with similar words of peace, blessing, and commission. In each case, a word of God – words of Jesus – open up a future that seemed impossible. Words of peace, forgiveness, commissioning, and love don't just reflect new possibilities - they create them. In the tradition of the Jewish prophets before him, Jesus spoke words of challenge and hope throughout his ministry, words that transformed lives: your sins are forgiven, your faith has saved you, come, follow me, stand up and walk.

The Emmaus narrative portrays how the words of a preacher can sustain or rekindle the hope of a community. Jesus, the preacher, first walks with the two disciples on their journey and listens to their story. He attends to their broken dreams, lost hopes, and words of anguish. But then he reframes their story in his rereading of the Scriptures. He reinterprets their understanding of God's fidelity to the promise by opening up a possibility that was beyond their imagination with the new metaphor of a suffering messiah. His resurrection reading of suffering and death opens up new possibilities for their own lives – an experience that shapes them into witnesses to the resurrection who are impelled to return to Jerusalem to tell their own story of new life.

Preachers of the resurrection – then and now – have only words of faith, testimony from our experience that the crucified one lives, that death is not the end, that no sin is unforgivable, that God's spirit can heal and empower us even in our deepest grief, that God is present and active in our lives in the most desperate of circumstances. But if our words are not to be dismissed as literally incredible, there must be traces of the Creator God's work, soundings of the Spirit, and witnesses to the risen one among us still today. We do not announce an event that happened 2000 years ago and is over. Rather, we believe that event included the pouring out of the Spirit on the disciples - then and now. In that unprecedented act of God, the Spirit who has been at work from the beginning of creation and who was the source of Jesus' own energy and power is released in a new and definitive way.

The resurrection promises that the Spirit of God is at work renewing the face of the earth in spite of our limits, and even beyond human betrayal of our kinship with the rest of creation and with the Earth itself. In the words of the poet Gerard Manley Hopkins:

> The world is charged with the grandeur of God
> It will flame out, like shining from shook foil;
> It gathers to a greatness, like the ooze of oil
> Crushed. Why do men then now not reck his rod?
> Generations have trod, have trod, have trod;
> And all is seared with trade; bleared, smeared with toil;
> And wears man's smudge and shares man's;
> smell: the soil
> Is bare now, nor can foot feel, being shod.
> And for all this, nature is never spent'
> There lives the dearest freshness deep down things
> And though the last lights off the black West went
> Oh, morning, at the brown brink eastward, springs -
> Because the Holy Ghost over the bent
> World broods with warm breast and with ah! bright wings.
> (Hopkins, 'God's Grandeur,' in *The Mentor Book of Major British Poets*, p. 349.)

But there is another aspect to the mystery of resurrection as well. The victory of God over the forces of sin and death was at the same time a commissioning of the disciples to make that good news known to the ends of the earth. The news of God's saving presence at work in our world can't be shared in words alone, no matter how poetic or prophetic. The proclamation that the crucified one has undone death, that God's justice will prevail, that the Spirit is at work sustaining life in the face of death, is the kind message that we can only tell as Jesus did - with his life, even unto death.

The Easter appearance stories are, among other things, also called narratives summoning those who have encountered the risen one to let him 'Easter in us' to paraphrase another of Hopkins' poems ('The Wreck of the Deutschland'). The Creator God's decision to act in and through creation, to undo evil and death by taking on our lot, does not end with the cross. Rather the Risen One proclaims: 'Whose sins you shall forgive, they are forgiven; whose sins you hold bound, they are held bound'; 'Do you love me? Feed my sheep'; 'Do not cling. Go and tell your brothers ... '

The concrete work of reconciliation, of feeding the hungry, of telling the good news that the crucified one lives, is the mission of the Church. To preach resurrection is to announce with confidence that the reign of God that Jesus proclaimed and embodied is meant for all, and to preach that with our lives. As Jon Sobrino reflects on what it means to proclaim resurrection hope in solidarity with those who are the victims of history,

> Putting oneself at the service of the resurrection means work-
> ing continually, often against hope, in the service of eschato-
> logical ideals: justice, peace, solidarity, the life of the weak
> community, dignity, celebration, and so on. And these partial

'resurrections' can generate hope in the final resurrection, the conviction that God did indeed perform the impossible, gave life to one crucified and will give life to all the crucified (Sobrino, *Christ the Liberator,* p. 49).

Theologians often dispute over whether our experience of the risen one is the same as that of the first disciples. But we miss the point if we focus on what kind of visual phenomenon they experienced. Matthew 25 makes it clear where we will encounter the risen one. When did we see you? ... 'For I was hungry and you gave me food. I was thirsty and you gave me drink. I was a stranger and you welcomed me, naked and you clothed me. I was ill and you comforted me, in prison and you came to visit me ... as often as you did it for one of my least brothers or sisters, you did it for me' (Mt 25:35-40). The greatest challenge in preaching the resurrection is that like the first disciples we have yet to recognize the presence of the risen one in our midst.

In the end the vocation of the preacher is to speak words of grace that help us to see and that move us to act. Preachers reinterpret the world and our human story through the lens of the gospel; they are bold enough to declare promises in the name of God and to summon us to 'step out on the promise' as the Black spiritual says. Theology is necessary to make preaching as difficult as it needs to be. But preaching - the testimony of faith - is even more necessary if hope is to be possible in a secular and suffering world. Like Magdalene, preachers are called to speak words that will be considered nonsense by many - not about amino acids, but about presence, power and possibility, about fidelity and future, about God and grace. In a real way the preacher's words share in the power of resurrection - they 'make a way where there is no way' to cite another of the Black spirituals. The word of preaching has the power to open up hope, possibility, and the future, in spite of all the evidence to the contrary. Preachers celebrate the fragments of grace already in our midst, but they also promise more. In the face of sin and death, preachers proclaim that 'all the evidence is not yet in.' God will have the final word and it will be the word spoken from the beginning and spoken anew in the resurrection of Jesus: 'let there be life.'

REFERENCES

1. Elizabeth A. Johnson, *Friends of God and Prophets: A Feminist Theological Reading of the Communion of Saints*, 1998, New York, Continuum.
2. Karl Rahner, 'Easter: A Faith that Loves the Earth,' *The Great Church Year*, 1993, New York, Crossroad, pp. 192-97.
3. Paul Tillich, 'Is There Any Word from the Lord?' in *The New Being*, 1955, New York, Charles Scribner's Sons, pp. 114-124.
4. John Updike, 'Seven Stanzas at Easter,' *Collected Poems 1953-1993*, 1993, New York, Alfred A. Knopf, pp. 20-21.

'HE TAUGHT THEM AS ONE WHO HAD AUTHORITY'
Matthew 7:29

TIMOTHY RADCLIFFE, O.P.

I learned much about and from Damian by being with him during three General Chapters: Oakland in 1989, Mexico in 1992 and Caleruega in 1995. Sadly, his premature death deprived subsequent chapters of the benefit of his immense wisdom and experience, and I would have enjoyed the company of another ex-Master! I discovered Damian's care for words, for their proper and accurate use. Words mattered, as they should for any preacher. He recognized the authority of words, first of all the words of the Word of God, but also of our words, the words of our Chapters, and the words that we preach. He remembered the words that we had voted in previous Chapters and ensured that they were borne in mind, even if only to be revised. He often reminded us of the four priorities of the Order. It is with them that he began his last *Relatio de Statu Ordinis* for the General Chapter of Mexico. This was not just because he had embraced them so fully but also because they had been solemnly voted in General Chapter and so have authority for us.

I remember, as a young Provincial at Oakland, sharing my concern with him. Do these words make any difference? Will anyone ever read them? Must we spend so many hours fighting over formulations that will soon be forgotten? He replied that these words do matter and that in his experience it takes about three General Chapters for them to filter down and penetrate the lives and the consciousness of the brethren. It was this care for words that gave Damian's own words such weight. He spoke, like Jesus, with authority and not like the scribes and the Pharisees. When he spoke we listened. When, as Master, I visited a

Province I always began by reading the letters written by Damian or his collaborators after the previous visitations. I often saw how these letters, which are such a labour to write, do eventually have an effect, of encouraging, challenging, and stimulating the brethren. Sometimes, after Damian had died and the letters that he had written appeared to have been forgotten, I discovered that they had borne fruit, even if he had never lived to know this.

As preachers the power of words is of first concern for us. Boring and ineffectual preaching has been a problem from the very beginning. Indeed Webster's Dictionary defines to preach as 'to give moral or religious advice, especially in a tiresome manner.' When I am discouraged by my own preaching I console myself by remembering that St Paul droned on at such length that Eutyches fell asleep and dropped to his death. At least so far my preaching has not killed anyone, as far as I know. Humbert of Romans talked about the preached word as sharing in God's power to raise the dead; often today it is more likely to send the living to sleep.[1] When St Caesarius of Arles preached, his sermons were so tedious that the doors had to be locked to stop the people from fleeing. John Donne, the Anglican preacher and poet, said that the Puritans preached for so long since they would not stop until the congregation had woken up again!

I believe that at this time we face more than the enduring problem of boring preaching. It is forging a discourse for the proclamation of our faith by the whole Dominican Family that is in question. Our society, which gives such value to images and symbols, is perhaps less responsive to the power of words than previous societies. We do not grow up nurtured by the poems, songs, proverbs and stories of our ancestors and communities; we

---

1. Ed. Simon Tugwell, O.P., *Early Dominicans: Selected Writings*, 1982, New York, Paulist Press, p. 201

do not seek life and vitality so much in the spoken and written word. There is a general doubt as to the possibility of attaining truth through words. Words have lost much their authority. No doubt this means that as an Order of Preachers we must find other forms of expression; we must find symbols and images with which to share our faith. We must dare to try other media: film, television, music, painting, the internet, etc. Yet surely words must always remain central to our vocation, and so we need to care for them and seek ways of renewing their power, authority and vitality. St Dominic faced such a crisis of preaching in the thirteenth century. He responded by creating a way of life that would sustain the first brethren as preachers, and sending them to the great Universities to be formed to face the questions of the time. What must we do?

In the last century theologians such as Semmelroth, Rahner and Schillebeeckx wrote much about the relationship between the proclaimed and preached word and the consecration of the body and blood of Christ.[2] They talked of the 'sacramentality of the word', since the preached word should be transformative of our hearts and minds as are the words of consecration of the bread and wine.[3] This is a beautiful theory; our concern is that it is not often so. But the drama of the Last Supper may suggest some of the ways in which our preached words can be renewed and revitalized. Our words need to be animated by the same dynamism of that event. I suggest that there are three elements of that 'happening' which should also mark our preaching.

1. Jesus reaches out to the disciples in their silence and puzzlement.

2. Cf Paul Janowiak S.J., *The Holy Preaching: The Sacramentality of the Word in the Liturgical Assembly,* 2000, Collegeville MN, The Liturgical Press.
3. I gave a talk on 'the sacramentality of the word' for an international congress of Jesuit liturgists in June 2002, which was a first attempt to grapple with the issues raised in this chapter.

2. He gathers them into communion through his words of truth.

3. He reaches out beyond this community to the fullness of the Kingdom.

How can our preaching needs to be animated by this same dynamic and so be transformative and have authority?

REACHING OUT TO EMBRACE THE SILENCE AND PUZZLEMENT OF THE DISCIPLES

In John's account of the Last Supper the disciples are portrayed as profoundly confused. They did not understand what was happening: 'Lord, do you wash my feet?' (13:6); 'Lord, we do not know where you are going; how can we know the way?' (14:5); 'Lord, show us the Father and we shall be satisfied.' (14:8). Jesus labours to help them understand. But they do not and they are reduced to silence: 'We do not know what he means' (16:18). The whole text is marked by puzzlement, misunderstanding and silence. This is where preaching begins.

For every generation the Eucharist remains a mystery beyond our words reducing us to silence. But surely in our time there is not just the silence of awe, faced with what is beyond the grasp of our words. There is an earlier and more befuddled silence, that of not having any idea of what is going. It is especially hard for those formed by modernity to get any grip with what is happening. It is an event that is more radically at odds with the presuppositions of our culture than that of our ancestors. So, like those first disciples, we are bewildered. Take the words of Jesus in Luke's account: 'This is my body which is given for you. Do this in remembrance of me.' (22:19). The presuppositions of those words run contrary to the grain of contemporary culture.

1. It is a gift. For most cultures, the exchange of gifts is a

profoundly important expression of one's belonging to a community. Our community is founded on the market place, in which every thing has a price, and is to be sold and bought. Even the most fundamental elements of creation, that have always been seen as the common possession of humanity – air, the fertility of seeds, even the very DNA of our bodies – are being claimed, patented and marketed.

2. Jesus gives his body. This is a gesture that relies upon an understanding of our corporeality that is being subverted, of the body as presence, the place of communion. For our society the body is increasingly just another object that we own and may dispose of like any other property. I came across a book on the human body published by a company that usually produces car manuals. It is called: *Man: 12,000 BC to Present Day. All Models, Shapes, Sizes and Colours. Haynes Owners Workshop Manual.*

3. Jesus asks his disciples to repeat this ritual gesture of gift. But we live in a society that has little conception of ritual.

4. It is the establishment of a new community, which challenges the profound individualism of our time.

This is not to criticize modernity, as if it were especially irreligious. In many ways it is marked by deep gospel values such as tolerance, generosity, a sense of the dignity of every human being, the rejection of all racialism and so on. I just wish to suggest why it is that Jesus' self-gift at the Last Supper may be profoundly bewildering to our contemporaries. And not just to them but to us, for we too are modern men and women. Unless we face the extent to which we share the incomprehension of our culture faced with the gospel, then we shall have no words to speak that have authority and power. 'Karl Barth said of the enormous *Yes* at the centre of Mozart's music, that it has weight and significance because it overpowers and contains a *No*.'[4] This can also be said of the Last Supper. The power of the new covenant that Jesus enacted that night lies precisely in its embrace of all that contradicts it, humanity's great *No* to God. It is a story that includes all our puzzlement and misunderstanding faced with Jesus.

The beginning of our preaching is embracing that incomprehension, sharing humanity's silence in the face of the gospel. Barbara Brown Taylor wrote: 'In each of the gospels, the Word comes forth from silence. For John, it is the silence at the beginning of creation. For Luke, it is the silence of poor old Zechariah, struck dumb by the angel Gabriel for doubting that Elizabeth would bear a child. For Matthew, it is the awkward silence between Joseph and Mary when she tells him her prenuptial news. And for Mark, it is the voice of one crying in the wilderness – the long-forgotten voice of prophecy puncturing the silence of the desert and of time.'[5] Mark, above all, is the gospel of silence, culminating in the silence of Jesus on the cross and ending originally with the silence of the women as they flee from the tomb, 'and they said nothing to anyone, for they were afraid' (16:8).

Our preaching begins in silence. We must let ourselves be silenced by the text, not knowing what it means, letting it escape our mastery and possession. It is the word that we cannot domesticate and tame. We will have nothing to say until we find that we do have nothing to say. Then we turn to God and beg for a word. Dominic wished that the Order of Preachers be a community of beggars.

The word that we are to preach may be given in a moment.

4. Seamus Heaney, *The Redress of Poetry*, 1995, New York, p. 169.
5. *When God Is Silent*, 1998, Boston, Cowley Publications, p. 73.

Einstein compared having a new idea to a chicken laying an egg: 'Cheep – and all at once there it is' ('*Keeks – auf einmal ist es da*').[6] Most of us are not like Einstein and we have to struggle to understand. The struggle is part of the preaching. The bringing to birth of the word is what we share with our hearers, often that which is most important. We are with them, modern men and women who are puzzled, labouring to understand, awaiting the gift of insight.

Annie Dillard captures well the combination of gift and hard grind that is involved in all creative writing: 'At its best, the sensation of writing is that of any unmerited grace. It is handed to you, but only if you look for it. You search, you break your heart, your back, your brain and then – and only then – it is handed to you. From the corner of your eye you can see motion. Something is moving the air and headed your way'.[7]

The words that appear effortlessly, like Einstein's chicken's egg, may seem to be too polished and finished for our hearers. The preaching is not so much the announcement of the good news as the sharing of its gift, and God usually gives through our beating our heads against the limits of our understanding. As William Hill, O.P., wrote, 'God cannot do without the stammering ways in which we strive to give utterance to that Word.'[8] Our stuttering words can speak more than well-rounded phrases because they are those of someone receiving a gift rather than sharing a possession.

Cornelius Ernst, O.P., wrote that 'budding is more illuminatingly the moment of the real than the flower or the soil out of which it grows: the genetic moment is the prime moment of the

---

6. Quoted by Annie Dillard in *Writing Life*, 1990, New York, p. 76.
7. ibid. p. 75
8. 'Preaching as a "Moment" in Theology', p. 186, in ed. Mary Catherine Hilkert, 1992, New York, Crossroad. Quoted by Janowiak *op. cit.* 187

real, the moment of truth'.[9] Our proclamation of the faith should be a budding, the coming to be of an insight, its flowering. We begin with the silence, then the struggle and then often there is granted an astonishing word. We share that astonishment. The novelist Louise Erdrich describes herself as 'a writer only, a woman constantly surprised.'[10] The preacher may share that constant surprise. The word is given. As Yann Martel writes: 'No thundering from a pulpit, no condemnation from bad churches, no peer pressure, just a book of scriptures quietly waiting to say hello, as gentle and powerful as a little girl's kiss on your cheek.'[11]

GATHERING INTO COMMUNION

In the old refectory of the Dominican Priory in Milan, there is the most reproduced picture in the world, Leonardo da Vinci's Last Supper. The disciples are in four loose groups, held together only by their common gaze on the solitary figure at the centre. The disciples did not form a united community. They were divided among themselves. When Jesus announced that one of them was to betray him, the reaction of each was for himself: 'Lord, is it I?' Jesus offers them the gift of the new covenant of his blood, but this is a community that must be created. The disciples are gathered in, freed from the solitude that surrounds each of them in this moment of crisis.

Our proclamation not only goes out to meet each person in his or her solitude and bewilderment. It gathers into communion. Preaching makes peace. One of the earliest great preaching missions of the Order in collaboration with the Franciscans was 'The Great Devotion' of 1233.[12] Most of the cities of northern

---

9. *The Theology of Grace*, 1974, Dublin, Mercier Press, p. 74
10. *The Blue Jay's Dance: A Birth Year.* 1995, London, HarperCollins, p. x
11. *The Life of Pi*, 2002, Edinburgh, Canongate, p. 208..
12. Cf. Augustine Thompson, O.P., *Revival Preachers and Politics in Thirteenth-Century Italy: The Great Devotion of 1233,* 1992, Oxford, Oxford University Press.

Italy were suffering from clashes between factions and were virtually in civil war. 'The Great Devotion' was a preaching of peace. Often the climax of the sermon was a ritual kiss of peace exchanged between enemies. As preachers, the friars were often authorized to ordain the release of prisoners, the forgiveness of debts, and even to rewrite the civil statutes. This was the power and authority of the preached word. So the branch of the Dominican Family in England which is called 'Dominican Peace Action', and which preaches against all forms of violence, expresses a fundamental and original aspect of our mission. Our Church needs such a proclamation of the faith. Especially in the West the Church is often split and polarized by divisions of left and right. Women feel excluded, and ethnic minorities marginalized. The authority of our proclamation will be evident if it bears fruit in peace. How can this happen?

Strife and polarization are usually evident in the language that we use. Our discourses are marked by ideological options through which we express our identity and our identification with a group. Every one of us is in danger of being confined by languages that are too narrow for the community that God is bringing into being: of the left or the right, patriarchal or feminist. We need to forge a language which is hospitable to aspirations and insights of others to whom we do not belong. We need to let the breadth and diversity of our Church inform and transform our words, so that ideological barriers are broken down, and the 'wall of hostility' (Eph 2:14) is demolished. The communion to which I belong must burst open the confines of my own discourse, that of a middle-aged, white, vaguely liberal Englishman. A Catholic word needs to be born. The preacher is stretched to embrace ways of thinking, believing and being that are not his or her own. The most radical example is that of St

Francis making peace between the citizens of Gubbio and the wolf. He mediates, accepting the verbal pledge of the citizens and non-verbal language of the wolf: 'the wolf knelt down and bowed its head, and by twisting its body and wagging its tail and ears it clearly showed to everyone that it would keep the pact it had promised.'[13]

Most of us are not called to such radical mediation! One of the most beautiful experiences that I ever had of the link between peace and preaching was during a meeting of the Dominican Family in Tucuman, in the north of Argentina. I had not realized that it was Malvinas Day, when the whole of Argentina commits itself to win back the Malvinas Islands – what the British call the Falklands – from the invaders. The city was filled with Argentinean flags. At first I felt rather alone. But when I arrived at the hall to meet a thousand of my brothers and sisters, there was a little Union Jack on the desk awaiting me. I concelebrated the Eucharist with the Provincial, and we prayed for all the dead, Argentinean and British. By providence I had chosen to preach that day on nonviolence. It was a moment of grace.

This is the challenge not just for the priest or deacon who preaches after the gospel at the Eucharist but for every proclamation of our faith. This is not the muting of our deepest convictions so as not to hurt 'the others'. Quite the contrary, it is the truthful preaching that is open to the reality of what others live.

This belongs to the very meaning of the offering of the bread and wine. Geoffrey Preston, O.P., wrote:

Think of the domination, exploitation and pollution of man and nature that goes with bread, all the bitterness of competition and class struggle, all the organized selfishness of tariffs

13. *St Francis of Assisi, Writings and Early Biographies: English Omnibus of the Sources for the life of St Francis*, ed. Marion A. Habig, 1972, Chicago, 1350 – 1.

and price-rings, all the wicked oddity of a world distribution
that brings plenty to some and malnutrition to others, bringing them to that symbol of poverty we call the bread line. And
wine too – fruit of the vine and work of human hands, the wine
of holidays and weddings. ...This wine is also the bottle, the
source of some of the most tragic forms of human degradation:
drunkenness, broken homes, sensuality, and debt. What Christ
bodies himself into is bread and wine like this, and he manages
to make sense of it, to humanize it. Nothing human is alien to
him. If we bring bread and wine to the Lord's Table, we are
implicating ourselves in being prepared to bring to God all
that bread and wine mean. We are implicating ourselves in
bringing to God, for him to make sense of, all which is broken
and unlovely. We are implicating ourselves in the sorrow as
well as the joy of the world.[14]

Our words gather into communion not by fudging issues,
pretending that conflicts do not exist or by a woolly generalized
benevolence. They may make a home in which all may belong
only if they tell the truth. They must say it as it is. At the Last
Supper, Jesus begins the process of gathering in the disciples into
unity by painfully telling them the truth. One of them will betray
him; they will all flee and be scattered; he will suffer and die; he
will rise again and the Holy Spirit with be sent. 'Because I have
said these things to you, sorrow has filled your hearts. Nevertheless I tell you the truth' (Jn 16:6); 'Sanctify them in the truth; thy
word is truth' (Jn 17:7). There is no communion without truth. It
is in the truth that we meet each other face to face. The new
covenant is born in this new truth telling.

If our words lack authority and power then it is because so
often we fear to tell the truth. As Mary Catherine Hilkert, O.P.,

14. *God's Way to be Man,* 1978, London, Darton, Longman and Todd, p. 84.

writes, we fear to name the grace and the dis-grace at work in our world.[15] We hesitate to bring to shared word the raw experience of those with whom we live. Our communities include young people struggling to reconcile their hormones and the teaching of the Church on sex, and perhaps failing to do so, the married and the divorced and remarried, the straight and the gay, old people facing retirement and solitude, those for whom the Church's doctrines seem incomprehensible, people filled with anger at the Church and others with what they see as the betrayal of the tradition, people facing sickness and death. Are our words touched by their experiences? Do we dare to speak aloud what they live so that they may recognize their experience in our words and so know that they belong?

Barbara Brown Taylor reports the complaint: 'I wish preachers did not lie so much'.[16] It is not so much that preachers tell blatant lies. It is rather that sometimes we fear to grapple with the complexity of human experience. If we really acknowledge the joys and the sorrows of humanity, then we will find ourselves lost for easy words. Our ecclesiastical language will appear threadbare and inadequate. We may find ourselves drawn into discussions that alarm us. We may become involved in controversy that split the community. We may open 'cans of worms' and be accused of 'rocking the boat'. And so for the sake of peace and unity, it may appear safer to keep quiet. Thus we loose that bold truthfulness of the early preaching, the *parrhesia* of the apostles (Acts 4:29; 28:31). But there is no true communion except in the truth. Damian was a truth-teller, even when it was uncomfortable.

If we test what we say against the reality of people's lives, then

15. *Naming Grace: Preaching and the Sacramental Imagination,* 1997, New York, Continuum.
16. op. cit., p. 107.

maybe our homilies will be more modest. The temptation of preachers is to make great and vague claims that must make our hearers smile to themselves. I dread the ecclesiastical indicative, such as 'Married couples, living in complete unity and perfect love, express the love of Christ'. Really? Try asking some of my friends! Our words will be more powerful if we say less. An old Eskimo woman was asked why the songs of her tribe were so short. She replied, 'Because we know so much.' [17]

REACHING OUT FOR THE KINGDOM

The Last Supper and every celebration of the Eucharist are marked by a tension that is summed up in the words of consecration of the wine: 'It will be shed for you and for all.' Every Eucharist is both the gathering of this particular community around the altar, and also points forward to the unimaginable vastness of the Kingdom in which all of humanity will find its home.

We have already looked at how our proclamation should gather into community as Jesus gathered his disciples around him and called them his friends. This requires of us that our words be hospitable to the experiences and faith of those whom we address. It asks of us truth telling. But the Last Supper is also marked by another dynamic, which is the reaching out to the Kingdom. Around the altar we are both a particular community of the disciples of the Lord, and also, as *Lumen Gentium* proclaimed, the sacrament of the unity of humanity. This is an abiding tension at the heart of the life of the Church and of our preaching of the gospel. A further reason for the contemporary crisis of preaching is the challenge of finding words that reach out to the Kingdom, to 'what no eye has seen, nor ear heard, nor the

17. Heaney, op. cit. p. 175.

human heart conceived, what God has prepared for those who love him' (1 Cor 2:9). Why is this? I will suggest two reasons.

First of all, the Church's double identity as a particular community and also a sign of the Kingdom requires of her occasional vast sea changes in her self-understanding. This is when the community of Church has to be prised open so as to welcome in strangers with other cultures and traditions. This is part of the pilgrimage of the Church. Each time this happens, then we must go through a little death and resurrection. In doing so, then we point beyond ourselves towards that Kingdom whose inclusion is beyond the reach of our words. We are living through such a moment now. The most dramatic such transformation lay between the Last Supper and our accounts of it in the gospels, the welcoming of the Gentiles. It is almost impossible for us to imagine what a profound experience of crucifixion and resurrection that was for the early Church. It required a reforging of the Church's theological language and self-understanding. If it had refused this dying and rising, then the Church would have become just a little Jewish sect, pointing towards nothing other than itself.

Another such moment was the arrival of Europeans in the Americas, bringing their faith and culture. This asked of the Church a radical transformation, and another welcoming of the stranger. It was the beginning of another small death and resurrection. It is a crisis that is dramatically captured by the words of Antonio de Montesinos on that First Sunday of Advent in 1511, when he rebuked the Spaniards of Hispaniola for their treatment of the indigenous people. 'Are they not human? Do they not have rational souls? With what right do you make war upon them? Are you not obliged to love them as yourselves?' The community that was gathered around the altar had to die to its established identity, be opened up beyond itself; otherwise, it would cease to be a sacrament of the vastness of the Kingdom and just become a sign of European culture.

It is debatable whether the global village in which we now live is just the culmination of a process that began in the sixteenth century or something new. It is not important. The Church is faced with the massive challenge of becoming for the first time in her history a truly multicultural community, a communion of cultures. In the Dominican General Council, which at the end of my term as Master had fourteen members of fourteen nationalities from five continents, we could just begin to glimpse what challenges lie ahead. How often we discovered the hidden agenda concealed in a theological language and self-understanding inherited from Europe! What languages are needed for us to express our unity and diversity? To what dying and rising does the Lord now call us? How are we to find new words for this Church that is coming to be and for its faith?

This brings me to the second reason why proclaiming the gospel faces such a radical challenge today. We have already seen how the gathering into the community requires a grappling with the complexity of human experience. We must dare to tell the truth, and this we often fear to do in the Church. But reaching out to the unimaginable plenitude of the Kingdom confronts us with another challenge for we seek to speak of what is beyond the grasp of our language.

Truthfulness demands of the preacher here not boldness but humility. The mystery defeats our words. Herbert McCabe, O.P., wrote:

> Our language does not encompass but simply strains towards the mystery that we encounter in Christ.... The theologian uses a word by stretching it to breaking point, and it is precisely

as it breaks that the communication, if any, is achieved. [18]

Stretching language to breaking point is a poetic task. It is poetry that renews our language by pushing it beyond what can be said easily and literally. This is beautifully described by Seamus Heaney who writes of 'its function as an agent of possible transformation, of evolution towards that more radiant and generous life which the imagination desires'.[19] He describes a poem by Dylan Thomas as giving 'the sensation of language on the move towards a destination in knowledge'.[20] We can preach the Kingdom in language that is on the move towards a destination in knowledge, as we stretch our minds and words towards a fullness that cannot be captured. Heaney even describes this poetic function in a way that is highly evocative of the Eucharist itself: 'We go to poetry, we go to literature in general, to be forwarded within ourselves. The best it can do is to give us an experience that is like foreknowledge of certain things which we already seem to be remembering. What is at work in this most original and illuminating poetry is the mind's capacity to conceive a new plane of regard for itself, a new scope for its own activity.'[21] This foreknowledge, which is also a remembering, suggests the dynamic of the Eucharist which is both a remembrance – 'Do this in memory of me' – and also a promise of an unsayable future.

So our preaching of the Kingdom requires the renewal of our language by poets and artists. Not every preacher is a poet but we need language that is kept alive, electric, tense and vibrant by poets. And this is a profound reason for the crisis of preaching

18. *God Matters*, 1987, London, Geoffrey Chapman, p. 177.
19. *The Redress of Poetry*, 1995, London, Faber and Faber, p. 113f
20. ibid. p. 141.
21. ibid. p. 159.

today. The poetic imagination is marginal within our dominant scientific culture which tends towards a deadening literalism, a 'dry yeastless factuality'. [22] In most traditional societies, poetry, myth, song and music have been central to the culture. In our society these have often been reduced to mere entertainment. The hunger for the transcendent is still there in the human heart. As St Augustine said, it is restless until it rests in God. But in our society it is harder for the preacher to evoke that ultimate human destiny which transcends our words. If the preaching of the word of God is to flourish, then we need poets and artists, singers and musicians who keep alive that intuition of our ultimate destiny. The Church needs these singers of the transcendent to nurture her life and her preaching.

CONCLUSION

In this volume we honour the memory of Damian. One way we may do this is by recalling that he was a man who spoke with authority. He respected words and believed in their power. The renewal of our preaching requires that we find words that have authority, that are powerful and transformative. So often ecclesiastical words are lukewarm, ineffectual and touch no one's heart or mind. There is a crisis of preaching. Such crises occur from time to time in the history of the Church. It was one such that led to the foundation of the Order, and the renewal of the Order requires us to face another.

I have suggested that to understand the nature of this crisis it is helpful to look at the Last Supper and its dynamic. It is not only the central act at the heart of our Christian life. It is also the primary example of a word that transforms, a sacramental word that makes the bread and wine become the body and blood of our

22. Yann Martel, op. cit, p. 64

Lord. The dynamism of that event can help us to see how to renew our preaching so that it may live from the same dynamism. There are at least three moments in that drama which our preaching must echo. Each offers us a different challenge.

The disciples are bewildered by what Jesus is doing at the Last Supper. They do not understand. Preaching begins in joining them in that puzzlement and silence and there labouring to forge a word that makes sense. We face a particular challenge in doing this because in some ways modernity, which forms us all, is at odds with many of the presuppositions of Jesus' bold, creative self-gift in the Eucharist. But if we are to preach a strong word, then we must dare to face that incomprehension. We must face the doubts of our contemporaries and perhaps own them as our own. We must be reduced to silence, and then struggle to bring a new word to birth.

The second moment in this drama is the gathering into communion. Jesus makes of these scattered and fearful people a new community that will survive even their flight. I suggest that this unity requires that we speak truthfully. It is only in the truth that we may meet each other. Here we face another challenge, which is that in the Church we are often too fearful of grappling with the complexity of human experience. We need to give each other courage to be faithful to our motto, *Veritas*. And in a Church that is so often split by party and ideology, I suspect that this is not the thundering proclamation of slogans, the denunciation of the 'others', but the courage to move beyond party politics. We need to speak a truth that is hospitable to others and their concerns.

Finally, Jesus does not only gather in the disciples into community. He also disperses them. He reaches out for the unimaginable inclusion of the Kingdom. We need poets and artists who can help us as we struggle to speak of that which is beyond the grasp of our words. We need to be liberated from the scientific literalism that so often suffocates our attempts to speak of the transcendent.

None of us can face all these challenges alone. Some are better at entering the silence and incomprehension of our culture faced with the gospel. Others are able to speak boldly and truthfully about what we live. Others have the gift of a poetic preaching. Not every proclamation will bear the marks of all these three moments in the Eucharistic drama, but they should be present in the shared preaching of the whole Church. And this is why no one individual can achieve the renewal of our preaching but it is the task of the whole Dominican family.

Two final remarks: There is a rhythm to these three moments, like the tempo of breathing. We reach out to people, gather them in and then reach out to the Kingdom, like lungs that are emptied, filled and then emptied again. Humanity's history is like breathing. The vital moments of our history are always moments of humanity's lungs. God breathes into the lungs of Adam at the beginning, then Christ breathes out his last breath at the climax of salvation, and then the Holy Spirit is breathed upon us at Pentecost. Our preaching will be powerful if it lives by the rhythm of this breathing, humanity's own breathing giving oxygen to our blood, and God's deep breathing within us. Clement of Alexandria wrote, 'Breathing together is properly said of the Church. For the sacrifice of the Church is the word breathing as incense from holy souls, the sacrifice and the whole mind being at the same time unveiled in God'.[23]

Notice, finally, that this dramatic event of the Last Supper moves us from the silence of incomprehension to the silence of the

23. *Stromata* VII. 6, *Ante-Nicene Fathers* 2:526f quoted by Janowiak op. cit. p. 15

mystery, from an empty silence to a plenary silence. We go from the silence of the disciples who understand nothing, to the silence of those who cannot find words for what they have glimpsed. The preacher lives within that space, begging for words. It is the gift of God's grace, what the early Dominicans called the *gratia praedicationis*, that propels us from that silence of poverty to that silence that is full.

PART 3

The Homiletic Dynamic

THE RECEPTION OF PREACHING: AN INSTANCE IN HISTORY

ROLANDO V. DE LA ROSA, O.P.

At the end of his term as Master of the Order, Damian Byrne gave the brethren an interesting insight on preaching. At the 1992 General Chapter in Mexico, he wrote: 'I asked a brother who is a producer on a national TV network which of the students he would select for training in his field. He replied: "Any one of them, as long as he is a good theologian. Anyone can learn the necessary techniques, but a religious who is not a good theologian has nothing to say." ' [1]

For Damian Byrne, content is of utmost importance in the act of preaching. He then proposed to the brethren a model for preaching as he recalled the pioneering work of the evangelizers of the New World. He wrote:

> The story of the first missionaries in the New World under-lines the need for scholarship, a collective approach, expert help, and witness. These four lessons can be taken from the consequences of the Advent sermon of Antonio Montesino in 1511. [2]

Byrne's allusion to Montesino was not arbitrary. The year 1992 marked the five hundredth anniversary of the discovery of America. Antonio Montesino [3] figured prominently in its history

---

1. Damian Byrne, O.P., *'Relatio de Statu Ordinis'* in *Acta Capituli Generalis Electivi Ordinis Fratrum Praedicatorum,* (1992, Rome, Curia Generalitia), p. 189. Henceforth, *Relatio.*
2. Ibid.
3. Antonio Montesino, O.P. (1486-1530) was already in the Island of Española together with another Dominican, Pedro de Cordoba, even before the formal evangelization of Latin America began. There, he took up the cause of the natives by preaching against slavery. His advent sermon was called *el primer grito* against the abuses of the Spanish colonizers. Recalled to Spain several times, he pleaded before the Spanish parliament for the just treatment of the natives.

of evangelization while Mexico served as the focal point of all missionary activities in the region. Byrne thought that Montesino was an excellent model of Dominican preaching because his sermon was derived from prayer and assiduous study, nurtured in community, enriched by the insights and discoveries of other experts, and reinforced or empowered by the witness of his life and his community. In the words of Byrne:

> He was respected as a theologian and his words had an impact. When the Councillors of the King wanted to refute him we are told that they brought twenty times more Masters in Theology to the meeting in Burgos than the Dominicans could assemble. We must learn from them and not let rhetoric overcome serious analysis if we are to be truly evangelizers.

The brothers acted as a group. When complaints were made to the Superior, Pedro de Cordoba, about Montesino's sermon, he replied that the community had preached the sermon. One of our historians once told me that he believed the community restrained Montesino somewhat by approaching the matter as a group. There is added lesson here, too!

They sought outside help. They realized that they did not have all the answers and had recourse to their Professors in Salamanca. Francisco de Vitoria's studies on the controversy led him to formulate the world's first Charter of Human Rights.[4] There will be many occasions when we will need expert help, not only from our scholars but from other experts

4. Francisco de Vitoria, O.P. (1483-1546) was a professor of Theology at Salamanca from 1526-1544. Like the famous *Apostle to the Indios,* Bartolome de las Casas (1474-1566), he wrote extensively on the humane treatment of natives in conquered territories. He also wrote treatises on international law as well as on the obligation of the non-Christians to embrace the Catholic faith. He argued that the Christian faith must be preached diligently and zealously to the natives with proper demonstration, reasonable arguments, and the witness of an upright life, in order to bind the natives to receive it under pain of mortal sin.

in economics and the social sciences.

They gave special importance to poverty in their lives. This allowed them the freedom to preach without fear of the consequences. They sought by their voluntary suffering to join themselves to the Passion of Christ and the suffering of the Indian people. They gave a living witness to those who thought only of finding more and more silver and gold. [5]

But lest we forget, the Advent sermon of Montesino alluded to by Byrne was directed not to the indigenous people of Latin America, but to his fellow Spaniards. He might have been quite effective in re-evangelizing his fellow Spaniards, but how did he fare in his preaching ministry to the natives? How was his preaching and that of the other missionaries in Latin America received by the natives whom they hoped to evangelize?

In his other communications to the Order, Byrne showed his sensitivity to the importance of reception in the task of preaching. The 1990 commemorative card issued by the Dominican Province of the Philippines in celebration of its nineteenth anniversary contains a passage taken from a letter of the Master. It goes:

> Our preaching must spring from an attentiveness to the needs and experiences of those whom we address ... This imposes on us the obligation of listening, an alertness to the movements which are taking place in our society. [6]

Though he did not explicitly mention the element of reception as one of his criteria for considering Montesino as a model preacher, he was certainly aware that it shapes not only the way preachers preach but more so, the content of preaching.

---

5. *Relatio*, pp. 189-190.
6. Damian Byrne, 'We are Preachers' in *Nineteenth Anniversary Commemorative Card*, (1990, Quezon City, Dominican Province of the Philippines).

I. THE RECEPTION OF PREACHING

Today, preachers can no longer just rely on scholarship, however sound and extensive it may be, nor on their eloquence and quality of witnessing. Neither can the effectiveness of the preacher be gauged solely in terms of the authenticity of sources used, the relevance of the message and the medium, nor by the extent of preparation. Ample literature has been written about the crucial part the audience plays, not only in the actual event of preaching but also in its composition.

In a way, both the preacher and the listener are actively constructing a meaning: the preacher, in the preparation and delivery of the homily; the listener, in the attempt to understand what was heard. To one familiar with scholastic philosophy and theology, this is but a re-affirmation of the axiom: *quidquid recipitur ad modum recipientis recipitur.*

Preaching involves a participative *making.* The preacher is, first of all, a receiver. The act of composing a homily or a sermon is itself a reception that proceeds out of the horizon of questions from which the preacher intends to communicate meaningful answers. Horizons of questions vary from person to person and from culture to culture, so the preacher's original reception of God's word may not coincide with the listener's own reception of it. The listener, to whom preaching is directed, concretizes in a particular context what was only presented by the preacher in a general way. What was merely virtual in the homily becomes actual or concrete by the listener's appropriation of it.

The act of preaching becomes a dialogic point where the preacher's own reception of revelation is brought to expression, while the listener's reception of the homily is brought to bear on the listener's particular situation. This dialogical nature of the homily itself invites future interpretation and application of the homily not foreseen or anticipated by the preacher. Indeed, preaching as a hermeneutical *event* leads to the *advent* of unforeseen and unexpected meanings.

The retrieval of reception as a significant theological category gave impetus to a gradual evolution of the way it is understood: from mere passive acceptance to creative transformation of what is received. Indeed, reception shapes, not only the way a preacher transmits the message, but also the *content* of preaching.

I(a). A Background Theory: Yves Congar's Idea of Reception

Yves Congar's idea of reception[7] can serve as our background theory for highlighting its importance in the task of preaching. Although his seminal study of reception was done within the context of the transmission and preservation of Christian tradition, his insights and conclusions could apply *mutatis mutandis* to preaching. Congar's description of tradition as 'not merely a transmission followed by a passive, mechanical reception but entails the making present in a human consciousness of a saving truth'[8] aptly describes the preaching event as well.

Congar developed his idea of reception as a way of extending the previously very narrow understanding of it. He demonstrated the pervasiveness of the reception phenomenon within ecclesial life in general. He set our to present this category not in the limited sense of reception of doctrine as taught by a conciliar body, but as an ecclesiological reality.[9] First, he rejects any approach that would restrict reception to a process of submitting

---

7. Cf. Yves Congar, O.P., *Tradition and Traditions*, trans. Michael Naseby and Thomas Rainborough (1966, London, Burns & Oates Ltd. and Macmillan Co.). Henceforth, *Traditions*.
8. Ibid., p. 253.
9. Cf. Yves Congar, O.P., 'Reception as an Ecclesiological Reality' in *Concilium*, Vol. 77 (1977) 43-68. Henceforth *Reception*. This a shortened version of 'La Réception comme réalité ecclésiologique' published in *Revue des sciences philosophiques et theologiques*, Vol 56 (1972) 369-403. Henceforth *La Réception*.

one's will to authority's legitimate precepts. Reception is not mere acceptance or obedience. He then searched for the areas of Church life where reception plays a role, namely: the councils, the formation of the canon, the exchange of synodal letters, the liturgical life of the Church, and Church discipline. After examining all these, he wrote:

> History offers an enormous array of actual *receptions,* and theories of reception within the Church. [10]

For Congar, the degree of importance enjoyed by the category of reception depends on the ecclesiology operative in the Church. He observed that during the first millennium, the prevailing idea of the Church was that of *communion*, with the Holy Spirit binding all the faithful together in unity, and who resides in all churches as guide and guarantor of truth and fidelity to tradition. In this context, not only the preacher, but also the listener (whether as individual or as local community) played a major role towards the transmission of Christian faith, and establishing consensus and unanimity in the Church.

In an ecclesiological model pervaded by communion, the transmission of the Christian faith occurs in a dialogical way. Congar compared this to human conversation:

> Every word or communication from one being to another needs to be received. A word is intended to make some impression; for the person to whom it is addressed it is a call, a challenge or stimulus, and it creates, virtually, an interpersonal relationship. [11]

Furthermore, this conversation takes place in human history. Human beings live *in history;* human beings *have a history.*

---

10. *La Réception*, p. 370.
11. *Traditions*, p. 253.

Human beings not only live in a particular point of time, but move through time. They search to integrate into a meaningful whole their past and present, leading into a meaningful future. In Congar's words:

> Saving faith is received by minds which ... must "receive" faith in an active way, in a manner which befits their nature. They are human minds, discursive intellects which perceive successively and only partially; hence also, minds fulfilling themselves only when in contact with other minds; lastly, minds living in a cosmic biological and temporal continuum. Historicity is an essential character of the human mind. [12]

Congar nostalgically looked back to the time when the original deposit of faith, carried through time in the memory of the Church, found continual rejuvenation not only in its transmission, but in the various modes of its reception. His thought echoed that of St Ireneaus' who wrote:

> The preaching of the Church presents in every respect an unshakeable stability, remains identical to itself and benefits, as we have shown, from the witness of the prophets, apostles, and all their disciples, a witness which embraces 'the beginning, the middle, and the end', in brief, the totality of the 'economy' of God and his operation infallibly ordained for the salvation of man and establishing our faith. From then on, this faith, which we have received from the Church, we preserve it with care, for unceasingly, through the action of the Spirit of God, such a deposit of great price enclosed in an excellent vessel, rejuvenates and causes a rejuvenation of the very vessel which contains it. [13]

12. Ibid, p. 256.
13. Quoted in J.M.R. Tillard, *Church of Churches. The Ecclesiology of Communion*, 1991, Collegeville MN, The Litrugical Press, p. 144.

Preaching bears the evident mark of *catholicity,* i.e., it makes the saving Word of God understandable and appropriable in diverse times and places. But such *catholicity* belongs primarily to the nature of the Word, for the same Word demands that it be expressed not only in a single tradition but also in several traditions so that it can be the message of salvation for all.[14]

In summary, Congar's idea of reception demonstrated how, during the first millennium of the Church, reception was a dynamic of the inner life of a church, the transmission of doctrine, as well as a dynamic of oral or written communication between persons and communities. To be initiated as a Christian is to be received in a communion. Reception helped maintain not only the continuity of the past to the present, but also its catholicity, by permitting it to expand in a new context.

In the second millennium, an ecclesiology gradually developed which became more and more hierarchical, and the notion of the Church as a communion as well as the idea of reception receded into the background. Congar wrote:

> The notion of reception –but not its whole reality, since life is resistant to theories – is excluded (or even expressly rejected) when for all the foregoing [interrelated theologies] there is substituted a wholly pyramidal conception of the Church as a mass totally determined by its summit, in which ... there is hardly any mention of the Holy Spirit other than as the guarantor of an infallibility of hierarchical courts ... [15]

Along with the shift from communion to hierarchy, was a parallel shift in the understanding of tradition, its transmission and preservation. For the early Church, authority resided in the demonstration of fidelity to the original apostolic tradition. The

14. Ibid., p. 141.
15. *Reception*, p. 60.

whole Church was understood to possess the grace and mission to exercise that authority. In the second millennium the emphasis was placed more and more on fidelity to WHO IS transmitting rather than on fidelity to WHAT is being transmitted. Consequently, 'there occurred a transition from a primacy of truthful content which it was the grace and mission of the whole Church to protect, to the primacy of authority.'[16]

A shift from discernment to obedience was consequent to this transition. For Congar, this was unfortunate because it further diminished the role of reception in the development and transmission of doctrine:

> If an authority relative to the content of truth as such is attributed to the ministry, one argues upon the juridical level, and the only permissible connection is one of obedience. If the content of truth and of good is taken into account, the faithful, and, better, the ecclesia may be allowed a certain activity of discernment and reception.[17]

This shift became even more pronounced when the Church was confronted with the crises of discipline and orthodoxy occasioned by the Protestant movements and the expansionist tendencies in the West. The obsession for orthodoxy elevated the philosophico-theological articulation of doctrine to a surrogate of religion itself. Christianity was viewed as a super religion that was all of a piece, absolutely coherent, did not contradict itself, left no loose ends, and could always cope with unexpected twists and turns. Many Church leaders and preachers substituted for Christian faith the *logical scheme* with which they, compelled by methodological and cultural stipulation, sought to define it.

It can also be added that the role of reception receded into the

16. *Reception*, p. 61.
17. Ibid.

background when culture was viewed in a classicist perspective. Western culture was regarded as the superior culture that transcended and, at the same time, must purify all other cultures. Preaching was thus a sort of a reducing agent, or a means to level off with other cultural expressions of faith, or at worst, a tool for the imperialism of a single interpretation of the Word that anathematized *ab initio* all other interpretations.

With this background theory on the study of reception in preaching, we now examine one historical instance of reception, an instance triggered by Byrne's allusion to the Latin American preachers, notably Montesino, in his *Relatio*.

II. PREACHING TO THE NATIVES: THE PLATICAS

We have no compilation of the sermons of Montesino but the *Platicas* compiled by Fray Bernardino de Sahagún, discovered and published in 1924, are representative of the style and content of preaching used by missionaries in the sixteenth century and onwards. These sermons were used for pre-baptismal instruction and other liturgical celebrations. Originally in Spanish, these sermons were collected by Sahagún and translated into *Nahuatl,* the native language of the Aztecs, at his direction.[18]

The *Platicas* were to have filled two books. Sahagún wrote that the first book was composed of thirty chapters containing ser-

---

18. The *Platicas* are discussed in R. Ricard, *The Spiritual Conquest of Mexico*, (1966), California, University of California Press), pp. 85-88; pp. 286-88. Henceforth, *Ricard*. He writes that since the missionaries methodically pooled their resources and procedures in the work of evangelization, theologians of the Franciscans, Augustinians, and Dominicans periodically met to assure uniformity in preaching and catechesis. Bernardino de Sahagún (1512-1590) was among the pioneer Franciscan missionaries. He came to Mexico in 1529 and devoted himself mainly to the most methodical and detailed ethnographic study of the natives. Most of his works were lost. A glimpse of his labours can be found in B. de Sahagún, *Historia general de las cosas de Nueva España*. The fourth edition of this work was published in Mexico in 1979.

mons and discourses which were delivered up to the moment when the natives 'very insistently demanded baptism'.[19] The second book contained a catechism of Christian doctrine.

As an aside, there had been many collections of sermons (*sermonarios*) and catechisms (*doctrinas*) published by the missionaries but these were not for distribution to the natives. The high cost of printing and the use of fragile rice paper ruled out the feasibility of instruction by means of written materials. The transmission of doctrine, therefore, was mainly oral (*through preaching and teaching*), and the catechisms were printed for the Spanish missionaries who needed uniform translations of complex doctrinal concepts that theologians had taken centuries to define.

The *Platicas* are extremely interesting. These showed the apologetic schemes and rhetorical structures common in Spain in those times. These sermons were often developed in a threefold movement corresponding to the Ciceronian requirements of the orator – *ut probet, ut delected, ut flectat*.[20] Accordingly the sermons aimed first, to arrest attention by the appeal to novelty, erudition, or intellectual superiority; second, to delight both senses and intellect with imaginative illustrations, lucid arguments, and suavity of diction; and third, to engage the emotions of the congregation in order to move them to embrace the doctrine or way of life that was preached. The words were carefully chosen, not only for rhetorical effect but also in compliance to Francisco de Vitoria's injunction that the Christian message had to be preached in a way that the hearers are placed under the moral obligation to accept it.

Their first sermon, addressed to the Lords of Mexico began

19. Ricard, p. 286.
20. For a typology of sermons during this time, see Hilary Dansey Smith, *Preaching in the Spanish Golden Age*, 1978, Oxford, Oxford University Press.

with an introduction of who they were, an indication of what Congar referred to earlier as an ecclesiology focused on hierarchy and authority.

> Fear not, we are men as you are. We are only messengers sent to you by a great Lord called the Holy Father (the Pope), who is the spiritual head of the world, and who is filled with pain and sadness by the state of your souls. These are the souls he has charged us to search out and save. [21]

'Salvation of souls' was the over-riding interest of the sermons. This reflected the missionary principle *extra ecclesiam nulla salus*[22] prevailing at the time. The discovery of the New World shattered the medieval assumption that the world as they knew it was co-extensive with Christianity. The theologians faced the problem of reconciling God's univeral salvific will with the immense number of people in newly-discovered lands, who, without their fault, could not have an explicit desire to be saved and to belong to the Catholic Church. Preaching and baptism were thus seen as the most potent instruments to bring those *extra ecclesiam* within the Catholic fold.

The current of spirituality sweeping Europe during the age of colonization added a sense of urgency to the task of converting non-Christians. Missionaries were influence by the twelfth cen-

21. Ricard, p. 86.
22. 'Outside the Church there is no salvation' was formulated by St. Cyprian in his *De Lapsis* addressed to Christians who have lapsed to heresy. This formula was found in the profession of faith imposed on the Waldensians by Innocent III but its clearest statement was in the bull *Unam Sanctam* of Boniface VIII. Although this formula was later applied to non-Christians Vatican I clarified this by declaring: 'For someone to obtain eternal salvation, it is not always required that he is in fact incorporated into the Church as a member, but he is required to be united to it by desire.' (Denz. 3870). Today, this axiom is understood as a way of expressing the ecclesiological principle that the Church is the sacrament of salvation. Cf. Karl Rahner (ed.) *Encyclopedia of Theology. A Concise Sacramentum Mundi.* (1977, London, Burns and Oates) pp. 230-231.

tury millenniarist thinker, Gioacchino de Fiore [23] who dreamt of
a forthcoming Golden Age, the historical realization of the
messianic reign of God. Since the end of the world was believed
to be imminent, it was necessary to act in a hurry and baptize as
many people as possible, to guarantee their eternal salvation. The
fact that the Gospel had reached the ends of the earth was itself
considered a sign of the imminent *parousia*. Spain was the new
Israel, and it was God who sent the missionaries to pagan lands.
The time of fulfillment had finally come.

So, in their sermons, the missionaries took pains to explain
why the natives must immediately convert to Christianity and
why they must belong to a Church headed by the Pope to whom
kings and emperors pledge obedience. The Pope was described
as the source of the missionaries' power to receive into his Church
those who desire to belong to it and are ready to renounce the cult
of the false gods. They then pictured in vivid color the stark
difference between the Christian God and the gods of the Aztecs,
unwittingly reducing the latter into demons:

> You have a god, you say, whose worship has been taught to you
> by your ancestors and your kings. Not so! You have a multi-
> tude of gods, each with his function. And you yourselves
> recognize that they deceive you … what they demand of you
> in sacrifice is your blood, your heart. Their images are loath-
> some. On the other hand, the true and universal God, our Lord
> and Creator and Dispenser of being and life, as we have been
> telling you in our sermons, has a character different from that
> of your gods. He does not deceive; he lies not, He hates no one,
> despises no one; there is nothing evil in Him. He regards all

23. For more information about this visionary, see F.E. Manuel and F.P. Manuel,
Utopian Thoughts in the Western World, (1979, Cambridge, The Belknap Press of
Harvard University Press) pp. 56-58.

wickedness with the greatest horror, forbids and interdicts it, for he is perfectly good. He is the deep well of all good things. He is the essence of love, compassion, and mercy. And He showed His infinite mercy when he made Himself Man here on earth like us; humble and poor, like us. He died for us and spilled his precious blood to redeem us and free us from the power of evil spirits. This true God is called Jesus Christ, true God and true man, dispenser of being and life, redeemer and savior of the world. Being God, he has no beginning; He is eternal. He created heaven and earth and hell. He created us, all the men in the world and he also created the devils whom you hold to be gods, and whom you call gods. This true God is everywhere. He sees all, knows all. He is altogether admirable. As man, He is in the His royal palace, and here below on earth he has his Kingdom, which He began with the beginning of the world. He would have you enter it now, and for this you should consider yourselves blessed. [24]

The *Platicas* also dealt with the creation of the angels, the revolt of Lucifer, the part played by the devils and the good angels, the creation of the world and human beings. The last page contained the titles of the missing pages that supposedly discussed the following: original sin, the death of Abel, the confusion of tongues, the Church, and divine justice.

The vehemently apologetic style of the *Platicas* followed a missionary strategy that characterized the evangelization of Latin America: the *tabula rasa* approach.[25] The missionaries generally saw in the native religions nothing that was worth salvaging. This is understandable if we consider the fact that the missionaries came from a nation that has always been extremely

24. Ricard, p. 86.
25. Ricard, p. 286.

hostile to heterodoxy and in which the Inquisition had gone farther than elsewhere. King Philip II, who came to the throne at the onset of the spiritual conquest of Latin America, thought of himself as the champion of the true faith in the world.[26]

Also, the Christianization of Latin America coincided with the Counter Reformation. It is easy to see why the phobia for heresy that raged in Spain was exaggerated in Latin America among the missionaries who saw first hand the non-Christian civilization. So far from considering native practices and rituals similar to Christian practices as heavy with hope and promise, the missionaries regarded these as demoniacal parodies from which they recoiled in horror. They avoided any accommodation, in ritual or dogma, and stubbornly prohibited practices and beliefs that are perceived as pagan in nature. They also caused the disappearance of a great number of native monuments, sacred places, and antiquities. The first Bishop of Mexico, Juan de Zumarraga wrote on June 12, 1531 that he had destroyed more than five hundred temples and twenty thousand idols.[27] Similar claims were made by other ecclesiastics and religious.

The missionaries insisted on presenting Christianity, not as perfecting or fulfilling the native religions, but as something entirely new, which meant an absolute and complete rupture with the whole past. The *tabula rasa* approach aimed precisely at achieving this.

It is interesting to know that one of the ways by which the missionaries applied this strategy was through what is now known as *evangelization by children*.[28]

26. For ample discussion on the role of the Spanish monarchs in the task of evangeli-zation, see W. E. Shiels, SJ, *King and Church,* (1961, Chicago, Loyola University Press).
27. Ricard, p. 37-38.
28. Ricard, 286. See also R. Trexler, 'From the Mouth of Babes: Christianization by Children in the 16th Century New Spain' in *Church and Community 1200-1600:*

II(a) The 'Preaching Children' Phenomenon

From the very start, the missionaries devoted themselves to the formation of native children not only because these represented the temporal and spiritual future of Latin America, but also because they saw in these youths their surest and most active auxiliaries in the task of spreading God's word.[29]

Many missionaries did not hesitate to attribute to these native children the greater part of the merit in the Christianization of Mexico. Without these child preachers, the religious admitted they would have been as helpless as molting falcons. Mendieta went so far as to entitle one of his chapters 'How the Conversion of the Indians was Done through the Preaching of Children'.[30]

The missionaries wrote that some of these children even taught the catechism to adults[31] and they revealed to the religious the secret superstitions of their relatives.[32] They also acted as interpreters when the need arose, repeating the missionaries sermons 'with the most profound convictions and persuasive warmth'[33]. In 1531 the Audiencia of Mexico acknowledged the use of child preachers and this practice received in 1558 the implicit approval of the Viceroy Luis de Velasco.[34]

But how were these children formed to become preachers and catechists? Their training itself mirrored the *tabula rasa approach*. First of all, they were interned in the convents for many

---

Studies in the History of Florence and New Spain, Storia e Letteratura, Vol. 168 (1987): 549-573. Henceforth, *Trexler*. Trexler traced this phenomenon to the radical juvenile experiment in Florence by Savonarola from 1496-1498.

29. Ricard, p. 224.

30. G. Mendieta, *Historia ecclesiatica Indiana,* (1971, Mexico), 222. Quoted in *Trexler*, p. 557.

31. Ricard, p. 99.

32. Ibid.

33. Ricard, p. 100.

34. 'Letter of Luis de Velasco to Philip II, September 30, 1558' in *Archivo General de Indias, Audiencia de Mexico, 58, 3-8.* Quoted in *Ricard*, p. 100.

years. One obvious outcome of this obligatory detention was the children's attachment to the missionaries whom they, for want of a paternal image, began to regard as surrogate fathers. By capitalizing on the inter-generational conflicts within the native society itself, the missionaries created a socio-cultural break that would sever the connection between the old and new generation of natives. The child preacher was, indeed, the veritable *tabula rasa* receptive of any imprint the missionaries might leave there.

The hoped-for native Christian society, totally free of any vestiges of an idolatrous past, did not materialize, however. The phenomenon of preaching children did not create the necessary break from the old to the new. Neither did this group develop into the future native clergy who would lead a truly indigenous church.[35] It seemed that the natives' reception of the missionary preaching was not commensurate to the benevolence shining through the missionaries' noble enterprise.

III. THE RECEPTION OF THE PLATICAS

As narrated in the summary of the *Platicas,* when the missionaries preached to the natives, their chiefs were at first stupefied, they found no argument to counter the missionaries' claims so they consulted their own priests. The priests deliberated among themselves and expressed great fear of the revenge of the gods should they prove faithless. They replied:

> What we know about our gods came to us from our forefathers. Our ways of worship were shaped by our tradition. Our gods have always served us in the past. Only disaster can come from our abandonment of the gods; their wrath will surely fall upon us. It is not salvation but death that you bring us. Oh what can we do who are mortals and dejected? Let us die if we have

35. Ricard, p. 224.

to die. If we are to perish, let us perish, because truly our gods
have died. [36]

Such eloquence must have been evoked by a great sense of loss.
For the natives, the acceptance of the Christian God in exchange
for their deities threatened not only the end of their tribal
organization but also their traditional *credenda* and *agenda*. It was
like the death of their way of life as they had known it.

Sahagún wrote that the chiefs and the Aztec priests, after
listening to the sermons, eventually asked to be baptized. He saw
in this a manifestation of God's grace, the effectiveness of their
preaching, and the natives' acceptance of it. A modern reader
would, however, wonder whether the natives' desire to be baptized was a proof of efficacious reception of the *Platicas,* or simply
practical capitulation to a foreign power.

In the first place, most of the concepts in the sermons of the
missionaries had no surrogates in the natives' system of thought.
Even when the missionaries showed sincere efforts at translating
their sermons into the native language, much of this was done by
forcibly inserting European words (either in Latin or in the
language of the missionary) into the native texts. From the point
of view of orthodoxy, this was deemed safe. Besides, there was
repeated warning from the Crown against the use of any term[37]
that might cause confusion in the minds of the natives, that is why
religious texts in native languages are sprinkled with many
Spanish and Latin words, such as *Dios, Apostoles, Yglesia, Misa,
Sanctus Spiritus, Santisima Trinidad,* and so on.

But even granting that Christian terms were adequately translated and the natives wanted to appropriate the missionaries'
credenda and *agenda,* their understanding of the depths and

36. Ricard, p. 266-267.
37. Ricard, p. 287.

subtleties of very Western and scholastic concepts would have been insufficient.

For instance, the missionaries praised the readiness with which their new converts streamed to confession after the former had preached the necessity of this sacrament. But the natives' reaction could also be construed as a desperate need for religious guidance as a result of the disappearance of their native priestly class. The unaccustomed freedom from the dreaded power of the offended idols was translated into eagerness to confess one's sins as an act of propitiation. The inadequate understanding of the sacrament explains the later observation of the missionaries that the natives slipped readily into a completely external view of the moral life and came to depend upon the priest as the absolute arbiter of their conduct.

The reception of the missionaries' preaching would have been greatly enhanced by the preaching children whom the missionaries trained as effective auxiliaries. Sad to say, they served more as the backbone of the new paternalism ushered in by coming of the Europeans, a paternalism that had nothing in common with the former patriarchal structure of the ancient indigenous society. It was a paternalism which, in spite of its good will, had one main flaw: it refused the children the right to grow up. It was a paternalism that regarded them as perennial children.[38]

This partially explains why, despite the almost unanimous judgment of the missionaries that the native children were effective preachers and teachers of the faith, the latter never developed into a full-fledged native clergy. In the first place, the religious did not teach the native masses the Spanish language. Ignorance of Castilian had the immediate advantage of shielding the natives from the dangerous contact of the European, but it

38. Ricard, p. 291.

also created a gulf that rendered difficult and even impossible the adequate reception of Christian doctrine. The evolution of this corps of preaching children into a full-fledged native clergy was also not supported by the Spanish Crown. It was regarded as nonsensical, running counter to the system of tutelage .

In the summary of the *Platicas,* the superiority of the Christian God was presented to the natives through many arguments. But the decisive argument given to the natives why they should embrace the Catholic religion was the missionaries' observation that the natives had not been supported in the slightest by their gods, while the Christian God, in proving his omnipotence, had allowed his faithful servants, the Spaniards to conquer the natives.[39]

This argument indicates clearly that the evangelization of Latin America was inescapably tied to conquest. Evangelization involved not only the adoption of the creed as preached, but also submission to a foreign power. For the missionaries, conquest was instrumental to evangelization; for the colonists and not a few priests, evangelization was instrumental to conquest and stability of Spanish rule. These conflicting motives produced disintegrative consequences for the colonized population, especially as regards the quality of their reception of missionary preaching and teaching.

As a native, one remained within the traditional world of the indigenous culture, whose practices – linguistic, religious, familial, vocational – affirmed the form and content of one's personal identity. At the same time, as a colonial subject one was connected into an administrative system, including guidelines, norms, expectations, rewards and punishment that amounted to a second nature.

39. Ricard, p. 267.

It is impossible to superimpose consistently these two images of oneself without damage to one's sense of identity and religiosity. The native thus became vulnerable to the existential crises that remained unresolved through the centuries. Many contemporary Third World authors now write about these as split-level morality, tendency towards syncretism, re-appearance of folk-religiosity as superstitious practices and beliefs.[40]

What aggravated this self-estrangement were the inconsistent policies and ambiguous or unattainable objectives presented by both the colonizers and evangelizers. It is a mistake to attribute too much clarity, unit, or consistency to the structures that promoted colonization and evangelization. A colonial regime typically resembles less a closed and smoothly contoured hegemonic edifice than an unstable assembly of partial discourses and practices. It's prime concern was the molding of the new colonial society in the image of the mother country's own traditions. When the missionary and the colonizer clashed over the ways in which this enterprise could best be fulfilled, the loser was generally the native over whom they quarreled, and the Christian message whose effective reception is hampered by such conflicts.

CONCLUSION

The early Spanish missionaries, undoubtedly exceptional and dedicated men like Sahagún and Montesino, had had the good fortune of seeing much of native civilization in Latin America still intact. Their preaching was a sincere attempt to convert the natives and bring them to the catholic fold. They also took pains

---

40. See for instance, R. Baglow, *The Crisis of Self in the Age of Information*, (1994, London, Routledge), pp. 139-141. He dealt in these pages on the logic of colonial organization which had detrimental effects on the native psyche persisting up to the present.

to remind their fellow Europeans that the native was a human person with inherent rights and not a natural slave.

But after the middle of the sixteenth century, the solidification of colonial life and accumulation of missionary precedents had hardened the arteries of Spanish spiritual enterprise. The native leadership, initially christianized by the missionaries receded to the background. This was followed by an almost brutal decimation of the native population and a continuous wave of European migration to Latin America.

Many contemporary historians today contend that the christianization of Latin America was not accomplished through a process of evangelization but through the emergence, two generations after the conquest, of a *mestizo* race with its own religion and culture, displacing the natives who receded further to the periphery of society.

Present-day missionaries had learned from the past. In the age of religious pluralism and inter-faith dialogue, missionary preaching is no longer primarily geared towards converting people to Catholicism. Still, many missionaries sincerely trying to update their methods are overly focused on the theological, psychological, sociological, linguistic, and communication theories that must mould their preaching, the politically correct ways of expressing the content of preaching, the dialogical methods to be used to effect understanding on the part of the non-believers, etc.

A study of the history of reception of preaching can complement these efforts. As mentioned earlier, reception refers not only to the way a listener listens, but how the listener shapes the content of the preacher's message. A study of the history of reception need not immerse the message in the relativism of its various receptions, but affirms the rich potential of the message to effect new meanings through the audience's active reception of it. Interest on the historicity of preaching can help modern preachers realistically gauge the conditioning factors of a homily's original production and reception, how these factors shape and are shaped by the history of its later receptions, and the consequent effects on the various receivers.

A study of the history of reception, furthermore, would highlight the reality of the *sensus fidelium*, which in turn affirms the presence of the Holy Spirit who works in all and through all, towards universal salvation. As Congar has written, and history has proven, when the Church acknowledges that it is the Spirit that moves the heart to listen, preaching ceases to be a monologue, a tool for imperialism and domination, but an instrument for understanding and conversion.

THIS GLORIOUS AND
TRANSCENDENT PLACE

JAMES P. DONLEAVY, O.P.

The research for this chapter occurred over a span of forty years preaching parish missions, retreats, Sunday and week-day homilies. The first parish mission I gave was in Carrick-on-Shannon, Co. Leitrim, with Fr Damian Byrne. I would, publicly, like to acknowledge his kindness and encouragement to me on that occasion as I took my first tentative steps in preaching.

No one can teach you to preach. It is craft that can be learned only by practice, listening, and self-criticism. Indeed, as in prayer, it is only by opening oneself to the Holy Spirit that one can proclaim the Good News. This *prima facie* principle underpins all that is said in this chapter.

Nevertheless, we can receive helpful tips from others, constructive criticism, and encouragement. We can see how others 'do it' and learn something from them. We can learn from other speaking trades – politicians or trade union speakers, barristers or actors. We may feel some hesitancy in regarding actors as helps because they do not necessarily believe what they say – they are 'putting it on' – yet a good actor is a good communicator and we humbly and gratefully listen.

THE SAME OLD THING OR SOMETHING NEW?

Sitting by a limestone lake on a calm day in May, watching those beautifully attractive insects, the Mayfly (*Ephemera danica*), I think of the sermons or homilies we give. These lovely insects are at least two years in the nymph state and yet their mature life is so short – hence the name 'Ephemera'. Sermons can take years to craft and create yet they are a brief breath on the face of eternity. A sermon 'like the snow falls on the river a moment white – then melts for ever'.[1] Never again can this sermon be given; its unique life passes with its close, although we devoutly hope that some good effects will remain. Material will be used over and over as we continue to tell the Gospel story. Yet there is a freshness and newness about each sermon as we breathe new life into it – otherwise it is dead.

Perhaps the most acute (and critical) accounts of sermons have been given by Chaucer in his *Canterbury Tales*, and how damning is, for example, the Pardoner's boast:

> 'My lords,' he said, 'in churches where I preach
> I cultivate a haughty kind of speech
> And ring it out as roundly as a bell;
> I've got it all by heart, this tale I tell.
> I have a text, it always is the same
> And always has been, since I learnt the game,
> Old as the hills and fresher than the grass,
> Radix malorum est cupiditas.'[2]

Those gloriously cynical lines should be sufficient to teach preachers the need for living sermons rather than dead parrot preaching.

Perhaps we did sail close to the wind in this matter. 'A carefully prepared mission can be used again and again, since each mission is preached to a different congregation.'[3] Today's custom, however, in great measure precludes that danger. In the missions of yesteryear it was the missioner who decided the

1. Tam O'Shanter, *Poems and Songs of Robert Burns*, Collins, London and Glasgow, 1964.
2. Geoffrey Chaucer, *The Canterbury Tales*, Penguin Classics, London, 1977.
3. *Vade-mecum Missionale: Handbook for Parish Missions*, private circulation within the Order.

subjects for the mission.[4] Now, however, the scene is different. Visits are paid to the parish and different groups are met. A questionnaire goes out to every household regarding the mission, and one section deals with the topics the parishioners feel should be covered. This has always worked out remarkably well. The earlier custom seemed to think that only the priest had access to the Holy Spirit whereas today we recognise more explicitly that the Holy Spirit breathes abroad in the parish.

THE TRINITY OF CREATIVITY

It is quite clear that whenever a human being puts hand or mind to creation the Trinity is involved. All our preaching is Trinitarian: an earthly trinity to match the heavenly.

> First there is the Creative Idea; passionless, timeless, beholding the whole work complete at once, the end and the beginning; and this is the image of the Father. Second: there is the Creative Energy, begotten of that Idea, working in time from the beginning to the end, with sweat and passion, being incarnate in the bonds of matter; and this is the image of the Word. Third: there is the Creative Power, the meaning of the work and its response in the lively soul; and this is the image of the indwelling Spirit. And these three are one, each equally in itself the whole work, whereof none can exist without the other; and this is the image of the Trinity.[5]

The Father is the moment of vision for the preacher. The Son is the long, often arduous incarnation of that vision, which in its culmination awakens those feelings of power and joy that drove the Father to begin the process. The Holy Spirit is that power and

4. Ibid.
5. *The Zeal of Thy House*, a play for Canterbury Cathedral, by Dorothy L. Sayers, Gollancz, London, 1937.

joy being communicated. These three – Father, Son, and Holy Spirit: inspiration, incarnation, joyful power – are inseparable: three persons, one God, three aspects of one creative act.

To what extent any preacher, at any given time, is overtly aware of the trinitarian nature of creating the preaching moment is immaterial. The theological and spiritual facts remain that all preaching issues from and returns to the Triune God. As years go on, this truth becomes more ingrained into the soul of the preacher and embedded into the heart and soul of his/her being.

This trinitarian foundation of every sermon is also mirrored in the transcendent past, the chronological present, and the eschatological future. We touch the Word that was 'in the beginning', the contemporary temporal word, and the future hope. For every sermon is a Paschal proclamation: Christ has died. Christ is risen. Christ will come again

THE PASSIONATE PREACHER

When I started on the itinerant road, forty years ago, preaching was essentially an intellectual activity. You were there to put before the people the Truth (as we saw it) and a very black-and-white commodity it was. The theory was that this platonic presentation of truth forced people of good will to recognise the value and saving power of the message. Even deeply moving sermons on Good Friday were graphic descriptions of the suffering of Christ, but the preacher's sufferings were not on show. At parish missions there were men who could simulate great anger or sadness over sin, but we knew it was an affected part of the presentation. As we read James Joyce's account of his school retreat in *A Portrait of the Artist as a Young Man*, and as we ourselves sat through frightening descriptions of death, judgement, damnation, and hell, we did wonder was the preacher as scared as he would hope his listeners were. It was passion, but an ersatz passion.

Then we discovered (or admitted) the attributes of the Right Brain: a capacity for surprise, a tolerance for ambiguity, an ability to depart from irrelevant rules, a heart that can see more deeply than the words can express, and a hospitality so broad that it can embrace the troubles and difficulties and hopes of the people whom God sends my way.

A balance is needed. To appreciate the Right Brain characteristics does not mean we dispense with the intellectual content: the habit of intellectual integrity is at once the foundation and result of scholarship. I believe that a solo unbridled Right Brain approach would have us charge, with gadarene abandonment, over the edge of the cliff just as ignoring the Right Brain would leave us propounding a sterile theology as cold as mathematics.

It is part of the following of Christ that we live with the ambiguity: that we can live with sin and still love God. Juliana of Norwich wrote/spoke with great feeling as she had experience of Christ in the *Shewings*: 'in this delight I was filled full of everlasting surety, powerfully secured without any painful fear … sin is necessary but all will be well … for we need to fall and we need to see it; for if we did not fall, we should not know how feeble we are in ourselves; nor too, should we know so completely the wonderful love of our Creator.'[6]

Having the temerity to speak from personal feeling allows us to remind people that Christianity is not about spiritual success but about redeeming failure. Robert Louis Stevenson was, perhaps, nearer the truth than many professional writers when he glibly stated that the saint is the sinner who never stopped trying.

6. Juliana of Norwich, *Shewings*. The Classics of Western Spirituality, Paulist Press, New York, 1978. See Chapters 27 and 61.

Man is born broken,
Life is mending,
God is glue.[7]

Passion and feeling are essential constituents in any sermon tempered by thoughtful and prayerful reflection,

COUNTER CULTURE

As the police say, fighting the drug culture is like standing waist deep in a fast flowing river and trying to keep the water back with one's bare hands. Preaching today can seem like that: the flood of the material-value world in which everything has to be sacrificed on the altar of wealth, success, and 'getting on', makes the work we are engaged in seem a pretty hopeless task. Add to this the loss of credibility (and probity) on account of abuse cases, and it is little wonder that there can be a crisis of confidence and low morale among preachers.

The resultant lack of inspiration is partly our own fault. Certainly there is a great challenge to our personal faith. If we are looking for a remedy against the present sickness of our society we need go no further than the words of Jesus who reckoned that there are forms of evil that can only be cast out by prayer, fasting, and penance. One can quote apposite scriptural passages: 'I can do all things in him', 'It is when I am weak that I am strong' … The challenge is whether or not we believe these sentiments and live them in a practical way in the pilgrim journey we are all making.

Preaching today needs to rediscover the compassionate and uncompromising Jesus who was, in fact and truth, the God 'by whom all things were made'. He was not a kind of demon pretending to be human; he was in every respect a genuine

7. Eugene O'Neill, *The Iceman Cometh*, New York, 1946.

human being. He was not merely a man so good as 'to be like God' – he was God. We have managed to tame Jesus and make him boring.

> We have very efficiently pared the claws of the Lion of Judah, certified him meek and mild, and recommended him as a fitting household pet for pale curates and pious old ladies. To those who knew him, however, he in no way suggests a mild-and-water person; they objected to him as a dangerous fire-brand. True, he was tender to the unfortunate, patient with the honest inquirers, and humble before heaven; but he insulted respectable clergymen by calling them hypocrites. He referred to King Herod as 'that fox'; he went to parties in disreputable company and was looked upon as a 'gluttonous man and a winebibber, a friend of publicans and sinners'; he assaulted indignant tradesmen and threw them and their belongings out of the temple; he drove a coach-and-horses through a number of sacrosanct and hoary regulations; he showed no proper deference for wealth and social position; when confronted with neat dialectical traps, he displayed a paradoxical humour that affronted serious minded people, and he retorted by asking disagreeably searching questions that could not be answered by rule of thumb. [8]

Jesus certainly was not a pallid or boring individual but one who gave zest and energy to his preaching and care of people.

A counter-culture motto: in a former Methodist seminary in Headingly Yorkshire, there is a mighty oak pulpit on which is engraved a constant reminder to preachers – the request the Greeks made to some of the apostles: 'We would like to see Jesus.' (Jn 12:21)

8. Dorothy L Sayers, 'The Greatest Drama ever Staged', *The Sunday Times*, April 3, 1938.

THE SYMBIOTIC DYNAMIC

We have all experienced it. The shuffle of itchy feet; the furtive glance at the watch; the vacant gazing at the stucco work on the ceiling; or just plain blankness, like a cow looking into an empty bucket. There is a dynamic here, albeit a rather negative one. Weary preacher, uninterested preacher, unprepared preacher and the same then can be said of the congregation. Who started the process? The preacher or the people?

At the other end of the spectrum, we know when the feeling is electric, like the high voltage of an arc when the electricity jumps across. Both terminals are contributing and both receive a high blast.

Preaching requires three parties: the Holy Spirit, the preacher, and the congregation. Should one of the three not be involved in an active and creative way much of the sermon will founder. Nor is it a matter of everyone agreeing with the preacher and all thinking the same way. How accurately and amusingly was such an antagonistic moment captured by Anthony Trollope as he described the fateful sermon of Mr Slope in the cathedral at Barchester.

> There was, at any rate, no tedium felt listening to Mr Slope on the occasion in question. His subject came too home to his audience to be dull; and, to tell the truth, Mr Slope had a gift of using words forcibly. He was heard through the thirty minutes of eloquence with mute attention and open ears; but with angry eyes, which glared round from one enraged parson to another, with widespread nostrils from which already burst forth fumes of indignation, and with many shufflings of feet and uneasy motions of body, which betokened minds disturbed, and hearts not at peace with the world.
>
> At last, the bishop, who of all the congregation had been

most surprised, and whose hair almost stood on end with
terror, gave the blessing in a manner not at all equal to that in
which he had long been practising in his own study, and the
congregation was free to go their way.[9]

There are times when you can hear an audience listening to
you – not simply quiet (they might in that case be all asleep) but
the active creative listening in which the Spirit, through the
preacher, speaks in a special way to this people.

The contribution of the people adds enormously to the effectiveness of the sermon and can bring the sermon to a height that
the preacher alone could not attain. The preacher too is a cause in
bringing about this effect.

For the preacher it is essential he/she knows his/her people.
Sermons are frequently criticised for 'not being relevant', for not
talking to the people but rather at the people. While we need to
have an intellectual exegesis of the text, a prayerful (*lectio divina*)
reflection of how I am converted by this piece of gospel, we also
need to have an exegesis of our congregation. For those of us who
are fortunate to preach Sunday after Sunday in the same church,
I perform a little exercise, which may seem naive, but to me is
extremely helpful.

Knowing what Mass you are saying the following Sunday and
knowing that people tend to come to the same Mass every Sunday
and sit in the same seat – these are prerequisites for an exercise in
exegising the congregation. When the church is closed – or empty
– I go into the church and sit in the seat a family – let's call them
the *A*s – always occupy. Imagine their week and the difficulties
that family (or that individual) is trying to grapple with; there
may be great sadness and worry and anger. At the introduction
to the Preface, when they are invited to 'Lift up their hearts' it

9. Anthony Trollope, *Barchester Towers,* Everyman's Library, London, 1906, p. 53.

may be a very weary and depressed heart they raise to the Lord. You look up at the pulpit and ask the questions they will ask: 'Has he anything to say to us? As we leave here are we strengthened and renewed in our faith and hope?' So, on to where the *B*s roost. The same procedure and the same questions. They may be full of joy and gratitude over recovery from illness or the birth of a longed-for baby or success in examinations. And they too will look up and wonder can the preacher express, in some way, their joy and Eucharist.

I find that an hour or two in prayerful reflection of the people with whom we expect to share the Word and the Sacrament forces one to cut out the peripherals and get to the core of the matter.

To be able to work over the Scriptures with a group prior to preaching can be an obvious help. It is necessary to be on one's guard lest the group become cliquish or patronising. But whatever helps the preacher to listen and reflect is good for the sermon

·

HUMOUR, JOY, AND POWER

We have good news. The first word of the story of the Incarnation, uttered by Gabriel to Mary, was: 'Rejoice'. And later we read of an effect of the Incarnation: 'the child in my womb leapt for joy'; and the shepherds were told, 'We bring you news of great joy'. As preachers, our vocation is to bring joy through hope and redemption to the community of which we are part.

Groucho Marx once received a letter from a clergyman who congratulated Groucho on his great ability as a comedian and thanked him for all the joy and happiness he had brought into the world. Groucho graciously replied and said he was flattered by the compliments. 'Unfortunately,' he said, 'I have to thank many clergymen for all the joy and happiness they have taken *out* of the world!' What a terrible indictment of (some) preaching. Robert Louis Stevenson notes in his diary, as if it were a most unusual event: 'Went to church today and was not depressed'. Clovis G. Chappell says: 'No man has the right so to preach as to send his hearers away on flat tyres ... every discouraging sermon is a wicked sermon ... a discouraged person is not an asset but a liability'. Fr Eltin Griffin, a well-known Irish Carmelite, asked some young people to give advice to preachers. The short poignant answer: 'Give up giving out'. A term dear to the New Testament writers and used to describe the Word, was the Greek adjective *kalos*, translated by William Barclay as handsome, gracious, winsome.

Good news is contagious. Think of the two disciples on the road to Emmaus: having recognised Christ, though it was late in the day and seven miles from Jerusalem, they had to go back to share their good news with the others. Good news is energising. Think of Paul: so on fire with Christ, he was not daunted by the difficulties of travel, the antagonisms of people, or the legion of other hardships he endured, but travelled the known world proclaiming Jesus as Lord. Good news is uplifting and hopeful. The word *euaggelion* occurs 72 times in the New Testament and is at the very heart and centre of our Christian faith.

Good news binds people together. Come out from a football match after a great win and you will be amazed at the number of people you know, at least people you talk to and with whom you are delighted to share a great experience. Watch people coming out of Mass on Sunday. Do they walk out with a smile on their faces and a spring in their step? Can we say: here is an energised and enthusiastic people; people who have heard good news and want to share it with others; people who are aware they are redeemed and hopeful; people who are supported by the community with which they have just broken bread? Often, unfortunately, their body language says otherwise.

The power of the Spirit of Jesus is the real hope and desire of people. The best sermon is not a noetic teaching that can pass for preaching. It is not a matter of 'here is the Christian religion – the one respectable and authoritative rule of life, take it or leave it'. It's much more a matter of 'here is a muddling and muddled state of affairs we call Life'. In spite of all the apparent contradictions, a state of affairs that can bring happiness and hope and whole-ness. We do not point to any theory but to the practical experi-ence. When the early members of Alcoholics Anonymous were asked to write down their recipe for successful sobriety, they did not give a list of rules or recommendations. They simply wrote: this is what we did – steps 1 to 12 – and we never found anyone who followed these steps sincerely, failed.[10] St Paul had a similar plan: look at me and follow my example. Preaching must be grounded and rooted in life.

Arising from our joy and confidence in the Good News comes a gentle humour. William Hazlitt, the essayist, says, I believe, that man is the only creature to laugh and cry because he is the only creature who knows the difference between what things are and what things ought to be. We are realists and see things as they are, but that realism brings us further because we believe in a loving compassionate God. We take things seriously but not too seriously; it does not all depend on me. Preaching needs humour – not crude or ridiculing, not flippant or facetious, but a whole-some humour that can be joyous in God.

We are not in the pulpit to be comedians but to excite people's imagination, to let them see what is and what could be – and this can lead to go(o)dly laughter. I believe in something far beyond my paltry efforts and thoughts:

10. See *Alcoholics Anonymous*, Alcoholics Anonymous World Services Inc., New York, 1976, p. 58.

And is it true? And is it true?
This most amazing tale of all!
A baby in an ox's stall.
And is it true? And is it true?
That God was man in Palestine
And lives today in bread and wine. [11]

We are overcome with awe and, like a child full of surprise, we are very close to laughter; and laughter is the language of joyous wonder.

THE NUTS AND BOLTS ... PERFECTING THE CRAFT

Rhetoric has been held in high esteem by many civilizations – Greek, Roman, Mediaeval. They would all have held that, while some people are gifted more than others, yet, it is a craft that can be learned and perfected by practice. The same is true today. There is a transcultural story of Bob Hope going for a short walk before he appeared in the Command Performance at the London Palladium. As he strolled along, someone stopped him and asked: 'Do you know how to get to the Palladium?' 'Practice! Practice! And more Practice,' replied Bob. (This story is told of the Carnegie Hall and many performers.) Legions of examples can be given of professionals at the zenith of their skill and power (musicians, sports people, actors or whatever) who constantly practise. As preachers, we too need to be thankful to God for this most wonderful of instruments – our voices – and show that gratitude by caring for it and using it as well as possible. I wonder how many preachers do appreciate this gift and continually try to improve their vocal ability.

Priests talk much about the importance of training readers for the liturgy, and rightly so. But what of priests themselves? Any

11. John Betjeman, 'Advent', quoted in many anthologies.

discipline which interests us will have its own place in our bookcase, and so too with the voice. We are fortunate in having the book, *Your Voice and How to Use It*, by Cicely Berry, voice director of the Royal Shakespeare Company and world-famous voice teacher, in which she deals with relaxation and breathing, clarity of diction and vocal flexibility – everything you need, to produce good speech.

I just quote a few sentences to raise the question: Do we even recognise the league professional speakers are in compared with many of today's preachers?

> [B]e conscious of the sweep of inflections. Notice, for instance, if you start a new thought with a different note, or whether you tend to start it on the same note as you finished the previous sentence. You should get a sense of your voice moving on, that there is something further to come, and this involves keeping us in suspense.[12]

That sort of challenge and expected standard usually passes us by.

No matter how good a book is, you cannot learn the violin or a language or golf just from a book. You pick up tips, you develop a suggested discipline, and altogether profit by studying a good manual. But there is no substitute for a good teacher (or coach). There is no substitute for a small tape-recorder that enables us to listen critically to ourselves and learn from our presentations. To be able to develop a keen self-critical sense is a great asset in developing one's skill. The skill we are talking about is the power to produce one's voice well and effectively and to have the capacity to express oneself articulately and pleasantly. An old saying goes: 'to err is human': but to err – err – err is unforgivable.

12. *Your Voice and how to Use It*, Cicely Berry, Virgin Books, London, 1994. We would also recommend Elsie Harden, *In Celebration of God's Word*, St Paul's, Maynooth, 1995.

The argumentative reader has already sprung to the attack to remind us that St Paul did not come with any show of rhetoric. I will accept that argument when I meet a preacher who has the same dedication, ruthless commitment, and fearless passion as Paul. And, anyway, how do we know Paul didn't practise?

WORDS, WORDS, AND MORE WORDS

When God wanted to become 'one of us', the act was described as 'the Word became flesh'. When God wanted to become 'one of us', the act was described as 'the Word became flesh'. Although Chesterton maintained 'Art is the signature of man',[13] we may prefer to say that 'word' is the signature of man. Word is that unique and intimate way of being human. Other animals can, to some extent, communicate with their own kind, but humans alone can formulate speech which is different, no only by way of complexity but by way of its very nature, from animals' communication. Speech is unique to humans. (It is when we appreciate the power of speech that we understand something of the great suffering of those – who for one reason or another – lack the power to articulate their thoughts and feelings.)

In preaching, the Word and the word are at the heart of the communication. Strangely enough, in various books on preaching, the human word receives scant attention. We presume – wrongly – that because a person can speak whatever language he/ she is using, that having marshalled the thoughts, the suitable words will automatically follow. This is a serious flaw in the attitude of the preacher.

People categorise themselves into various classes, not by their wealth or their position in the community, but, as *Pygmalion* reminded us, by the way they speak. We do not mean by this

13. See G. K. Chesterton, *The Everlasting Man*, Hodder and Stoughton, London, 1953, p. 37.

whether they speak with an upper class accent or a drawl or a pleasant lilt or whatever.

In the last twenty or thirty years much valuable work has been done for preachers, in a technical, scientific way, by the study of socio-linguistics. We could profitably give a whole chapter to this topic but a few broad outlines will have to surface.

The way we speak is indicative of the way we feel and think. Naom Chomsky has demonstrated this, and his pioneering work is the subject of much theory and research today.[14] One class of people will think in the immediate short-term time module. They are people of immediate response. Often you will see it in the way they deal with their children: there is no doubt about their love for them, they can be extremely affectionate at one moment and yet come in with immediate punishment for a misdemeanour.

This is not to criticise this sub-culture – but for those who do not belong, it is difficult to understand. Such people will tend to use short sentences, concrete nouns, active verbs. They will be convinced more by *ad hominem* arguments than reasons and will be at home with a sermon that is more a montage than an orderly argument. On the other hand, there is another sub-culture group – mentioned in a non-judgemental way – for whom reason, detachment, and the long term is more conducive to its mind-set. Abstract terms will be used (with the grammatical implications) and progressive reasoning appreciated. Without caricaturing this group, I often wonder is their idea of a good sermon a holy syllogism.

14. See Naom Chomsky, *Language and Mind* (revised edition), New York, Harcourt Brace Jovanovich, 1972; *Reflections on Language*, New York, Pantehon Books, 1975. For discussion of origins and formulation of language, see Victoria Fromkin and Robert Rodman, *An Introduction to Language*, New York, Harcourt Brace Jovanovich, 1993; Robert J.Sternberg, *Cognitive Psychology* (Chapters 9 and 10), New York, Harcourt Brace College Publishers, 1996.

Allowing this is a brief inadequate overview of two classes, the dilemma for the preacher is immediately evident. How do we cope when words – and hence thought pattern – are so diverse?

In trying to come to terms with this difficulty, we need to listen – listen to people on the bus, at football matches, in shops, or wherever. It will eventually dawn on the would-be preacher that (total) difference exists. Suddenly, we may understand why the criticism that 'sermons are not relevant' has worth and meaning. Because people are hearing a different language from the one they live, its saving value is minimal. This is certainly true of the class we call 'young people' who have a different mind-set and vocabulary from the older generation.

A sermon has to be carefully crafted. It is like baking a cake. The right amounts of different ingredients are blended together and mixed and the final product may be taken as a parable for the Church – many, many ingredients resulting in the manifestation of one harmonious (or not so harmonious) whole.

Thankfully, many of our congregations are still like a stew – made up of bits of everything. We need to cater for the 'everything'. Jesus was a good blender and mixer of words and mind-sets. Short practical everyday examples rested easily with abstract sermons (as at the Last Supper). Perhaps that is why St Dominic was so keen on St Matthew's Gospel. There, we find story, followed by reflection, followed by story.

Nor should we be too keen to finish every sermon nice and clean and tidy with no loose ends. It takes confidence and courage to leave questions unanswered or slightly obscure. 'And the disciples came to Jesus and said: what did you mean ... ?' (Mt 13:10.36) One of the most encouraging results of a sermon is when you are accosted in the street a few days later and someone asks: 'What did you mean? We were just talking about it?' People listened, are wondering, and want to know – the preacher has brought them a long way.

Whatever class you belong to, there is one universal interest. We all love to hear a story. Preaching is storytelling. (Jesus being a Jewish Rabbi taught by means of story: 'And who is my neighbour?' He told a story. 'Decide between my brother and me'. He told a story). St Benedict in the Prologue to his Rule answers the unasked question: what are the monks doing when they pray/preach/ work? His answer is that they glorify God at work in their lives (*magnificant Dominum in se operantem*). That involves telling our story and seeing Emmanuel – God is with us. We tell other people's stories, too, identifying with their hopes and fears and sorrows and joy and humour.

Our congregations need to hear the word that speaks for them: the truthful word, the encouraging and supporting word; the word of forgiveness, and the word of healing. The Word was made flesh and we must be on our guard that we do not make it word again: our words must be rooted in our living experience.

TO SEE OURSELVES OTHERS SEE US

Robbie Burns cannot have been too interested in the sermon when, seated behind a 'woman of quality', he spied a louse on her bonnet. So, to relieve the boredom of the droning minister, he gave himself to composing a poem and left us with some of the most often quoted lines:

> O wad power the giftie gie us
> To see oursels as others see us?
> It wad frae many a blunder free us
> > And foolish notion.[15]

With modern technology we have many ways of seeing our-

15. Robert Burns, 'To a Louse', Tam O'Shanter, *op. cit.*

selves. But the rub is: do we see ourselves as others see us? We all need help to position our preaching in the context of our congregations. Whether it is by a professional 'assessor' or discussing regularly the content and trend of our preaching with soul friend, an *anam cara*, we can all derive immense help from this humbling yet profitable practice. Over the years, I have discovered that we can, imperceptibly, veer to an extreme one way or another. We may not recognise that our preaching has become, for example, totally supernaturalised to the exclusion of 'the world' or, on the other hand ,our whole thrust is an extreme form of Christian anthropology. We need this to be pointed out to us.

Our accent, the way we frame phrases, the whole speech act is so intimate to each individual that it can prove embarrassing and humbling to open ourselves in so personal a way: criticism in this area can appear to be a criticism of our very being.

There is a strange convention in some parts of the Order that we do not listen to each other's sermons. Hence we don't comment (good or bad) on the pulpit work of the brethren. But how will we ever learn? How be helped? How encouraged? In the early days of the Order the convent was known as a *praedicatio* and the preaching was the preaching of the community, not of individuals. Perhaps there is need to revert to this tradition for both preaching and the presentation of liturgy, for we do not see ourselves as others see us.

A PARADIGM FOR FAILURE

Not all sermons are successful in human terms. We may have tried and prayed and worked and yet the sermon falls flat on its face. This is experience is not only for the preacher but for the listeners too. Perhaps the listeners' hopeful disappointment was never better captured than in the encouraging words of George Herbert who could, I'm sure, chalk up his human failings in the pulpit, when he wrote:

> God calleth preaching folly.[16] Do not grudge
> To pick out treasures from an earthen pot.[17]
> The worst speak something good: if all want sense,
> God takes a text, and preacheth patience.[18]

It is, however, deeply part of the preacher's spirituality to believe that the divine Word, spoken with sincerity and truth, does not fall on barren soil. Humanly speaking, we may look on a sermon as a disaster; but good news does not go unheeded. We know from our own experience, and the anecdotal evidence of others, that often it is not the great theme of our sermon that 'gets home' but the aside or more incidental element. When we seem to fail we are brought to our knees afterwards and pray that someone was helped somehow even in one small way. Maybe we are called to dismantle the high-blown structures we thought would be so impressive and look at the Lord with humility.

> Now that my ladder's gone,
> I must lie down where all the ladders start,
> In the foul rag-and-bone shop of the heart.[19]

I love Fr Vincent McNabb's whimsical thought on the Pharisee and Publican. When asked, all the Publican could say was: 'I am a sinner'. Fr Vincent imaginatively asked him: 'And what do you know about Prayer?' 'Oh, I know nothing about prayer. If you want to know about prayer ask that Pharisee ... he's very well up in prayer ... he'll tell you how to pray.' And the Publican

16. See 1 Corinthians 1:21
17. See 2 Corinthians 4:7
18. George Herbert, 'The Church Porch', lines 429-32 in *The Country Parson, The Temple*, Classics of Western Spirituality, Paulist Press, New York, 1981.
19. W. B. Yeats: 'The Circus Animals' Desertion', *Collected Poems*, Macmillan, London, 1969.

went to his home 'justified' and he didn't know he was justified.

The paradigm when faced with failure is faith, hope, patience, and humility. What more does the preacher need on such occasions?

CONCLUSION

Preaching is a craft that is at once rewarding and difficult, energising and draining, humbling and inspiring. We are graced to be preachers trying to fulfil the command of Jesus: 'Go out and proclaim the Good News.' Great people have gone before us and, with God's help, great people will come after us. But *carpe diem*. As far as our human ability allows, we fervently hope there will be prayerful, reflective, and great preaching today.

> In your desire to be of use to the souls of your neighbours, you must first of all have recourse to God with all your heart, and simply make this request to him. Ask him in his goodness to pour into you that love which is the sum of all virtues, through which you may be able to achieve what you desire.[20]

The Pulpit is indeed a glorious and transcendent place.

> Lord, how can man preach thy eternal word?
>   He is a brittle and crazy glass:
> Yet in thy temple thou dost him afford
>   This glorious and transcendent place,
>   To be a window, through thy grace.[21]

---

20. Breviary, Second Lesson for Feast of St Vincent Ferrer.
21. George Herbert, 'The Windows from the Church', lines 1-5, in *The Country Parson, The Temple*, Classics of Western Spirituality, Paulist Press, New York, 1981.

THE ROLE OF 'THE QUESTION' IN PREACHING: ADULT EDUCATIONAL MODELS

CATHLEEN M. GOING, O.P.

I. INTRODUCTION

I drove to Brattleboro to read poems at the new church there, in a state of dread and exhaustion. How to summon the vitality needed? I had made an arrangement of religious poems ... I suppose it went all right – at least it was not a disaster – but I felt (perhaps I am wrong) that the kind, intelligent people gathered in the big room looking out on pine trees did not really want to think about God, His absence or His presence. – May Sarton[1]

To illuminate from one angle the preacher's task, this chapter affirms the primacy of questions – in human development generally, and specifically in education and in the preaching effort.

Are the contexts and goals of preacher and teacher sufficiently similar that such important common ground can be affirmed? Recall the preacher's spontaneously negative references to matters 'academic' or 'intellectual'; recall also the educator's spontaneous aversion for 'preaching to' students. Even when there is mutual admiration and respect, the difference of roles may seem clearer than their commonality, as the following imaginable exchange expresses:

'Preachers, we educators envy you, especially in your liturgical assemblies. The atmosphere is solemn; those present expect something from you and they expect something from God. What you say usually is not immediately challenged; those in

1. *Journal of a Solitude* (1973, New York, Norton), p. 95.

attendance bring silence to your meeting, and you bring words. In the gathering is a variety of lived experience, an intergenerational and intercultural mix, which, together with your contribution, makes a rich weave. You have powerful resources: you can call to conversion and count on the impact of that call on feelings and decisions. We envy you the expectant, holistic, integrally human character of the liturgical assembly before you.'

And in turn:

'Teachers, we preachers envy you, especially you educators of older adults. You do not have to persuade your people to action; rather, you invite them to a time of reflection, of getting the issues straight. You can 'build,' you can count on accumulation of insights – for six months, for a year. Your groups have been created by an interest rather than by a need, and are to that extent both free and focused. Questions can flow easily among you, and insights, and laughter. It is not only you who must prepare for your meetings; you ask the others to prepare also. We envy you the differentiated, participative nature of your project, and the opportunity you have to follow together wherever the search for understanding may lead.'

As for the topic of questions: which of the many kinds of question are meant in our opening affirmation? We know about questions that ask for something other than an answer: those which are delaying tactics, or tests, or exclamations or some other emotional move on the part of the questioners. We know that some questions want only the understanding needed for manipulating concepts (the appropriate talent of twelve-year-olds, as Piaget taught us). We know there are 'canned' questions, formulated for discussion with no group concretely in view –

'generic brand,' we might call them. Because of the gifts of Maria
Montessori we know rather a lot about children's questions. In
fact, to understand development, we might rest with the profound Montessori insights were there not urgent voices [2] asking
that we take adults, rather than children, as the model, the 'axis,'
for our educational planning.

We know also about questions in which it is the wish to
understand that is dominant: the contemplative, the 'useless'
questions. These 'pure questions' are without pressure, without
dynamic external to themselves (though they may ask about very
practical matters and about crucial decisions). We know, in other
words, about questions that are real – not simply tactical – and
really our own. Some have affected us disturbingly, and marked
us in an important way.

Evoking some of the data on questions may have half-won the
day for us in establishing their primacy. Already we can recognize that questions are bound up with our going beyond ourselves, with the entry of something new within our horizon, and
with horizon shifts. They are like the growing tips of an ever-
green. We will spend time later with confirmations of our idea.
Here we clarify that we are taking 'question' in a full-bodied
sense: as heading for moral and religious as well as intellectual
self-transcendence. Our confidence in questions does not ignore
the fact of our stunted growth and interior divisions; it is simply
taking that fact as being neither normative nor explanatory for us
in regard to the role of intelligence in our lives. It is the whole tree
that grows.

From our preoccupation with questions, there is a recommendation awaiting the reader and it can be told in advance: not to

---

2. For U.S. Catholics there were urgent voices in the 1960s (e.g., Gabriel Moran, *Vision
and Tactics: Toward an Adult Church* [1968]), and in the pastoral meeting of the US
Catholic Bishops Conference on adult faith formation (1999).

make a large increase in the number of explicit questions we address to an assembly, but to make a shift of horizon to reflecting on what we ourselves are doing.[3] Preachers and teachers already know that what they learn in their preparation for a presentation is likely to appear chiefly in what they do not say, or by the choice of an adverb, or in the deletion of a 'never' or an 'always.'

II. THE CENTRAL AFFIRMATION: QUESTIONS HAVE A PRIMARY ROLE IN HUMAN PROCESS, HENCE ALSO IN TEACHING AND PREACHING.

And what is this God? I asked the earth and it answered: 'I am not He'; and all things that are in the earth made the same confession.... My question was my gazing upon them, and their answer was their beauty ... Is not the face of the earth clearly seen by all whose senses function properly? Then why does it not give the same answer to all? ... If one man [sic] merely sees the world, while another not only sees but interrogates it, the world does not change its speech ... but presenting exactly the same face to each, it says nothing to the one, but gives answer to the other – Augustine.[4]

The affirmation is an emphasis, strongly expressed, on a factor which may seem more obviously important in education than in preaching. We can select two ways to justify the emphasis.

II.1. First we adapt to our purposes the notion of the question as operator.[5]

What gets us on the move, under way, on the road again, when

3. Perhaps a few more questions would be good? We listeners appreciate the occasional question we hear, and we do sometimes 'think about it during the day'.
4. *Confessions*, Bk X, vi, (trans. F. Sheed, 1943, New York, Sheed and Ward, pp. 216-7).
5. See Bernard Lonergan, *Insight*, 1957, *Collected Works* [CW] 3 (1992, Toronto: University of Toronto Press): 'Clearly, despite the imposing name, transcendence

we have settled into a position or an attitude? What opens up past experience to new light?

What makes us aware of error? What starts to unravel a stand we have taken?

What questions do we suppress?

What controls the power of our images? What liberates our imaginations?

What happens in dialogue when we are contradicted, and yet are interested in more than saving face?

The answer to all the above? The 'operator' that is a question: some concretization of wonder, the question one allows to emerge into consciousness. As one theorist of preaching put it:

> In so far as we open ourselves to a whole series of questions ... to the extent that we search for understanding in what we do not yet understand ... we attune the ear of our own self-understanding.[6]

A question is part of a structure that is dynamic. It pivots: it presupposes, and then inquires into experiences, images, and insights. (What Augustine said about the questioning of creation – quoted above – applies to the very data of our consciousness too.) Further, every real question heads for the 'known un-

---

is the elementary matter of raising further questions' (p. 658). '[T]he immanent source of transcendence in man [sic] is his detached, disinterested, unrestricted desire to know. As it is the origin of all his questions, it is the origin of the radical further questions that take him beyond the defined limits of particular issues. Nor is it solely the operator of his cognitional development. ... [T]he knowledge it yields demands of his will the endeavour to develop in willingness and so make his doing consistent with his knowing' (pp. 659-660). Specifically on the notion of 'operator' – a mathematical and biological analogy – see pp. 488-504, including: 'the emergence of the further question effects [the] transition [of higher system] into the operator' (pp. 493-4).

6. Gabriel Chico, O.P. (Province of Mexico), 'Temps salvifique et prédication chrétienne,' *Science et Esprit* [Dominican bilingual journal], 53/3 (2001), 452 [Tr. C. M. Going]. See also p. 457.

known' – a formulation centuries old which shows us a marvel: our questions already give us a direction and at least the shape of the answers to them.

'Mere' questions? Too 'intellectual' an approach to be interesting for preaching? If we worry in this way, we may be understanding ourselves from the viewpoint of the pathology of consciousness – that is where 'mere' intellect is rightly considered and feared – or from the viewpoint of 'faculty psychology' which often betrays its inadequacy.[7]

II.2. A question is a correlate of mystery

We [must] show that the Word we proclaim does not just stand over and against us. It is more intimate to our being than any word we could speak; it made us and it enters the darkest places of the human heart and offers us a home. – Timothy Radcliffe, O.P.[8]

A second aspect of 'question,' which, besides 'operator,' indicates a primacy of questioning in development, and hence in preaching and teaching efforts, is the inner movement and receding horizon which we experience. The unrestricted character of our desire to understand and to be loving, is our experience (not yet our knowledge) of mystery. Question is a correlate of mystery. If the native flood and persistence of questions causes some people (as Bernard Lonergan pointed out [9]) to think that relativist tenets deserve belief, the same flood causes others to think that there are some answers to questions, that to ever further questions there is eventually an unconditional answer,

7. See, for example, the tortuous formulations, engendered and trapped by faculty psychology, of Thomas Philippe, O.P., in *The Contemplative Life*, (1991, N.Y.: Crossroad), especially Chapter 3.
8. *I Call You Friends* (2001, New York and London, Con-tinuum), p. 175.
9. See *Insight*, p. 369.

and that it is partly our questioning that reveals us to ourselves as heading for God. Question pulls us toward mystery.

Problems

If our affirmation is clear, namely that a question is an operator of development and a correlate of mystery, still there are problems with it. Recall: 'Our preaching of the gospel ... was carried on in the Holy Spirit and out of complete conviction' (1 Thess 1:5, NAB). The dialectic of questions and convictions which this passage sets in motion, lays open a major tension in religion (revelation or discovery; virtue or grace), in learning (tentative starting-points in comparison with grounded judgments), and in preaching (convictions mean no questions? questions mean no mission, no good news to share?). Emphasis on questions in our development may seem to run counter to the 'grace' and 'gift' which are central to religious vocabulary.

Further, whatever may be the case with students, the Eucharistic Assembly of the Christian community seems to come together because of a conviction, not because of a question. Surely for everyone, it is answers that have the primacy? understanding? truth? Whether we are preachers or teachers, can we responsibly export questions? We owe people sound doctrine, enlightenment, truth, sureness, confidence, clarity. Why emphasize questions?[10]

Authenticity

Moving within the dialectic of conviction-and-question, we are en route toward fresh realization of the variegated character

10. As though raising the opposite question, namely, 'Why answers?' Northrop Frye, literary critic, wrote that the questioner's advance in understanding is blocked by any answer given; answers consolidate the mental level at which questions were asked. (In terms we have been using: answers are not operators but integrators.) Irony was his recommendation. See *The Great Code* (1982, Toronto: Academic Press Canada), p. xv.

of our human consciousness. As the old story has it, Proteus of the sea was very resourceful in slipping from one shape to another to escape answering a questioner. But if anyone could hold him still, long enough to get a question across to him, he would answer. What if our polymorphic, protean consciousness, with its shifting perceptions of reality, would hold still long enough to be accosted by a real question and persuaded to assume a stable shape to meet that challenge? We might then recognize that our convictions are the residue [11] of processes at the origin of which were our own questions. We could rediscover those original questions to which our doctrines, insights, and commitments were the answers – the living moments of the birth of our convictions.

Authenticity is prepared for us by rediscovery of the origins of our convictions, and by finding our own continuing questions. Preacher or teacher can play uselessly at discerning the needs of hearers: which is the 'right line in'? Which wavelengths are common, or suitable, or up-to-date, or inculturated? The first authentic thing that can be done is the hard work of identifying our own real questions about the matter/text/situation at hand. Once insights and convictions emerge for ourselves from these questions, they can be told to others as a story is told, until the others can appropriate their own equivalents. What we will have shared will be authentic, and more a method than a content, or, to say it better: a limited content and a versatile method.

III. CONFIRMATION OF THE CENTRAL IDEA

The Church ... does not always have a ready answer to every question.

Vatican Council II, *Gaudium et Spes* 33

11. Chico (cf. note 6 above) speaks of 'sedimentation' and 'significant residue' (p. 452).

What confirmation have we for our notion that questions have a primacy for us in our own development, and hence also for those whom we address? First of all, the ground for such confirmation is cleared wherever preachers are trying to elaborate increasingly sublating, holistic accounts of the role in religion of 'intelligence' and 'intellect' – an effort complementary to the emphases made by partisans of the 'heart' who, in discussing religion and spirituality, often speak in anti-intellectual terms.

Confirming factors surround us in the present climate of dialogue, interview, discussion, and even communal research,[12] because this climate has been created by questions. There is confirmation in the writings of persons as diverse as Heidegger (language as the house of Being), Aquinas (his dialectic), Sertillanges (relaxed, loving inquiry), and Thérèse of Lisieux.[13] There are 'whispering witnesses' (Chico, 451, n. 3) among those of our contemporaries who have written about preaching in a way that fosters inquiry.[14] Writing as Master of the Order of Preachers, Damian Byrne was very clear: 'We must be struggling with significant issues for the Gospel to be powerfully proclaimed.'[15]

Lonergan

[F]rom an experience of love focused on mystery there wells forth longing for knowledge, while love itself is a longing for

---

12. This is an idea which we expect in 'hard' science but may still find surprising in the social sciences and humanities. See the presentation in M. Gergen and K. Gergen, 'Qualitative Inquiry,' *Handbook of Qualitative Research,* ed. Denzin and Lincoln, 2000, London: Sage Pubs., Inc.

13. The reference to Thérèse may need explanation. Thérèse – a Doctor, but not usually invoked as a patron of the intellectual life – was heard to say in her last suffering days, 'I have always sought only the truth.' ('Je ne jamais cherché que la verité.') Doubtless it was her thinking about humility that occasioned the remark.

14. Dominicans Carla May Streeter, Mary Catherine Hilkert, Gabriel Chico (quoted above), and Simon Tugwell are explicitly in mind here.

15. Damian Byrne, O.P., *A Pilgrimage of Faith* (1991, Dublin, Dominican Publications).

union; so for the lover of the unknown beloved the concept of bliss is knowledge of him and union with him, however they may be achieved.[16]

With the notion of operator (used earlier), and with other characteristics of questions adopted from Lonergan's work (see the Indices of the *Collected Works*), we have already involved him in our topic in a confirming way. For the correlation of question with 'mystery,' we call on him also. 'God is the eternal rapture glimpsed in every Archimedean cry of "eureka".'[17]

On education Lonergan wrote and lectured,[18] but he repeatedly and explicitly left to the adult-educationists whom he knew, the concrete implementation in education of transcendental method. Preaching he located within 'communications' as a 'functional specialty'.[19] The brevity of that presentation was partly due to the technical reason that the more one approaches the concrete, the less can helpfully be said in advance.[20] But many themes elsewhere in his work illuminate the preacher's task. For special mention here: his description of sensibility held open for the higher integration which is mystery; 'mutual self-mediation' as a description of the task of preaching; 'emergent probability' as naming world process (within which the act of preaching occurs), and in his cognitional theory, the 'four levels' of conscious intentionality (virtually a directory for preachers and teachers).[21] But

---

16. Bernard Lonergan, *Method in Theology* (1972, New York, Herder and Herder, p. 109). (*CW* 14, forthcoming)

17. Bernard Lonergan, *Insight*, p. 706. It is interesting that Damian Byrne agreed with Lonergan that the 'failure' of the traditional proofs for the existence of God is a failure to consult religious experience (in elaborating or repeating those proofs). See *A Pilgrimage of Faith,* (1991, Dublin: Dominican Publications), pp. 124-125.

18. See Bernard Lonergan, *Topics in Education,* 1993, (CW, 10).

19. *Method in Theology*, Chapter 13.

20. Ibid., pp. 355-6.

21. Pertinent to the preacher also are Lonergan's designation of dialectic as the occurrence of encounter between persons, his awareness of persons as in their own

let us pause at 'communications,' the eighth and last of his functional specialties in theology.

'Communications' is the moment when the whole cycle of the specialties will start again freshly because in the altered situation brought about by collaborative method, experience now flows in a different way. It is new, and we move forward again with Augustine to questioning this altered experience: 'if one person asks it questions, it says nothing to the one who does not ask, but gives answer to the other ... ' Lonergan's location of preaching within the last functional specialty recalls, in a scriptural text favoured by Dominicans, the reality of the Word coming down like rain and not returning fruitless to its source – an image for the way the whole process of history, individual and communal (and including the preacher's efforts), opens out again and again, as good seed sown in the ground and watered, grows, and eventually puts forth fruit.

Voegelin

We will borrow from Eric Voegelin's work,[22] later in this chapter, two images of the preaching effort. Here, in relation to what we have thought of as 'the question as operator,' and 'the question as correlate of mystery,' confirmation from Voegelin includes the following passages which now speak for themselves:

Still, the order of creation does not lead by itself to the creator,

---

way originating values, and the intense exchange on wisdom which occurred in the last interview of *Caring about Meaning* (1982, ed. P. Lambert, C. Tansey, C. M. Going. Montreal: Thomas More Institute), pp. 244-256.

22. Eric Voegelin was professor at Munich (and in the USA at: Bennington College, Louisiana State, the Hoover Institution at Stanford University). His five-volume *Order in History* (Baton Rouge: Louisiana State U. Press) is a profound meditation on The Question and on Mystery, within a study of the order of human existence in society. See especially vol. 4, *The Ecumenic Age* (1974) cited here, on the following page. He saw such meditation as an act of resistance in a time of disorder, as – so he taught us – Plato's meditations were.

but does so only if in creation there is a 'heart' in search of God. The 'mind of the heart,' in the Apocalypse [of Abraham], is the Aramaic equivalent to the Platonic-Aristotelian *psyche* and the Augustinian *anima animi* as the term designating the site of the search ... the tension of God seeking man, and man seeking God – the mutuality of seeking and finding one another ... Since God is present even in the confusion of the heart, preceding and motivating the search itself, the divine Beyond is at the same time a divine Within (324).

[T]he structures in reality are experienced not as givens beyond question, but as raising the questions in search of answers. [One of these structures is] the experience of questioning as the constituent of humanity (326).

The Question capitalized is not a question concerning the nature of this or that object in the external world, but a structure inherent to the experience of reality (317).

Such reflections [e.g., his five volumes on order in history] ... are an act of open participation in the process of both history and the Whole (335).

[T]he Mystery ... becomes luminous in the acts of questioning (330).

An adult-education model

A special kind of university education offers strong confirmation of the primacy of the question in human development: university studies for older adults in the liberal arts tradition. It does so because this kind of education proceeds best by way of formal discussion – where 'formal' means: with leaders who surface their own real questions about a writing or situation, and thus demonstrate an authentic method of approaching a common study.[23]

The reference to 'older' adults is important because it suggests some educational circumstances that are especially favourable to the pure questions, the contemplative questions, the real questions. The 'older adult' is usually someone who has settled the urgent matters of making a living, has made basic commitments, and come through to some integrated living. Life has been full of questions and answers, presented in classroom and Church. What will alter the horizon for that person? More information, yes; but once the anxiety about having less information than one's grandchildren is assuaged, or the need is met for keeping up-to-date at work, deeper questions are likely to emerge and the process becomes intensely participative for all. After the first identity-declarations made in a new group, there begins, for all present, a self-transcending preoccupation with what discussion leaders call 'the question in the middle of the table.' There begins the learner's *kenosis*.

A monastic-study model

In the Dominican family there is a conviction that belonging to the Order of Preachers entails respect for the intellectual life; attention to their Constitutions actually leads the Dominican cloistered nuns to study. But for them and for others similarly situated, is question in its proper dialogue form appropriate? For example, compare and contrast the team or group approach to learning, on the one hand, and monastic silence on the other. Some doubts about the suitability of adult-education procedures (including the key one, discussion) have been satisfied by adverting to the highly participative character of Dominican community

23. Consult the Great Books tradition, the nearly sixty-year experience of the Thomas More Institute in Montreal (where Lonergan first presented some of the basic ideas of *Insight*), and the most interesting of the programs offered by professors of University Evening Colleges.

life. Rather than disabling nuns for solitary study, discussion shows how to internalize the many voices of a group and thus activate healthily in solitude one's own many inner voices, for the sake of less inadequate data and richer perspective.[24]

Further monastic confirmation of the rightness of emphasizing questions, is the moral and social fittingness of the temperate speech and outlook which can grow in those accustomed to asking real questions. Fitting also to daily monastic life are: cultivation of tentativeness, learning about the ground of judgment, and understanding inner consistency. The purified and purifying real question – the question not powered by some alien drive – accords well with the ancient monastic ideal of *apatheia*.

Craddock

In one of his book titles, Professor Fred Craddock implicitly confirms the importance of questions within the preaching event: *As One without Authority*.[25] His 'inductive preaching' is tentative, inconclusive (p. 60). As to the question as operator: he reminds the preacher not to think for the assembly. The listeners finish the sermon (p. 54); preachers should allow them to be the priests they are (p. 56). He refers to the 'monological character' [of preaching] as a fundamental weakness in the preaching tradition (p. 18). He is aware of the fact of polymorphic consciousness, asking: 'How can she [the minister] preach with a changing mind?' (13; 68)[26] He knows the benefit of reading a great book for other than sermon purposes (p. 66). He warns that 'dialogical methods are rather easily postured' (p. 18). In relation to the authority title

24. The genuine problem for monastic persons, as for many a discussion group, with learning by discussion is not solitude or silence but excessive homogeneity in the group.
25. See Fred Craddock, *As One without Authority* (1967 and 2001, St Louis MO, Chalice Press). Fred B. Craddock is Professor Emeritus of Candler University, Atlanta, Georgia, USA; teacher of homiletics and once cited (*Newsweek*) as one of the 'twelve best living preachers'.

which he has given his book, he recognizes (quoting Bonhoeffer) that authority is present where 'a word from the deepest knowledge of my humanity encounters me here and now in all my reality' (p. 59).[27]

IV. TWO IMAGES

Offered here in the service of the preaching are two images. They come indirectly from the two adult-educational models of questioning cited earlier (i.e., 'older adults' and monastic learners). They correspond directly to two values which are the real treasure in the asking of questions: a heightening of the probabilities of development, and our intensifying participation in reality. These images as they occur in Eric Voegelin's work come from sources outside the Jewish and Christian revelations. They furnish an example of the Voegelin theme of the equivalences of experience and symbolization of the constants in reality – a theme familiar to the teacher of preaching who instructs students about relating the Bible and present-day experience.

The singer

Voegelin notices that Hesiod picks up not the Homeric image of the Seer, but that of the Singer.[28] The difference is reflective

26. In his view preachers should bring the assembly through the same process as they followed themselves in preparation of their sermon. (One of his tips for preachers, this is different from my own suggestion. See the section on 'Authenticity' above.)

27. In the discussion procedure, authority is earned by leaders who have taken the time to think out in advance what the important questions are in some portion of a great work. But chiefly it belongs to the great writings or achievements, and to their authors. Here should enter Bernard Lonergan's challenge about measuring up to the mind of an author, and what David Tracy has written about the role of the 'classic' – classics for monastics being, as for preachers, especially the Bible, the Fathers of the Church, Aquinas, and the important spirituality writers of our own day.

28. *Order and History*, vol V: *In Search of Order* (1987, Baton Rouge, LA: Louisiana State University Press), pp. 85-86. See also vol. II: *The World of the Polis*, pp. 93-103.

distance,[29] yet the singing comes consciously from deep within the process which the song celebrates. The Singer keeps the memories, lifts them up and hands them over, selected and embellished. Though it is not a point Voegelin was making, 'Singer' also suggests total personal-corporeal involvement, as well as the presence (at least in memory) of others who may know the melody and the words.[30] 'Singer' is a contemplative image. The theme of questions is not left behind. The singing, as though responding to hidden questions, is an act of interpretation. And it is an act of participation. In everything, Hesiod's Singer discerns the divine presence which is drawing us.

Saving the tale that saves us

At the very end of Plato's *Republic*, Socrates is telling the story of Er (who is the 'Everyone' of the piece). He uses 'saving the Tale that saves us' as a phrase already well known, and he goes on to say of the story: 'and it will save us if we believe it' (621c). As Voegelin comments,[31] the Tale needs to be saved from being deformed by drugging speech, deformed 'by the very forces of imagination and language which let truth break forth' (p. 372). The threat (p. 373-374) is from the 'public unconscious' – the affliction, perhaps, of 'those kind, intelligent people gathered in the big room ... [who] did not really want to think about God. His presence or his absence.'

The Tale itself reveals that all are offered the free choice of their destiny but not the wisdom to choose well – a desperate situation of soul. But there is hope in the fact that a message is sent

---

29. *Search*, p. 48.
30. To suggest that the preacher is Singer presupposes that preachers have already spent time with current reflection on 'word' in human affairs, and now are ready to think about what melody, and the singing of it, add to word.
31. 'Wisdom and the Magic of the Extreme: a Meditation,' *Collected Works* vol. 12, ed. E. Sandoz, *Published Essays 1966-1985* (1990, Baton Rouge, LA: Louisiana State University. Press), Chapter 13.

– brought by Er ascending from Hades (or by the philosopher descending into the Cave)[32] (62). The tale that saves 'must itself be saved from the death from which it emerges, if it is to become the living Word with the … power of salvation' (Wisdom, 335). With Christ, 'The saving tale is more than a tale of salvation; it is the tale that saves. Transfiguration in reality is real' ('Wisdom,' 370).

The two images coalesce, containing Question and Mystery. The Singer can dispel sorrow because he [sic] has 'discerned the divine presence as formatively moving in all things' (Chapter 5, p. 131), including the song. Or, in equivalent terms: Saving the tale that saves us heightens the probabilities for good within world process by that very participation. Or, in equivalent terms: We preachers have been promised participation in the redemption of the world.

V. CONCLUSION

'When the Son of Man comes, do you think he will find faith on earth?' – Lk 18:8

Was it a real question?
An operator of development?
A correlate of mystery?
A gift from a teacher to a preacher?

---

32. Vol. II, *Plato and Aristotle* (1957), p. 62.

PART 4

Preaching and Scripture

'BUT WHY DO WE HAVE TO KNOW THAT?': PREACHING AND CRITICAL BIBLICAL STUDY

BARBARA GREEN, O.P.

Resistance has emerged, recently and unexpectedly, to the critical study of Scripture that grounds seminary education in virtually all of the western world. Such academic study presumably undergirds not only preaching but the other crucial aspects of the life and prayer of professional ministry. There are many reasons for this unwillingness to engage in critical study and reflection, ranging from the inexcusable to the very understandable. Some students are lazy or bored with it, some confident that 'store-bought' assists will suffice for their preparation; others appear content to simply restate (or even reread) the biblical passages into homilies, or to harangue righteously about the surface meaning of a narrative. Others (as we move across the spectrum from inexcusable reluctance to engage biblical studies toward the more understandable qualms) are fearful that critical study and faith are fundamentally opposed, seem fearful that even a provisional commitment to criticism will slide down the slope to something worse; some students seem to sense that to ask questions about human cultural processes may somehow threaten the mysteries we call Revelation and Inspiration. Finally, there are the perennial problems of lack of time for sufficient study, a frustration with the arcane opacity of much of what is available, even a bewilderment at the rapid pace of change in biblical studies today. These diverse sentiments, uttered rebelliously, resentfully, suspiciously, or frustratedly, provide the title for this essay.

My supposition is that critical study is crucial for biblical preaching and that no one in graduate school in this third millennium CE may hold herself or himself excused from it. If it may be argued that a particular preacher does not feel in need of such information, still it is unlikely that they will never minister to someone who does. So though we all know of many people who are very close to God without ever having heard about critical methods, the times in which we live demand that those who will preach must be well-educated in biblical studies. Please understand that I am not advocating the exegetical homily – far from it. What I do want to promote and to demonstrate is the value for preaching available when one is able to draw on current study, also the likely deficit if the preacher is innocent of such information. Nor am I suggesting that such preaching will remain exclusively in the realm of the scholarly. It is my belief that our best preaching is about matters of deep existential concern to the preacher and those participating with him or her in reflecting on the Word of God. But since that word took shape in the distant past and has made its way through some 2,500 years of culture and consideration of various kinds, some appropriate attention to that past is required. Finally, though I will restrict myself here to the Old Testament, whose challenges are acute, what I am advocating goes, *mutatis mutandis*, for the New Testament as well.

I will use as my example the book of the prophet Jeremiah, whose texts feature in liturgy some fifty-one times, eighteen different chapters for a total of 165 verses (spread across Sundays, weekdays, and other regular set occasions). Though Isaiah appears more frequently and surely many Old Testament books are far more sparsely represented, Jeremiah makes a workable example. My plan is to offer five ways in which critical study of one sort or another (so the various types of historical study, certain aspects of literary study, and the several kinds of 'interested' or advocacy procedure or endeavours) is fruitful. In each case, I will cite Eucharistic liturgy texts, suggest what we need to know, indicate what risks happening if we overlook such information, and what may be possible if we have certain knowledge which critical study can offer.

1. WHAT IS HAPPENING?

The backdrop for Jeremiah's ministry is the most traumatic event (from our biblical text-oriented viewpoint) that befell Israel until at least six hundred years later: the imminent threat from imperial Babylon, which gathered strength in the end of the seventh century and culminated in exile (several deportations happened between 597 and 580 or so BCE); exile was preceded by siege, military defeat, destruction of the city Jerusalem, and by the devastation of Solomon's temple and of the cult long centred there.[1] The most likely comparison for us would be the gradual gathering of fascism's threat in Europe, culminating in World War II and its various culture-changing aftermaths. It is inconceivable to talk about situations in Europe between 1935 and 1949 without making the war a dominant backdrop. Even in countries where devastation did not touch so closely, such as the U.S.A. or Ireland, the war's shadow was focalizing and its frame-of-reference common to the lives of virtually all. All the biblical texts of the period are suffused with awareness of this experience of massive defeat.

Jeremiah's most consistent view on the looming Babylonian threat is that Israel (more precisely, the kingdom of Judah which alone by now remains of the larger entity) must go willingly and as soon as possible into captivity in the imperial region to the East,

1. A good summary of the period can be found in J. David Pleins, *The Social Visions of the Hebrew Bible: A Theological Introduction* (Louisville: Westminster John Knox Press, 2001) Chapters 7-8.

since that is God's implacable will (1:14-19). At the very moments
when the kings whom Jeremiah serves are advocating alliances
which might spare the people (and the king, even the monarchy
itself) from defeat and devastation, Jeremiah is urging submission. His words and viewpoint have to have appeared treasonous
in the extreme, defeatist, scandalous, even likely heretical. Though
it can become obvious, in retrospect, when strategic submission
is preferable to resistance, it is rarely clear at the time and surely
not to all. And so with Jeremiah: When invited – or ordered – to
the palace to give advice, Jeremiah's words will have split the
inevitable court factions in ways dangerous to his life, which we
can see in narratives like 28:1-17; 38:4-10; 20:10-13. Conversely,
as the ensuing devastation becomes more obvious even to those
who have tried to refuse it, Jeremiah shifts ground and proclaims
God's new covenant with Judah (31:1-9; 31-34). That is, as defeat
appears inevitable, Jeremiah talks of a new freedom. These
familiar words which likely cause us no trouble have to have
registered upon a shocked and angry people as the rankest insult,
parody, even treachery, perhaps as risky to call out as are some of
his words urging submission and promising defeat.

To understand and utilize such a context can provide opportunity to preach against automatic cohesion or collusion with the
political agendas of our day, should the preacher genuinely feel
those are to be resisted or at least questioned. Even should a
commander-in-chief enjoy an approval rating in the 80-plus
percentile points for his strategies of war and retaliation, such
popular policies may need prophetic cavil. And when circumstances appear menacing and dire, even hopeless to those about
to be swept away from their homes into captivity from which
they themselves will never return, hope may be held out for
another generation yet unborn, assuming that the preacher can

urge it with integrity of genuine vision. War is a complex situation and resists easy factoring into utter right and wrong. Jeremiah spends little time analysing the international politics of his day, is not very prone to seek the roots of some of the sins he cries out against in the very structure of an imperial neighbourhood. But his very silence on the more global reasons for the social inequities among classes and castes may prompt us to query them more closely. Wars lay bare lodes rich in self-knowledge, for individuals, groups, and nations, and many of them are nuanced rather than clear.

2. WHAT IS A PROPHET?

Most of us feel that we know at least what a prophet is, and of course to some extent that is the case. But once we examine our information, and especially if we dig a little deeper and nuance it with the results of contemporary cross-cultural study of the intermediation phenomenon as well as with careful attention to the particular situation of Jeremiah himself (not exactly the same as that of fellow-prophets Deborah, Elijah, Amos, Huldah, Haggai or Daniel), our views may become appropriately more complex.[2] From our macrocosmic study of prophecy we would likely learn that – far from being lone-ranger types, isolated and anomalous genius figures – prophets exist typically in tense relation with their communities, unable, sociologically speaking, to venture past what a critical mass of their audiences are able to be persuaded of. So Jeremiah is reliant upon and sustained by a community of those able to tolerate his radical preaching, even if somewhat unwillingly. That Jeremiah is invited back to the

2. For useful information on the phenomenon of intermediation see Thomas Overholt, *Prophecy in Cross-Cultural Perspective* (Atlanta: Scholars Press, 1986). For study more specific to Israel's prophets see Lester L. Grabbe, *Priests, Prophets, Diviners, Sages* (Valley Forge, PA: Trinity Press International, 1995) Chapters 4 and 7.

king's presence even when his advice is unlikely to please all
serves as a marker that it pleases someone, or may be used as
ballast against someone else. The corollary is that Jeremiah's
other 'constituency,' the divine partner in the prophet's shuttle-
diplomacy of intermediation, will not (sociologically speaking)
make demands of him that are too far-removed from or alien to
Jeremiah's politics. That is, Jeremiah is less counter-cultural than
we may suppose him to have been, if he shares the general
features of his kind that have been teased out in comparative
social-scientific study. And, toward the more local and micro-
end of the study scale, Jeremiah's ministry will have been distilled
from his own particular circumstances: born of a priestly family,
influential in royal circles, likely to be invited, in a way not true
for other prophets, to give the king advice.[3]

To attend to such cross-cultural and text-specific investiga-
tions saves the preacher from assuming that Jeremiah is a sort of
super-human, seeing calmly and confidently far down the line
ahead of all others, implanted mysteriously with a God's-eye
viewpoint that overrides his own cultural particulars. Such information may also help us see Jeremiah's prophetic opponent
Hananiah (28:1-17) as very similar to Jeremiah himself, though
espousing a slightly different point of view. In other words, it
would not have been so obvious that Jeremiah is the true prophet
and Hananiah the false one. In fact, what may strike us is that
they are quite similar, each one preaching 'on the war' in similar
tones, employing the same image of the yoke (with one thinking

---

3. In terms familiar to a US readership, Jeremiah resembles not so much Billy Graham
or Ralph Nader as Jesse Jackson. Graham has survived a number of presidential
administrations with his prestige intact (which Jeremiah did not); Nader is too
radical to be useful to mainline and high-up official. Jackson (and his mentor
Martin King) come closer to retracing the called-in-today/banished-tomorrow
experience of Jeremiah. To search for apt analogues is a good exercise for preachers
and teachers.

it will be broken off Judah's shoulders soon, the other saying not so). And, of course, each takes a different view of what leaders and people of Judah should do, what God requires of them, how the community must best respond to the imperial Babylonian threat.

A true prophet, and a false one, both exist to some extent in the eye of the retrospective beholder, and most easily when events are past and seem clear. In retrospect, Jeremiah was right and Hananiah wrong, the one true, the other consequently false. Such knowledge helps us read with sensitivity a passage like 38:4-10, where Jeremiah is indeed called to the palace to offer the king advice. The advice, though requested, is uncongenial for at least some, and so Jeremiah is dropped into a pit, ignominious though such treatment is for one of his particular role and status. However, he is not killed – not drowned or starved – but rescued by others who appreciate his value. No prophet can survive without a strong network of support.

What can such information prompt in our preaching? Any strategy that slow us a bit from vilifying our opponents seems a good thing, any insight which reminds us that they may differ from us, even substantially and painfully, without necessarily being malevolent. I think available here, as well, is the mystery of how a great prophet can be so right about some things, so wrong (retrospectively?) about certain others. If the model in which we cast our prophets (biblical and contemporary) presumes that they receive clear and largely unambiguous information and instruction from God (information conveyed only to 'true' prophets), then it is a mystery why they do not get matters more correct. If, on the other hand, the social circumstances of the prophet make significant edges to what he or she will be able to see, then odd blends are more understandable. Why, it is often asked, can

Martin Luther King have been so right, so sensitive about violence and racism but so blind and so insensitive about sexism?
How can a spiritual giant like John Paul II be so perspicacious
and creative about certain political situations – like the factors
constructing Poland in the period of the Cold War – and so
resistant to what seems obvious in many other eyes about the role
of women in the Church? A prophet will get only so far out in
front of his or her audiences, and such figures will not typically
be prophetic about what lies outside of their experience.

3. WHAT TO DO WHEN PROPHETS DISAGREE?

One of the things that emerges into the light of day in critical
study is the situation of serious disagreement among Old Testament 'true' prophets upon fundamentals. Isaiah of Jerusalem,
preaching a century earlier than Jeremiah, insists resolutely that
God will not abandon Zion – the mountain, the city, the temple,
the dynasty, the priesthood – no matter how loudly circumstances might seem to suggest that collapse and defeat are imminent. Isaiah stiffens the resistance of more than one king and
through more than one crisis with his words of confidence. And
we read in the scroll named for him, what he prophesies comes
to stand. But Jeremiah, scion of an Anathoth family of priests,
goes to the temple on a day of his choosing, stands prominently
within its gates, and preaches that people should put less confidence than they are doing in the 'temple of the Lord, temple of the
Lord, temple of the Lord' (7:4, elaborated there [verses 1-11, 23-
28] and in 26:1-9, 11-16, 24[4]). And the warp and weft of Jeremi-

---

4. I cannot resist the opportunity to point out that the habit in the lectionary of
snippeting intricately constructed passages is often, in part, responsible for their
being obscure and simplistic, a situation that may, at times, prompt useful preacherly
comment. It is not so lethal in Jeremiah as in story narratives (like Genesis), but it
is rarely worth the few seconds saved by skipping a few verses. Examples include:
Jer 15:10, 16-21; 26:1-9, 11-16, 24; 30:1-2, 12-15, 18-22; 31:1-9, 31-34.

ah's whole ministry is that God's preserving the city and its environs, the Ark of the Covenant and its Presence and contents (3:14-17), the temple and its denizens, the palace and its inhabitants is most definitely not to be presumed. To the contrary. Though it would not be impossible to reconcile these positions of Isaiah and Jeremiah, better that we do not.

Why do I say so? The natural assumption that (true) prophets will agree, that their words have a timeless and universal quality, may comfort us. It takes rise from leads back to the search for messages in the text. These little pellets, quite a staple in biblical preaching, are abstract apothegms, wee truisms, extracted and abstracted from narratives and made perennial, usually at the unacknowledged cost of ignoring a great deal else that does not support such easy stances. Next to a sort of sloppy allegorizing of texts (e.g., 'We, too, like Jeremiah, have been dropped into cisterns ... ') messages are favourite tracks for preachers to seek. An alternative title for this essay is 'There is No "The Message".' Messages are harvested at the cost of overriding the multiple contexts of the narrative and likely the situation of the preaching as well. Messages sand off nuance and particularity, reduce life and language to generalizations that actually hold up poorly when examined or relied upon. Aside from a few tenets (e.g., God wishes all creation well, God is reliable) messages are, in my opinion, to be eschewed.

A great deal has changed in the situation of biblical Judah between the time of Isaiah and his royal 'bosses' Ahaz or Hezekiah (eighth century) and the circumstances which Jeremiah addresses with his kings – Jehoiakim and Zedekiah, as the late seventh century turns into the top of the sixth. The point is not so much that God will or will not save the Zion enterprise. God will save, does care, and has stood by the project of the singularly beloved people. How that will be made actual cannot be smelted into a calf of gold (attractive though such an animal may be) or manipulated presumptuously to take certain contours of our preference. How God will stand by us is ever-fresh and always to be discerned, strugglously.

To advert to and even preach about prophetic disagreement gives us opportunity to discuss the challenge of reading the biblical texts much more creatively, deeply, and answerably than we may be accustomed to do. To resist messages is not to have arrived instantly into a state of chaos or relativism. But it hands back to our communal and personal negotiation some of the complexity that attends God and our relatedness with God. A passage like Jeremiah's 'temple sermon' (7, 26) gives us an occasion to open out the challenging question of God's commitments and reliability, even the question of change in God. It provides a wonderful opportunity to review that the Judeo-Christian anthropology of communication does not rise from verbatim dictées, attractive though such certainty may seem upon occasion. The prophetic disagreement gives us a window into the uncertainty of any of us claiming too easily to have cornered the truth about God's deep desires, invites us to a certain gentleness, not to say humility, about what we see over against 'our others'. And those are topics that can do with some exercise in preaching.

4. WHO IS TALKING?

It seems clear enough, especially in the professional and scholarly vernacular translations we use in liturgy and thus rely on for preaching, who is the speaker. That is the function of narrator tags and quotation marks: to ensure that we will understand without much trouble whose speech we are hearing. Textually, it is not always so certain, since Hebrew does not use quotation marks and rather enjoys blurring the edges between what we call reporting and reported speech.[5] So in fact, translations often simplify the matter for us, not inappropriately, but perhaps too tidily closing us out from other interpretive possibilities. And recent advances in literary theory and criticism have reminded us of the phenomenon of shared language.[6]

We can see this feature at work in a couple of different ways. First, intertextuality makes cousins (or closer) of a great deal of biblical language. Jeremiah's description of the persecution of the righteous one (18:16-20) can be brought into fruitful relationship with Wisdom 2; and Jeremiah's frequent image of the planted tree shares a world with Psalm 1 (and with many other 'tree texts'). It has all been said before, and to visit previous contexts where vital language has functioned adds texture and meaning, much as music can increase its capacity to stimulate and please us as we review all the places where we have savoured and drawn on its beauty and depth.

Additionally, interlocutors can borrow each others' language, a phenomenon that enriches and intensifies dialogue. Recall, if you will, what happens when people in long relationships (e.g., families and members of religious communities) rehearse topics of accumulated sensitivity. Language reused, especially in emotionally complex situations, becomes richly freighted with mean-

---

5. Reporting speech is usually the name given to that summarized by the narrator or another character; reported speech is cited directly. A spectrum reaching from reported to reporting would go like this: She asked, 'Are you sure?' She asked was he sure. She asked if he was sure. The differences seem unimportant when considered abstractly, but all of us can think of instances where our words have been taken over by another and shifted ever so slightly but with great effect.

6. One name for this phenomenon is intertextuality. Jewish Midrash is an ancient form of intertextuality. Another more complex (and interesting) theory can be found in the thought of Mikhail Bakhtin. If interested, investigate the phenomenon in Barbara Green, *Mikhail Bakhtin and Biblical Scholarship: An Introduction* (Atlanta: Scholars Press, 2000).

ing, beyond the dictionary sense of the words.

Where can this issue of language richness bring us with our prophetic texts? The confessions (so-called) of Jeremiah are wonderful places to preach, and several of them are included in the lectionary. These are heartfelt (com)plaints of the prophet to God, prayers that well up from the very toes of Jeremiah, from feet made sore and worn out by prophetic ministry. Jeremiah cries out to God, who remains verbally unresponsive. Like that of the deity in Job, silence here may seem to goad the human interlocutor to fresh efforts. Jeremiah accuses God of a variety of things, e.g., of being a deceitful brook (15:18).[7] And God remains, for all practical purposes, silent.

Whether we register it consciously or not, this apparent indifference of God to Jeremiah's pleas reinforces some aspects of the theistic figure who is described as 'omni-together': all-knowing, all-powerful, all-present − a far cry from what the Hebrew Scriptures draw of the divine character on page after page. In fact, if we rely too passively on the standard quotation marks, the God in Jeremiah reads as all-retaliatory, all-resentful, all-determined to punish (e.g., 18:1-6). God stands outside the human drama of Jeremiah's fifty-two chapters, except, first, to plan punishments and then perhaps to dust off the divine hands, to cross off items to do from the divine list. I doubt this is helpful, nor is it the only way to read.

If we open up the possibility that God and the prophet Jeremiah are such old and intimate friends, are so like an old couple, that as they go the rounds on their perennial topics, they share speech, finish each others' sentences, take each others' parts, we can hear their words as a counterpoint and polyphony difficult to

---

7. One of the most wonderful things to do in a long text like Jeremiah is to take water imagery that appears in many forms throughout the book and explore it for semantic significance.

disentwine. Suppose, as some scholars suggest, the confessions of Jeremiah are duets sung with God, so that the eyes that run with tears day and night are God's as well as the prophet's (14:17-26), that the sheep led persistently to the slaughter (18:18-20) is God's experience as well as Jeremiah's – as it is indeed said to be some pages past the Old Testament.

Is there room in our theology, in our spirituality, for a God who grieves at least as much as we do over the unreliability and perversion of the human heart (17:9-10)? What changes in our ministry, in our lives and in those of others, when our beloved conversation partner is no less pained that we are at the tragedies of the cosmos, who is perhaps patiently waiting for our eye to see and our heart to respond to what needs remedy? The old question – How can I believe in a God who would allow such suffering? – shifts at least a bit under the strategic sharing of the speech of the prophet. How do prophets like Jeremiah hear God's word? If it does not come in tidy message-nuggets or buff-coloured telegrams, if it comes from verbal wrestlings with a beloved until some clarity emerges, why should not our best words have started their journey in the heart of God (try 20:7-9)?

5. WHAT IS SHORED UP, WHAT UNDERCUT?

Finally, as we bring ancient prophetic texts into the contexts of our own lives, which is surely what we do when our preaching is at its best, we import with our biblical readings not abstract messages but powerful, if partly-submerged, ideological viewpoints, garbed at least minimally in the values of the times in which they were first uttered.

We need to examine critically, even suspiciously though also respectfully, the question of values built-in to the narratives, inscribed so deeply that they cannot be readily eliminated. There

was a time when we might have thought we could simply ignore
such features and they would go away or remain inoperative, or
that we could override such elements, perhaps explain them
away. But I think the problem is deeper than that. The two
support beams that are most dangerous in Jeremiah (and perhaps
in all the prophets) are first, the tendency (both) to disregard and
denigrate women (the female and the feminine), and second, the
tolerance (not to say enthusiasm for) of violence. We need minimally to admit that the prophet (indeed the whole Bible) is born
from a thoroughly patriarchal and androcentric culture and will
resist easy vaccination against it. It is not simply that we are liable
to overstress the males-only world of the biblical Jeremiah, or to
interpret too simplistically and disproportionately the stock negative imagery of idolatry/adultery which the prophets tend to
delight in, always showcasing the woman as the erring and
sluttish partner. The divine commander-in-chief leading the
people to slaughter – either of their enemies or themselves – is, as
we know afresh, harmful to our health. Nor, of course, can we
simply whisper the passages or even excise them. They are there,
stand within the canon and as part of liturgy; and if we proceed
naively in regard to them they are not thereby deterred from their
impact.

If we preach without ever addressing the surface and deeper
sexism of certain passages, without struggling to resituate the
angry and bellicose language characterizing God, we simply
reinforce it, whether our move is made consciously or not. When
we rehearse, typically without comment, the many places where
the language of election and specialness between God and Israel
pertains, we reinforce – with one impact or another – the question of God's preferences. Does God prefer one people to another? Is it we, whoever 'we' may be? Is it we now, and not the

Jews, and if so, because of our superior virtue? Is God's favourite the others and not we, due to our inherent unworthiness in God's eyes? Does God so distinguish one gender from the other, one race or caste from its fellows, that all we most prize flows from such constructions? These are not, to my way of thinking, useful tracks to be dug ever-deeper in the imaginations and consciousness of most people I know.[8]

These passages present us – almost commandeer and beg us – to raise the questions of how our insight into the mystery of God both recedes and increases over long time as well as in our individual lives. Such topics are not without precedent, nor are we without models in these difficult passages. It has become clear, even comfortable to us, that though there are passages in both testaments where slavery is condoned – enjoined – such is not compatible with our sense of God's radical goodness. That step will have been a much more difficult one in the eras when our particular societies struggled over that question (I am thinking specifically of the abolitionist movement in the U.S.A. in the middle of the nineteenth century, when the passages on slavery and the hierarchal society of Israel will have been far more troublesome in liturgy than at present). We have not eliminated the passages (though they are not so frequently read as the violence-laden ones I am thinking of here). If we conclude that God once condoned slavery but no longer does, can God make the same move with sexism, with violence? Or does that phrasing suggest that the problem needs restatement? How will we, studying, reading and preaching well, take appropriate respon-

8. An analogous situation in many New Testament texts which recur in liturgy, relates to the manner by which the evangelists name and describe the Jewish opponents of Jesus. The names can be changed to 'officials' rather than 'Pharisees,' but it strikes me that to comment helpfully on the complex issues involved (occasionally) is more helpful than a change in terminology that most hearers are unlikely to pick up on in any case.

sibility within our long tradition and wide circles of co-readers to ask the questions better? It is not a move that will be made in a hop; it is a topic that will need a long and slow tending. But it is time to start, and time to continue.

CONCLUDING CHALLENGES

Critical study aids preaching, prayer, self-knowledge, and compassion. The real challenge is how first to form our reading strategies and then how to continue to nourish them suitably. I am not willing to excuse the lazy or the bored, the smug or even now the fearful, who ought to use their education and formation as occasion to exercise and excise such dreads about critical study of Scripture and faith.

A challenge I would offer to biblical faculties of seminaries, my own included: Is it possible in these days of relatively easy communication to set up a network of biblical scholars and alumni/ae, where a regular, well-chosen, and user-friendly source of relevant information might go from the seminary or theologate to those preaching? I am thinking of a new genre, not a long disquisition on a text, not a finished product, but perhaps some crucial new piece of information that might be unfolded over time? It would make a nice link between schools and students, between professors and those with whom they have worked. The benefits, I suspect, would flow both ways.

PROPHETIC STORIES AS A PREACHING RESOURCE: THE ELISHA COLLECTION

MARK A. O'BRIEN, O.P.

When one thinks of Old Testament prophecy, the natural tendency is to turn to books like Isaiah and Jeremiah. These portray prophets as powerful preachers and master poets. The poetic form gives their preaching a vitality that has attracted the attention of generations of preachers and their listeners – and rightly so. Nevertheless, there is another form of prophecy that may be overlooked as one is swept along by the power and intensity of the poetic sermon. These are the stories about prophets, especially those in the books of Samuel and Kings. Prominent among them of course are the stories about Elijah and Elisha.

Prophetic poetry and prophetic story provide different opportunities and challenges for the preacher. With the former, one's focus is on the prophetic sermon and how poetry shapes the words to give them rhetorical power and impact. With the latter, the focus is more on the plot of the story and the portrayal of its characters. The point of a story, the depiction of a character, tends to be subtle and even elusive, yet the impact of a story can be just as powerful as a prophetic sermon.

There is no better text to illustrate this than the collection of stories and shorter anecdotes about Elisha. Of particular value is the story of Elisha and the Shunammite woman in 2 Kings 4:8-37.[1] If one pays attention to the way any story works, prophetic stories are a rich vein to be mined by the preacher. And not only prophetic stories: Old Testament stories, whether about Israel's

1. Comparison with other stories of women in the Old Testament who are promised a child is beyond the scope of this essay (e.g. Sarah in Genesis 18, or the wife of Manoah in Judges 13). Studies by feminist scholars, in particular, have contributed greatly to our understanding of such stories.

ancestors in Genesis, Moses in Exodus and Numbers, or Israel's leaders in the historical books, exemplify the biblical art of storytelling and offer a wealth of material for preaching.

THE ELISHA COLLECTION

The collection of stories about Elisha begins with 2 Kings 2 where he takes up the mantle of his master Elijah. It effectively concludes with 2 Kings 8:1-15 which revisits two prominent items in the collection – Elisha's resuscitation of the Shunammite woman's child and his relationship with the kingdom of Syria (Aram). The story of Jehu's revolution in 2 Kings 9–10 begins with Elisha dispatching a disciple to anoint Jehu king, but this is not a story about the prophet as such. Somewhat separated from the collection is a final episode about Elisha followed by the report of his death (2 Kgs 13:14-21).

Because of legendary and miraculous elements, critical scholars who sought to reconstruct the history of ancient Israel attached little value to these stories. Happily, recent study of narrative has opened our eyes to the literary and theological qualities of such stories. Furthermore, we now realize that one cannot expect such texts to be historical records of Elisha and his times. Ancient Israel's authors operated in an age and culture that was marked by dramatic and imaginative storytelling. Maintaining a clear distinction between story and historical report, as we conceive it, was probably not an issue. Nevertheless, for readers interested in historical questions, the stories do allow some insight into how those who composed them thought and worked, and how they portrayed figures in their tradition.

A brief tour of the collection will serve to introduce the types of story found there and provide a context for a closer look at one of its greatest treasures – the story of Elisha and the Shunammite woman in 4:8-37. In 2 Kings 2, what one might call the 'succession story', there are two seminal moments. The first is the figure of a lone Elisha, the mantle of his master in his hand, striking the Jordan twice and crying 'where is the Lord, the God of Elijah?' (v. 14). The second is that of the new prophet responding to a pressing 'pastoral need' – a community troubled by bad water and barren land (v. 19). The first moment evokes the powerful yet elusive nature of the prophetic spirit. Despite the experience of divine power associated with Elijah's 'departure', Elisha appears indecisive. His first words are a question, his first action uncertain. He strikes the Jordan twice, a distant echo of the doubting Moses who struck the rock twice in Numbers 20:10-12.[2] Even though the company of prophets proclaims that 'the spirit of Elijah' rests on Elisha, dispute erupts between him and the company over the whereabouts of Elijah. The second seminal moment serves to dispel any doubt about Elisha's prophetic status and it involves his response to a need. In contrast to his earlier uncertainty, he now acts decisively as a prophet to fix a community's water supply (vv. 20-22). Both his words and actions are effective.

The subsequent narrative explores the power and elusiveness of prophecy – its profound mystery – in a variety of ways, not all of them comforting to the modern reader.[3] Prophetic power and insight are prominent in the war stories of 2 Kings 3, 2 Kings 6-7 and 2 Kings 8:7-15. Elisha, not Israel's king and army, is the one

---

2. The Hebrew in 2 Kings 2:14 uses the same phrase twice: 'and he struck the water'. The NRSV obscures the repetition by translating 'and (he) struck the water … When he had struck the water…' For a discussion of this and other aspects of the story, see my 'The Portrayal of Prophets in 2 Kings 2,' *AusBR* 46 (1998) 1-16.

3. In 2 Kings 2:23-24 Elisha curses a gang of boys who ridicule him and they are mauled by bears. This episode warns that those who revile the prophet are cursed: by implication, those who revere him are blessed. The text is a reminder that the Bible comes from another age and culture and that it does not always conform to our expectations.

who by his words and deeds exemplifies the 'chariots of Israel and its horsemen' (cf. 2 Kings 2:12 with 2 Kings 3:7 [horses], 2 Kings 6:17, 2 Kings 7:6 and 2 Kings 13:14). One may describe these as anti-war stories because Elisha's intervention thwarts the war-like plans of kings and their armies. In 2 Kings 3, the king of Israel claims that his campaign against a recalcitrant vassal, Moab, is the will of God (vv. 10, 13). Elisha's prophecy initially seems to endorse the claim but, via a series of ironic twists, leads to the very reversal of what the king and his allies set out to do. The king of Moab escapes and Israel is obliged to withdraw. Even worse, instead of providing plunder for Israel, the campaign has destroyed the source of that plunder – the wealth of Moab (v. 25). The story implies that it is dangerous, especially for one in power, to presume to know the will of God.

The two stories in 6:8-23 and 6:24–7:20 tell how Elisha brings peace when kings and armies seek violence and death. In the first, Elisha temporally blinds a Syrian (Aramean) cohort sent to seize him, throws a party for them and then sends them home. There are no casualties. In the second story, he promises a peaceful end to a Syrian siege. A group of lepers, not soldiers, brings the good news of the enemy's flight. The only casualty is an army captain who doubts the prophet (7:2) – he is trampled to death in the stampede to plunder the enemy camp.

The legendary and miraculous elements in the stories should not detract from their value for the preacher. It is a mistake to eliminate such elements in an attempt to recover the historical core of a story. As they stand, the stories make an important faith claim; namely, that God turns what is hopeless and death-dealing into what is hope-filled and life-giving. God can make the impossible possible through the word of the prophet. The legendary elements add a light, sometimes humorous, touch to stories

that deal with the horror of war. It is a tribute to the skill and
sensitivity of Old Testament storytellers that they did not wallow
in violence and terror. Nor did they see the human condition as
tragic: they may paint it in sombre colours at times but overall
there is a sense of life and hope.[4]

In between these anti-war stories in 2 Kings 3 and 6-7, there is
the story of the 'Great Woman' of Shunem in 4:8-37 and the
'Great Man' Naaman the Syrian in 2 Kings 5. Each is preceded
and followed by an anecdote about Elisha the miracle worker
(4:1-7, 38-41, 42-44; 6:1-7). One gains the impression of a carefully
arranged structure but it is nevertheless a flexible one. 2 Kings 5
shares something of the anti-war stories in that Elisha intervenes
when the Israelite king sees Naaman's request as a veiled attempt
to pick a quarrel (v. 7-8). Nevertheless, the story seems equally at
home with the preceding accounts of Elisha's care for those in
need – Naaman is a leper seeking healing. It also devotes considerable attention to the character of Elisha's servant Gehazi who
features in the story of the Shunammite woman.

The arrangement of this material may in part be due to what
Alexander Rofé, professor at Hebrew University, Jerusalem,
calls 'associative order, i.e., the arrangement by external associa-
tions, such as similarity of words or phrases'.[5] According to Rofé,
this is a typical phenomenon in biblical texts. Elisha's assistance
for a woman and her sons in 4:1-7 may be linked to the following
story of the Shunammite woman by the presence of children in
each and because each woman refers to herself as 'your servant'
(4:2, 16). Similarly, the episode in 4:38-41 may have been placed

---

4. For an engaging treatment of the Bible as 'comic drama' not tragedy, see Francesca
    Aran Murphy, *The Comedy of Revelation: Paradise Lost and Paradise Regained in
    Biblical Narrative* (2000; Edinburgh: T. & T. Clark).
5. Alexander Rofé, *The Prophetical Stories. The Narratives about the Prophets in the
    Hebrew Bible. Their Literary Types and History* (1988; Jerusalem: The Magnes Press)
    p. 49.

after the story of the Shunammite woman because of a perceived association between the death of her child and the prophets' cry that there is 'death in the pot' (v. 40). The miracle of the loaves in 4:42-44 may have been placed after 4:38-41 because of the theme of food and Elisha's command to 'Serve it/give it to the people and let them eat' (vv. 41, 43). It may be associated with 2 Kings 5 because both the man from Baal-shalishah and Naaman come bearing gifts. The axe-head incident in 6:1-7 and the story of Naaman's healing are both associated with the Jordan river (5:10; 6:2).

The impression is of a delicate editorial touch in the arrangement of the present text. There are connections but they are not intrusive. The result is a bonus for the preacher: each text can be read as an independent piece; each can also be explored for its connection with others and its contribution to the portrait of Elisha.

A common thread in the stories and shorter anecdotes in 2 Kings 3-7 is the prophet as a life-giver for those in need. In the war stories, Elisha's intervention undoes the deadly plans of kings or brings peace where violence threatened. These frame texts in which he brings life-sustaining or life-giving power to a variety of domestic situations, which, from a human point of view, look hopeless or powerless.

The story of Elisha and the Shunammite woman occupies a special place in this company. Of all the narratives in the collection, this one alone tells how Elisha raised the dead – the ultimate sign of prophetic power.[6] Its importance is also signalled by 2 Kings 8:1-6 which provides a sequel to the story. Yet it is in the story of Elisha and the Shunammite woman that the elusive

6. The last mention of Elisha in 2 Kings 13:20-21 tells of the raising of a corpse through contact with his corpse.

nature of prophetic power, glimpsed initially in 2 Kings 2, is brought more to the fore. The interplay of these two powerful themes gives a special fascination and depth to this story and an array of possibilities for the preacher.

THE STORY OF ELISHA AND THE 'GREAT WOMAN'
OF SHUNEM (2 KINGS 4:8-37)[7]

One does not have to be a literary expert to appreciate this story. The customary tools of narrative criticism are as applicable here as to any other literary piece; we are familiar with them and use them regularly to enjoy the literature of our own culture. The following list is therefore simply a reminder – sensitivity to the way things are communicated (form) in order to grasp what is communicated (content); identification of the constituent parts of a text and their relationship to the whole; attention to the way characters are portrayed in a story; tracking the plot of a story and how this normally involves a situation, a complication, a crisis and its resolution.

Three specifically biblical items need to be added to this list. One concerns characteristic features of Old Testament storytelling such as reticence and economy of expression. Our awareness of these will develop as we become more familiar with Old Testament stories and the culture and history behind them. Another is that Old Testament texts are often the work of more than one hand. However, there seems little evidence of this in 2 Kings 4:8-37. A third is the need to be aware of the particular theology of inspiration that influences the way people interpret biblical texts. It is good to know where we, and those to whom we preach, are coming from. Some may regard this text as an

7.   The term 'great (woman)' is translated as 'wealthy' in the NRSV. It can have this sense (cf. Gen 26:13; 1 Sam 25:2; 2 Sam 19:33; Job 1:3). Nevertheless, within the context of this story, it seems to acquire a deeper meaning in relation to the woman.

accurate historical account: it is the Word of God and what it says must therefore be (historically) true. Others may see it as a dramatic composition by a storyteller drawing on traditional information, or as a work of fiction like the Book of Jonah or Jesus' parables. They believe that inspiration operates in the various ways people express themselves: a text does not have to be historically accurate to be inspired.

To demonstrate one position to the satisfaction of those holding others is probably out of the question. The only 'evidence' we have is the biblical text and it is on this limited evidence that we must base our interpretations. The only 'tools' we have to sift the evidence are our limited literary and associated skills. It is virtually impossible to be critically aware of all the factors involved in reading a text and to take them into account. My own preference is for the second position outlined: Israelite storytellers drew on the rich stock of their tradition but in a creative way that would engage and challenge their audience. They were like the scribe described in Matthew 13:52 'who brings out of his treasure what is new and what is old'.

Telling a story is a creative moment for a storyteller but it also imposes certain limitations. There is a plot to unfold and so some things need to be highlighted while others can receive only passing attention.[8] There are characters to portray and while one or two can be developed (the plot may require focus on a prophet), others serve to fill in the background. Historical and cultural distances between ancient authors and contemporary listeners/

8. Old Testament stories like those about Elisha can be read in a few minutes. This has led Antony F. Campbell to propose that the written text is an outline of the story, a guide for oral performance. In a performance, a storyteller could flesh out scenes in ways that were impossible to record with the methods then available. Choices would of course still need to be made, depending on the occasion, the audience, the storyteller's familiarity with the tale, etc ('The Reported Story: Midway Between Oral Performance and Literary Art,' *Semeia* 46 [1989] pp. 77-85).

readers may mean that some elements in a story will be seen as limitations or even offensive (the way Elisha addresses the Shunammite woman). These factors need to be kept in mind when evaluating a story and the characters it portrays.

The relationship between reader and text is a complex matter and complete agreement between readers is unlikely. Nevertheless, I am willing to assert that most readers would agree – with some fine-tuning here and there – that our story has the following constituent parts. There is the opening scene in 4:8-10 that tells how Elisha came to avail of the woman's hospitality. The next scene in vv. 11-16 involves the promise of a child with the fulfilment of that promise in v. 17. Verses 18-20 tell of the death of the child and vv. 21-37 the events that unfold as a result – the mother's reaction to the death and her dramatic encounter with Elisha (vv. 21-30); his servant Gehazi's unsuccessful attempt to revive the child in vv. 31; Elisha's successful attempt in vv. 32-37. Some readers may prefer a more detailed division. There is no hard and fast rule about this; readers have different perspectives and this will influence their assessment of the literary phenomena. It is noteworthy that three major parts of the above division, vv. 8-10, 11-17 and 18-20 (21-37) are introduced by the phrase 'one day'.[9] Each 'day' marks a significant stage in the unfolding of a story that reaches a turning point with the third occurrence – the day of the child's death.

The preceding text leads up to it – the woman's hospitality, Elisha's response and the promise of a child, the child's birth and death. The subsequent text looks back to it – the mother's reaction to the death, her encounter with Elisha, the resuscitation of the child. On this reading, the plot of the story looks relatively

9. Cf. Rofé, *The Prophetical Stories*, 27-28 and Robert L. Cohn, *2 Kings* (Berit Olam: Studies in Hebrew Narrative and Poetry; 2000; Collegeville: The Liturgical Press) pp. 27-28.

straightforward: the miraculous power of the prophet over life and death. He gives life and he restores life. This is true enough. But, blessed is the reader whose second thoughts come first: closer inspection reveals a more complex and subtle picture.

Stories normally unfold their plot by developing an initial situation (4:8-10) via a complication (vv. 11-17) that builds to a crisis (vv. 18-20; the death of the child). The remainder of the story tells how the crisis is resolved (vv. 21-37). Sometimes, the crisis may be only partly resolved, allowing for a further story or another chapter to a book. The mark of a great storyteller is to exploit the conventional form in a creative way. In my judgment, whoever composed this story did just that. The way the plot unfolds suggests that the death and resuscitation of the child is important but not central. The real interest of the story is not so much whether the child will be raised but how this will come about.[10]

An important component that drives the plot of this story is Elisha's promise of a child and the realization of that promise. Two miracles are associated with this component: the first is the gift of a child to the childless woman; the second is the resuscitation of her child. Given the miracle of the child's birth, it seems unlikely the story would end with its untimely death. This would make it a tragedy and, as pointed out earlier, the Bible does not have a tragic view of humanity. Rather, expectation is raised as to how the crisis of the child's death will be resolved. What further miracle may be worked? A tragic ending would also cast a very dark shadow over prophecy. Although this story does paint a critical portrait of the prophet, it believes in prophetic power.

10. 2 Kings 6:11-23 is somewhat similar. According to v. 12, Elisha knows the most secret plans of the King of Aram; hence he is well aware of the plot to kidnap him. There is no real crisis for Elisha; the focus of the story is on how he will handle an enemy about whom he knows all.

The portrayal of the two main characters in the story supports this interpretation. The woman's hospitality initially draws her and Elisha together. Ironically, his attempt to repay her has the opposite effect. The woman declines any favours for her hospitality (v. 13b) and does not welcome his promise of a child (v. 16b). After the child is born, there is no further reference to his visits or to her hospitality. A gap seems to have opened between them, arousing expectation as to how it might be bridged. The death of the child is the catalyst for a decisive reversal of 'direction', a bridging of the gap – superbly narrated as a dramatic dash by the woman to Mount Carmel and an equally dramatic encounter with Elisha there. As at the beginning, she takes the initiative. A reader senses that this second encounter will play a vital role in the fate of the child who lies dead on the man of God's bed.

In contrast to the woman, Elisha does not initiate hospitality. He accepts it and then insists on rewarding the woman where no such favour is sought. He maintains a certain distance, communicating with her via his servant Gehazi (vv. 12-16). When she objects to his promise of a child, Elisha offers no reply. One could say that he, rather than the woman, 'bears' responsibility for the child. If he has 'worked' the miracle of its birth, a reader can expect that he will work the miracle of restoring it to life. Nevertheless, there are some surprises in the portrayal of the man of God that create an element of uncertainty about how the crisis will be resolved.

Uncertainty is signalled early in the piece when Elisha does not know what Gehazi knows – that the woman is childless and her husband old (v. 14). Why should this be so for a prophet who can so confidently predict 'at this season, in due time, you shall embrace a son' (v. 16a)? The uncertainty becomes more pronounced as the plot unfolds. When the woman reaches him at

Mount Carmel, he confesses that God has hidden from him the cause of her 'bitter distress' (v. 27). Without the insight provided by God, prophets are ordinary folk like us and, like us, they miss things and bungle things. Elisha dispatches Gehazi with his staff to awaken the child. The mother senses this will not work because she refuses to leave Elisha. Her cry 'I will not leave you' (v. 30) is exactly what Elisha says three times to his master Elijah in 2 Kings 2:2, 4, 6.[11] At this point in the drama it seems that the Shunammite woman is cast as the prophet rather than Elisha. She has 'foreknowledge' that Gehazi will fail. In 2 Kings 2, Elijah plays the role of master to Elisha as disciple. One would expect that Elisha would play the role of master now that Elijah is gone. Instead, in an intriguing reversal, Elisha is cast as disciple to another 'master'. According to 4:30b, 'So he (Elisha) rose up and followed her'.

This subtle critique of the prophet is also signalled by the distribution of the man of God title in the story. Elisha is given this title by the woman in 4:9, 16, 22, and by the narrator in 4:21, 25 (bis), 27 (bis). After v. 27, where Elisha admits that God has hidden things from him, the title no longer occurs.

The elusive and unpredictable nature of prophecy is also evident in the account of the resuscitation of the child. Commentators have seen a magical quality in 4:34-35, arguing that Elisha recharges via his own senses the corresponding senses of the dead child. This may be so because magical elements occur in other prophetic stories. Nevertheless, the analysis so far suggests there may be more at work in this story than magic. Verses 34-35 report the second of two 'magical' moves to raise the child. The first is in vv. 30-31 where Gehazi is dispatched to lay his master's staff on

---

11. The NRSV has translated the same Hebrew phrase in 4:30 as 'I will not leave without you'. The RSV has the better translation 'I will not leave you'.

the face of the child and awaken it. The use of the master's staff recalls 2 Kings 2:13-14 where Elisha strikes the Jordan twice with his master's mantle and asks 'where is the Lord, the God of Elijah?' The water parts but Elisha's words and actions betray uncertainty. Compared to this, 4:29-31 indicates Elisha is confident that the touch of his staff will awaken the child. It fails. If this is a story about a prophet wielding magical power, the staff episode does not really help the cause.

Elisha's second and successful 'magical' attempt to raise the child is preceded by prayer (v. 33). This is the first time in the story that he prays to God. The combination of prayer followed by bodily gestures parallels 1 Kings 17:20-23 where Elijah in similar fashion raises a child from the dead. As v. 22 makes clear, he is successful because God heeds his prayer. Yet Elijah's bodily gestures must also be significant; otherwise why recount them? Presumably they are to be understood as part of the prophet's intercession – it involves his whole person. If this is the case, something similar can be assumed for Elisha. 2 Kings 4:32-35 also describes Elisha's actions in more detail than the account of Elijah. Within the context of the story, the intensity and intimacy of Elisha's actions evoke a sense of deep commitment to this child for whom he is, after all, more responsible than the woman who never asked for it.

Verses 33-35 create a poignant contrast when compared to Elisha's first encounter with the Shunammite woman in vv. 12-16. In this earlier scene there is a sense of distance as he speaks to her through Gehazi while she remains outside his room. This may well reflect customs in ancient Israel where people from different social strata knew their place. But such polite formalities are shattered when, in vv. 25-27, she brushes past Gehazi to prostrate herself before Elisha and grasp his feet. In response to this, it seems only fitting that this man of God should return with her to prostrate himself in prayer on the body of her dead son.

FROM STORY TO HOMILY

The step from story to homily is as creative and challenging a moment for the preacher as the creation of a story is for the story-teller. And, as with storytelling, it imposes certain limitations. Choices have to be made, one cannot preach on all aspects of a text. But, by paying attention to the dynamics of a biblical story, the preacher should be equipped to identify elements in it that will best serve the sermon to be given. For a particular sermon, the plot of a story may be judged the more important element to focus on. Alternatively, it may be one or more of the characters in a story that attracts the preacher's attention. There is little doubt that the characters of Elisha and the Shunammite woman loom large in our story. Indeed, the plot seems to have been shaped to highlight their respective roles.

In relation to Elisha, it is striking that a story, which celebrates the peak of the prophet's power – restoring the dead to life – can also be so critical in its portrayal of the prophet. Elisha is described by the woman as a 'holy man of God' in 4:9. Yet he makes no mention of God until v. 27 when he admits that God has concealed the cause of the woman's distress from him. He bungles the first attempt to restore her child and is obliged to follow her initiative rather than his own. A society that is able to portray a major figure in its tradition in such a way is one that has a mature and confident faith. It has moved beyond the need to accord hero status to Elisha or indeed any other prophet.[12]

Associated with this critical portrayal of Elisha is the mysteri-

---

12. It is significant that most of the major figures of the Old Testament are presented as limited, even flawed human beings, in need of God's mercy.

ous and elusive nature of the prophetic charism: it is not something the prophet has on his own terms. Just when Elisha needs
prophetic insight to respond to the bereaved mother, it is hidden
from him (4:27). Instead, it is manifest in the mother. Just when
he needs prophetic power to raise the dead child, it is not there (v.
31). He prays (v. 33) and it returns. But is prayer a requirement
for the exercise of such power? Earlier in the story, Elisha
successfully prophesied the birth of the child without recourse to
prayer.

A striking feature of the portrayal of the Shunammite woman
is her reaction to the death of the child. There is no mention of
mourning or weeping over the dead body; rather she is galva-
nized into a burst of purposeful activity. Her journey ends with
her prostrate before Elisha in what looks to be a dramatic gesture
of entreaty. One would expect a plea for help to follow; instead,
she asks two questions to which the prophet offers no answer
(4:28).

In one sense, there is no need to because the answers are
obvious to those who have listened to or read the story thus far.
In another sense however, her questions and the prophet's silence
imply deeper issues are running here. Are her questions an
accusation that Elisha has indeed deceived her, as she feared (v.
16)? He promised her new life but instead there is death and
grief. Do they imply that Elisha is the one responsible for her
child and so in some way responsible for its death? The elasticity
of the story is such that a reader would be unwise to settle for just
one answer to her questions.

If her questions are accusations against the man of God, what
implications do they have for the portrayal of God in the story?
Elisha is described several times as a man of God; yet, as already
noted, he acknowledges God only on two occasions (4:27, 33).

The woman invokes God once when she swears 'as the LORD lives … I will not leave you' (v. 30). God is not in the foreground of this story; the focus remains firmly fixed on the human players.

Nevertheless, one gains the impression that God responds to the woman's faith and the prophet's prayer to move the story to a happy conclusion. One might ask: Why would God bring about the birth of a child only to allow it to die so soon? On this question, the text is silent. For some, this will be seen as a weakness in the story. For others, it is a question the story does not answer because there is no theology that can offer a satisfactory answer.

Each Old Testament story has its unique shape and features, its strengths and limitations; as a result readers are likely to assess each story somewhat differently. The story of Elisha and the Shunammite woman explores a number of issues with sensitivity and skill. Other issues remain in the background or are passed over in silence – perhaps because words would be inappropriate. Despite their limitations, prophetic stories can have transforming power in the hands of a preacher. In the case of the stories about Elisha, the text actually provides an example of their transforming power – 2 Kings 8:1-6. In this passage the King of Israel, as a result of listening to what one may call 'the gospel of Elisha' from both Gehazi and the Shunammite woman, is moved to ensure that all she lost during a famine is restored to her.

PART 5

Dominican Preaching

A WINE OF ENCOURAGEMENT:
PREACHING IN A TIME OF DISILLUSION*

PAUL MURRAY, O.P.

In a lengthy but illuminating work entitled 'Treatise on the Formation of Preachers' composed by the medieval Dominican, Blessed Humbert of Romans, there is one line, one phrase, which leaps off the page – at least for me. Humbert writes: 'I became like a man who is drunk, like someone sodden with wine, from my encounter with the words of God'.[1]

That image of drinking or of being made drunk is worth noting for it is – I discovered a few years ago – an image which recurs over and over again in the writings of the early Dominican preachers, and not only in their theological writings and homilies but also in the stories they liked to tell about themselves. The image had been used before, of course, by other religious traditions within the Church in order to evoke aspects of the spiritual and apostolic life.[2] But Dominicans seem to have taken to this metaphor with a unique enthusiasm. In their conversations and homilies and writings the image of drinking or of being made drunk described not only the overwhelming impact the Word of God made on their interior lives but also the effect of that encounter on almost every other aspect of their lives as preachers.

In this brief essay I would like to do two things: first of all, to try to understand why the early Dominicans were instinctively drawn to the image of drinking, and in what way it served their

* This paper was originally delivered in May 2002 to an Assembly of the Irish Dominican Province. It is printed here in the 'spoken' form in which it was first given.

1. S. Tugwell O.P. ed. 'Treatise on the Formation of Preachers', no. 70, in *Early Dominicans: Selected Writings*, (New York 1982) p. 202. Humbert is echoing a passage from Jeremiah 23:9.

2. See 'Ivresse Spirituelle' in *Dictionaire de Spiritualité*, Vol VII (Paris 1971) pp. 2312-37.

understanding of prayer and preaching; and, then, to indicate the possible usefulness and relevance of this image at a time of crisis in the Irish Church and in our own Province.

DRUNK ON THE WORD

Many images have been used, over the centuries, to describe progress in the spiritual life, or to name the mysteries of faith-experience, the dark night, for example, or the ladder, or the steep ascent of a mountain. Why the first Dominican preachers should have chosen such an unexpected image as drinking is, I think, because it answered so well to their sense of the Gospel. Their spirituality was not something tense or introverted or self-preoccupied but rather joyous and expansive. And so the image of a group of friends or companions drinking together would naturally have appealed to them. Here is a line, for example, from one of Blessed Jordan of Saxony's homilies, a sentence which is typically down-to-earth and colloquial: 'Nowadays people say, "I think it would be great if you could come to me and have a drink". And it's just like that with the Lord. For he says to the soul: "Give me something to drink". O if only you knew the love of God which is saying to you, "I thirst"!'[3]

Drinking wine was, of course, such a common custom in the Middle Ages it might seem, perhaps, a mistake to read too much into the use made by Dominicans of this image. But if we compare the Dominican use of the image in the early years with the use made by the Franciscans, for example, our own particular enthusiasm becomes evident. In the *Fioretti* of St. Francis of Assisi, which can in some way be compared with our own *Vitae Fratrum*, there is only one brief passage that refers to drinking

3. 'Sermo de Sancto Johanne Evangelista', f. 90 va. See 'Three Sermons of Friar Jordan of Saxony, the Successor of St. Dominic', *The English Historical Review*, CCXIII (January 1939) p. 14.

whereas in the *Vitae Fratrum* the image of drinking occurs again and again.

One reason why Dominican preachers were drawn to talk and to write so much about drinking is that wine or drink is an image of the goodness or the sweetness of life. Whereas many of the ascetics of St. Dominic's day would have regarded it as something evil, Dominic himself, with his own deep understanding of the goodness of creation and his innate respect for every living thing, clearly accepted it – and with enthusiasm – as something good.

On one particular occasion, according to someone who knew Dominic well, as soon as the preacher had finished delivering a talk in a certain convent, he said to the sisters: 'It would be good, my daughters, to have something to drink'.[4] One of the brethren was asked to go and get some wine that was poured into a cup. Dominic was the first to take a drink. Then, the brethren, who were there, were encouraged to take a drink, and third and last, the sisters. Dominic said: 'I want all my daughters to have a drink'. In the text, as composed by Blessed Cecilia, we read: 'all the sisters drank as much as they wanted encouraged by St Dominic, who kept on saying, "Drink up, my daughters!" At that time there were 104 sisters there, and they all drank as much wine as they wanted.'[5]

The notion that drinking wine is not only something good but also something 'healthy for soul and body' is stated by Aquinas in a number of places.[6] But St Thomas always makes it clear that alcohol, though it may well be healthy, should not be over-indulged in, much less regarded as one's best friend or one's only solace. 'Wine', Thomas remarks dryly, 'does not love man the way man loves wine'! ('*Non enim vinum amat hominem, sicut*

4. *Miracula* 6 [by Blessed Cecilia]. See *Early Dominicans*, p. 391.
5. Ibid.
6. See, for example, II.II q.149 a.1

homo amat vinum').[7]

Another reason, and perhaps the most important, why the early Dominicans were drawn to the image of drinking was because it gave them a vivid way of speaking about preaching – about the need, first, to become 'drunk' on the Word, and then about the effects of that encounter with God: the ecstasy of self-forgetfulness, the grace of new joy, the compulsion to share that joy with others, and the gifts of renewed hope and courage. On one occasion, making use of the image of drinking or drunkenness to great effect, Humbert of Romans drew attention to an aspect of preaching which has often been overlooked. In spite of the manifest wisdom in our motto, '*contemplata aliis tradere*', [to pass on to others what we have contemplated], Humbert suggests that it is not always because of the preacher's own holiness or spiritual enthusiasm that the words of a particular homily catch fire, but rather because of the enthusiasm and awakened faith of God's people listening to the Word. It is because of them – the listeners – that the preacher is sometimes able, even while preaching, to enter into the fire of the Word. Humbert quotes *Proverbs*: 'He who makes others drunk will himself be made drunk too' (Prov 11:25). And then he comments: 'The one who makes his hearers drunk with the words of God will himself be made drunk with a draft of manifold blessing.'[8]

Among the best-known early Dominicans the one who strikes me as, by far, the most Irish in character and temperament is Blessed Jordan of Saxony. I say this, not simply because Jordan likes to cite the image of drinking more than anyone else, but because he had such a great sense of humor. According to the ancient account, Jordan 'overflowed with enthusiastic talk, bril-

7. *Sententia Libri Ethicorum*, VIII, 2, 1115 b 27 (Roma 1969) p. 446
8. 'Treatise on the Formation of Preachers', no. 34, p. 195. See also no. 176, p. 237, and no. 325, pp. 272-73.

liant with apt and powerful illustrations'.[9] What is more, he worked quite consciously, we are told, at getting his hearers 'drunk' on the Word. Once, when he was preaching at Padua, someone asked him why he had such manifest success with the Arts students, the students of Aristotle, but seemed to make little impact on the theologians and canonists. Jordan replied, speaking with his characteristic verve and sharp good humor:

> Arts men drink the plain water of Aristotle and the other philosophers all week so when they are offered the words of Christ or his disciples in a Sunday sermon or on a feast-day, they fall victim at once to the intoxication of the Holy Spirit's wine, and hand over to God not only their goods but themselves. But these theologians are always listening to the words of God, and they go the same way as a country sacristan who passes the altar so often that he loses his reverence for it and frequently turns his back on it, while outsiders bow reverently towards it.[10]

As a direct result of listening to Jordan, an amazing number of young men joined the Dominican Order. They had obviously become intoxicated with 'the Spirit's wine'. But Jordan's unique genius or 'tactic' with respect to vocations, was not always matched, it has to be said, by the recruitment practice of some the brethren. One report indicates that actual alcohol may have been employed, on one occasion, to 'encourage' a particular individual to join the Order! The source for this account is a letter sent by Pope Innocent IV in 1244. There was, at that time, apparently, at least the suspicion, that a number of friars actually got a schoolmaster from Asti drunk, and then forced a habit on him – not, obviously,

---

9. *Vitae Fratrum*, III, 11, p. 108. See *Early Dominicans*, p. 127.
10. *Libellus*, III, 42 ix, p. 141. See *Early Dominicans*, p. 130.

the kind of *spiritual* intoxication Jordan of Saxony had in mind! [11]

JORDAN AND THE WINE OF ENCOURAGEMENT

At one of the earliest chapters of the Order, held around the time of Pentecost – and we are at Pentecost now – the brethren were obviously feeling a bit discouraged. According to the *Lives of the Brethren*, they asked Blessed Jordan, although he was feeling really ill at the time, 'to say a few words of consolation'.[12] Jordan, more than anyone in his time, was the great encourager of the brethren. A sermon of his has survived in which he speaks memorably about what he calls 'the wine of hope'. It is, he says, that 'good wine which puts a man at his ease, and cheers him up so that he no longer feels his sorrows'.[13]

In his short address to the assembled brothers at the Pentecost assembly, Jordan referred to that passage in *The Acts of the Apostles* in which the first preachers of the Gospel, after they had come down from the upper room in the power of the Spirit, were accused of being 'drunk' or 'filled with new wine'. Jordan pointed out that it was precisely to people like the apostles, people who had been humbled by failure, and who were 'poor in spirit', to whom the fullness of the grace of Pentecost was given. In order to make his point vivid, Jordan uses the image of a goblet or a drinking-cup that had been completely emptied. 'My brothers, during this week [of Pentecost] we often say these words, "They were all filled with the Holy Spirit". You know that a drinking-

---

11. *Registrum*, no. 529. See *Early Dominicans*, p. 154, n. 27. My confrère, Austin Flannery, has drawn my attention to a comparable story reported by Thomas Cage in the se enteenth century. Cage claimed he had been recruited to the Order with copious drafts of sherry! See J.S. Cummins, *A Question of Rites: Friar Domingo Navarette and the Jesuits* (Aldershot, Hants., 1993) p. 222.
12. B.M. Reichert, O.P., ed. 'De Sancte Memorie Fratre Iordane', XLII, in *Vitae Fratrum*, (Louvain 1846) p. 142.
13. 'Sermon 5', 'Les Sermons de Jourdain de Saxe, Successeur de Saint Dominique', *Archivum Fratrum Praedicatorum.*, Vol LXVI, 1996, p. 205.

cup, once it is full, can hold no more. All that is poured in, only flows out again. On this account the holy apostles were filled with the Holy Spirit having been first emptied of their own spirit.'[14]

Emptied of their own spirit. We don't know the reason why, at that particular Pentecost assembly of Dominicans in the thirteenth century, the brethren were feeling so discouraged, or what precise circumstances had caused them to feel so empty in themselves and poor in spirit. But what is clear is that Jordan saw this new state or condition of emptiness – the fact of being and of feeling severely humbled – as an opportunity for grace. When they were full of themselves and sure of themselves, like a cup of wine filled to overflowing, they could receive little or no help from God, but once emptied and poor in spirit, they were able at last to receive the Spirit's grace, and drink in the new wine of hope, somehow finding courage again, in that 'drinking', to go out from their upper room of fear and preach the Word.

An observation Cardinal Newman makes about the preacher comes to mind here. If, by chance, he has never known great affliction in his life or oppression or humiliation, the preacher risks delivering very banal and superficial homilies, preaching himself rather than the Word. 'The most awful truths [of Scripture],' Newman says, 'are ... used by him ... for his own purposes'. 'But,' Newman goes on at once to note, and the phrase is memorable, 'let his heart at length be ploughed by some keen grief or deep anxiety, and Scripture is a new book to him.'[15] In the same passage, Newman writes: 'to the disconsolate, the tempted, the perplexed, the suffering, there comes, by means of their very trials, an enlargement of thought, which enables them to see in [Scripture] what they never saw before'.[16]

14. 'De Sancte Memorie Fratre Iordane', XLII, in *Vitae Fratrum*, p. 142.
15. *A Grammar of Assent* (New York 1955) pp. 79-80.
16. Ibid.

I think it is no exaggeration to say that, in the present crisis of the Church in Ireland and in the present crisis of the Province, most of us, if not all us, find ourselves among 'the disconsolate', 'the tempted' and 'the perplexed'. We feel hurt and bewildered, and for good reason, and you who are living in Ireland are more affected obviously than someone like myself living in Rome. But what both Jordan of Saxony and Cardinal Newman are saying about the life of preachers, is that opposition, humiliation, grief, embarrassment, or whatever it is which wounds us as a group and wounds us as individuals, that experience of being hurt, that wound itself, in spite of all the damage which it causes, can also somehow become a blessing, a purification, and an aid for better preaching. Somewhere, in one of his poems, the seventeenth century poet, Henry Vaughan, once shrewdly remarked:

> ... the poet, like bad priest,
> Is seldom good, but when oppressed.
> And wit as well as piety
> Doth thrive best in adversity.[17]

But these words are easy to say. What is wounding us and wounding the Church, in these months, is a betrayal of the Gospel and of Gospel witness, and a betrayal of the young, the effect of which is almost impossible to calculate When, day after day, we find ourselves confronting not just bad news on television, or in our newspapers, but truly horrendous news, we very quickly begin to feel paralyzed. We have no choice, it seems, but to take in the full sadness and the appalling horror of it all. But contemplating so much evil – the evil of sexual abuse for example within the priesthood and religious life – can very quickly sap the

---

17. 'To the Editor of the Matchless Orinda', in *Henry Vaughan: The Complete Poems* (Harmondsworth 1976) p. 345.

sources of our energy and our hope, and especially if we focus our attention, as we must in this area, on the plight of the victims. How are we to continue as preachers to take in so much bad news and yet still retain our hope?

BAD NEWS AND GOOD NEWS

In the present crisis, particularly in relation to the issue of sexual abuse, there are a number of important questions and issues which, obviously, I am unable to address in this short paper: the issue, for example, about being transparent, and the need for ourselves and our leaders never again to engage in any kind of 'cover-up'. But the question I want to raise here is simply this: How are we to continue, as men, as preachers, as believers, to drink in so much bad news every day and yet still retain our hope?

In almost every culture and civilization, this question has come to the fore in one form or other – the question, that is, about how to survive a direct confrontation with evil. One of the most powerful and important myths from the ancient world, one that grapples with this question, is the myth of Perseus. Perseus knows that he has to slay the evil Gorgon, Medusa, and he has to do it by cutting off her head. But he also knows that anyone who stares directly into the face of the evil Gorgon will at once be turned into stone. Perseus accepts as a gift from one of the gods a shining bronze shield. And this helps him to achieve his task. For, instead of staring directly into the face of Medusa as he slays her, he looks only at the image of the Gorgon reflected in his shield. So, he sees evil, he confronts it, but indirectly in a sense, and as a result he is not hypnotized by evil, not paralysed, not turned into stone.

One of the great prayers of the Irish tradition, 'St Patrick's

Breastplate', is concerned almost exclusively with the question of confronting evil. From the beginning to the end we are re-minded, by the words of the prayer, never to face evil on our own, but always to seek refuge in God and in God's strength. The prayer begins:

> I arise today
> Through a mighty strength, the invocation of the Trinity...
> I arise today
> Through God's strength to pilot me...
> God's hand to guard me,
> God's way to lie before me,
> God's shield to protect me,
> God's host to save me
> From snares of devils,
> From temptations of vices,
> From everyone who will wish me ill,
> Afar and near,
> Alone and in a multitude,
> I summon today all these powers between me and those
>   evils...against every knowledge
> that corrupts man's body and soul.
> Christ to shield me today...[18]

If out of pride or curiosity I allow myself to contemplate evil directly, without seeking refuge in God, if I contemplate it, day after day, week after week, either in the ordinary realm of the public media or in private gossip, gradually it will rob me of all my energy and hope. But if, when I have to confront evil, I have the humility to look at it only in the light of Christ my shield, then

18. S. Dwyer, ed. 'St Patrick's Breastplate', in *Playing With Fire: A Natural Selection of Religious Poetry* (Dublin 1980) pp.30-2.

my energy and my hope will not be taken from me.

There are two ways, I think, in which we can be turned to stone when confronting evil. The first is due to an over-load of bad news, the effect of which can be despair, a slow *petrifaction* of despair. That is something all of us will recognize in ourselves should it begin to happen. But the second is something far subtler. It is the hardening of our heart against those among our brothers whom we perceive to be touched in any way by evil, it is the projection of our own fears onto others, it is the sin of harsh judgment. This does not mean that I cannot name evil as evil, and fight that evil in order to protect the innocent. But I can never judge the person; I can judge only the deed. Final judgment is for God alone. I can never name as evil the inner heart of one of my brothers, no matter what evil he may appear to have done or what damage he may have caused.

Learning to look directly at that mirror which is Christ my shield, learning to see the evil around me, and the evil within me, in the light of Christ, is the best way, in fact the only sure way, to prevent my heart from being hardened into a stone by either fear or prejudice, despair or false judgment.

Journalists and social-commentators can give us innumerable facts; necessary facts; facts which are painful sometimes and which must be faced. But all the facts in the world don't add up to the saving truth of the Gospel. The Good News is more, far more, than the sum total of all the knowledge and information, which comes to us from the sciences, or from philosophy, or from the media, even though that knowledge may well be useful and illuminating in itself.

It is, I think, an amazing thing for us to realize that when God looks at us, he looks at much more than the facts of our lives. Catherine of Siena says that God is 'drunk with love for our good'.[19] And in one of her prayers, thinking about the mystery of our creation, she exclaims: 'O unutterable love, even though you saw all the evils that all your creatures would commit against your infinite goodness, you acted as if you did not see and set your eye only on the beauty of your creature with whom you fell in love, like one drunk and crazy with love. And in love you drew us out of yourself giving us being'.[20]

If we want to be preachers (the early Dominicans tell us over and over again) it is important – it is *necessary* – to drink in the knowledge that we, that you and I, are loved by God. The problem is, of course, that today we find ourselves drinking in a lot more bad news than good news. And the result is that we lose all confidence as preachers. As Catherine of Siena would say, we begin to lose even our voice! There are all kinds of nettles to be grasped, issues to be faced, in an assembly like this. But I am convinced that our fundamental task, as individuals and as a Province, is first and last to drink deep from the wine of God's mercy, and to find in Christ our true refuge, and to help others, in time, experience the same deep security in God's love, the same glad intoxication.

DOMINICANS DRINKING

In this talk I have been concerned, for the most part, to focus on the spiritual meaning that the early Dominicans gave to the idea of drinking. But I think it will come as no surprise to you to learn that the brothers were not always able to remain on that high spiritual level. As early as 1241,[21] there was a complaint from the Provincial Chapter of Provence about 'nocturnal dinners and

19. S. Noffke, trans. *The Dialogue*, (New York 1980) p. 55.
20. S. Noffke, trans. 'Prayer 13', in *The Prayers of St. Catherine of Siena*, (New York 1983) pp.112-13.
21. See Simon Tugwell, O.P., *The Way of the Preacher* (London 1979) p.57.

long confabulations' still going on after Compline. And, in the Roman Province, a special rule had to be introduced which declared that the brethren must say Compline again after their nightly wine-drinking sessions![22]

Before I end I want to underline one unexpected but profoundly wise statement in Aquinas, a statement which I find personally very challenging. When St Thomas is discussing the question of drunkenness in the *Summa* – a subject which, as you can imagine, he treats with great compassion – all of a sudden he surprises us by drawing attention to a vice or a failure the very opposite of drunken excess, a vice which he says has no name, but which, perhaps, we might call *the vice of being too sober*.[23] Now being too sober, in relation to actually drinking alcohol, is not perhaps our greatest problem as Dominicans! But, at the spiritual level, at the level of our prayer-life and our preaching, and in the areas of hard thinking and decision-making, we stand perhaps accused of being too sensible, too sober, or too safe.

Towards the end of his remarkable study, *Enthusiasm*, Ronald Knox writes: 'Men will not live without vision...If we are content with the humdrum, the second-best, the hand-over-hand, it will not be forgiven us'.[24] We need to do something more than merely sipping at the Word of God like the theologians and canonists described by Jordan of Saxony. We need prayerfully but urgently to drink in long draughts of what Jordan calls 'the sweet wine' which Christ himself gives to 'those whose soul is suffering bitterness'. '[T]hat noble wine', he calls it, 'the wine which makes man's heart glad'.[25]

22. Rome Chapter, 1251. See *The Way of the Preacher*, p.57.
23. II.II q.150 a.1 ad 1.
24. Knox, *Enthusiasm* (Oxford 1950) p. 591.
25. A Walz, O.P., ed. 'Epistola XXXV', in *Beati Jordani De Saxonia Epistulae, Monumenta Ordinis Fratrum Praedicatorum Historica* (Rome 1951) pp. 41-2. See Kathleen Pond, *Love Among the Saints* [Jordan's Letters] (London 1958) p. 17.

The Word itself is that wine. But, there is another 'wine of hope' which Christ has given each one of us as members of the Irish Dominican Province: it is the wine of the memory of fellowship in the Province, the wine of our own particular tradition and traditions, the good wine of the example given to us over the years by our co-operator brothers and by our brothers on the missions, the wine of wisdom and knowledge and friendship poured out for us in abundance since we were novices, the wine of many kindnesses received and mercies shown. It may be that, if we are to survive as preachers in the future, we must take time to drink in, not only the Word itself, but also the good wine of the memory of these things.

'Let us behave', Catherine of Siena exclaims, 'like the drunkard who doesn't think of himself but only of the wine he has drunk and of the wine that remains to be drunk'![26]

26. P. Misciattelli ed. Letter 29, *Le Lettere di Santa Caterina*, Vol I, (Florence 1940) p. 108.

PREACHING AND CONTEMPLATION

ALBERT NOLAN, O.P.

We honour Damian Byrne as the Master who recognised the critical importance for the whole Dominican Family of the preaching renewal in the Catholic Church since Vatican II. We Dominicans, especially the friars, had developed the reputation of being theologians and intellectuals rather than preachers.

In 2001, the Friars' General Chapter in Providence, Rhode Island, recognised the equally critical importance of the more recent renewal of interest in spirituality and contemplation (Acts nn. 202-244). We Dominicans have a long and powerful tradition of contemplative living. This too had been, until recently, somewhat neglected.

In the words of this 2001 General Chapter, 'Contemplation, situated in time and place, in relation to God and others, has always marked our Dominican life. The challenges of the present time only increase our taste for it and our need to return to it. The new generation wishes to put it at the heart of our common life. In fact, only an enriched contemplative life can ensure authentic witness.' (Acts n. 202)

The new emphasis on preaching and contemplation signals a return to our Dominican roots and a significant recovery of the relevance for today of our charism, our particular contribution to the Church and the world. If we were looking for a definition of what it means to be a Dominican at the beginning of the twenty-first century, I would suggest that we are, or should be, contemplative preachers.

A contemplative preacher is someone for whom, in the words of the friars' Fundamental Constitution, 'preaching and teaching … proceed from an abundance of contemplation' (LCO 1 iv). Thomas Aquinas describes this as the highest of all ideals (*Summa*

Theologiae, II II 188.6). He argues that while a life devoted to contemplation is better than one devoted to active ministries, the mixed life that combines the two in such a way that one's preaching and teaching is derived from an overflow of contemplation is the highest of all callings.

While today we would not wish to grade different ways of life or callings as higher and lower, there is a challenge here to all who feel called to be Dominicans or to anyone who wishes to preach really effectively. It is, in the famous words of Thomas Aquinas, to see our preaching as *contemplata aliis tradere* which we usually translate as 'giving to others the fruits of our contemplation' (II II 188.6).

This, then, is the preaching ideal that I would like to explore in this essay. As I understand it, contemplative preaching is the ideal and charism of all who belong to the Dominican Family, but it can also be seen as a challenge to anyone who is called to preach in any way at all. What does it mean, then, to be a contemplative preacher?

PREACHING TODAY

Contemplative preaching is by no means a new phenomenon. It has been the way of preaching of the prophets, the saints and the mystics through the ages. And even today it is the way of preaching of all really good and authentic preachers. They would not call it contemplative preaching. That is my word. In fact many truly holy and effective preachers may not even refer to their prayer life as contemplative.

While we will, of necessity, be referring frequently to the preacher as the one who stands up before an audience in a Church, contemplative preaching can happen in any number of other ways.

The teacher in the classroom and the professor in the lecture hall can give to their listeners the fruits of their contemplation. The author and the journalist can do the same. Discussion and dialogue in workshops and seminars could be places where the results of contemplative prayer are experienced.

A specially privileged place for this kind of communication, though, is the counselling session. *Contemplata aliis tradere* can happen very powerfully within the context of counselling or spiritual direction. But it can also happen in less obvious ways, like parents giving advice to their children, friends sharing their insights, leaders giving public addresses, and meetings in the work-place. To contemplate and to give to others the fruits of our contemplation is something that we are all challenged to do wherever and whenever we can – in season and out of season. Francis of Assisi is said to have told his friars to preach at all times and when necessary to use words.

We have all suffered under bad preachers in our churches, not only those who talk nonsense, those who never prepare and who preach more or less the same sermon every Sunday, but also those who just criticise, condemn and lay down the law. On the other hand, there are a growing number of preachers whose sermons are informative and interesting especially in their interpretation of Scripture and the teaching of the Church.

Contemplative preaching, however, does something more than this, something different. It is not merely a matter of *doctrina aliis tradere*, giving to others the teaching of the Church, its doctrines and dogmas. Nor is it a matter of *theologia aliis tradere,* handing on to others the latest theology or scriptural exegesis. *Contemplata aliis tradere* means communicating to others what we ourselves have learnt from our own experience of faith and contemplation.

We live in a post-modern world. On the whole people are no longer looking for doctrines and dogmas or grand systems of theology. The Age of the Enlightenment with its total reliance upon logic and rationality is over. Most people no longer believe that human beings will eventually overcome the world's problems and that progress is inevitable. That was modernity. What people believe in today is not reason and universal theories, but experience.

The world, as we experience it, is profoundly irrational. Things don't always make sense, and if we are going to be honest we must admit that often enough we have no explanation for the things we experience like massacres, torture, the sexual abuse of small children and the maiming of innocent people – to name but a few. Even the grand certainties of science are now being discovered to be mistaken. In quantum physics and astronomy as well as sciences like biology, scientists are coming face to face with the limits of human knowledge – with the mystery of it all.

Of course there are those who cannot cope with all this uncertainty and insecurity. They are the ones who seek a haven in fundamentalism of one kind or another – religious fundamentalism, scientific fundamentalism or even economic fundamentalism. They cling desperately to their absolute truths no matter what happens. They rely blindly on those they regard as authorities.

By and large, though, people today are suspicious of ideologies, dogmas, doctrines and any other absolute truths.

They are looking for authenticity rather than authority. They want to hear an honest and sincere witness rather than a certified authority. Recent scandals in the Church have only re-enforced this reluctance to put one's trust in the words of those who exercise authority.

Besides, with such a plurality of voices and 'authorities' competing with one another and even killing one another, the postmodern attitude has become one of tolerance. People have learnt to live with fragmentation and plurality. Difference and otherness are treated as interesting and informative rather than as a problem.

Postmodernism is not the latest philosophy of a few highly educated and disillusioned thinkers in the North. It is a general attitude of mind that is growing fast in the North and the South and especially amongst the youth whatever their cultural heritage might be. The only exceptions would be fundamentalists, the older generation, isolated rural communities and those who are so poor that survival is their sole preoccupation.

The post-modern attitude of mind is not necessarily an obstacle to the preaching of the Good News of Jesus Christ. In fact it could be seen as an unprecedented opportunity. It often leads to a greater interest than before in our Christian experience of spirituality, meditation, contemplation, prayer, mysticism and inner peace.

However, if the Good News is presented as *doctrina* or *theologia,* it will not be heard. Not because the *contemplata,* the things that have emerged from our contemplation, are totally different from *doctrina* and *theologia*, but because the message comes across quite differently when the preacher is not just a parrot repeating the doctrines and laws of the church or the latest theology found in books, but a man or woman of prayer who has internalised the Word of God and speaks from experience and with obvious sincerity.

But it is more than that. A life that is seriously committed to contemplation will produce fruits that will transform the whole experience of preaching – for the preacher and the listener. We will explore something of what this might mean for preaching after a brief look at contemplation today and especially the Dominican tradition of contemplation.

CONTEMPLATION TODAY

While originally contemplation was thought of as the calling of all Christians, for a long time now Catholics have regarded it as the special vocation of a chosen few: monks, nuns and hermits. The rest of us are said to be engaged in the active life.

Somewhere along the way the whole tradition of contemplative prayer was lost or at least badly neglected – even by monks and nuns. Today there is a very powerful movement throughout Christianity of returning to the Catholic tradition of contemplation and meditation. And what is even more important, this widespread movement includes the revival of the original tradition that contemplation is for everyone and not only for the privileged few. Today there are a growing number of lay-people, as well as religious and clergy, who meditate, practice centring prayer and give themselves to contemplation and mysticism.

This new movement has been deepened and developed by the discoveries of the new cosmology and by the emerging spirituality of the ecological movement. Contemplating the grandeur of God in the marvels of an expanding and evolving universe, of which we are such a tiny part, adds a new dimension to the experience of wonder and awe.

Much has been written about all of this, but what concerns us here is the effect the renewed practice of contemplation might have on preaching and on the Order of Preachers.

In his keynote address at the Friars General Chapter of 2001, Paul Murray pointed out that ' … fidelity to the life of prayer and contemplation has been a distinguishing mark of many of our best-known Dominican preachers and saints. But, within the Church, at least until recently, the Order has generally been noted more for its intellectual prowess than for its contemplative zeal. Today all that is beginning to change' (Acts p. 256).

For a very long time the Dominican Friars were best known for their Thomism. The most famous of our Dominican saints at that time was Thomas Aquinas. The more recent emphasis on preaching brought Dominic himself back into the limelight. When social justice and liberation became a major preoccupation, we focussed attention on Bartholomew de Las Casas. Today, when the accent is on mysticism or contemplation, the two Dominican saints who are most read and quoted, both within the Dominican Family and beyond it, are Catherine of Siena and Meister Eckhart.

When Richard Woods was asked to write about the Dominican tradition for a new series of books on Christian spirituality, he chose to use as examples of Dominican Spirituality (after Dominic and the early friars) Thomas, Eckhart and Catherine. He wrote about Thomas the mystic and entitled the book *Mysticism and Prophecy*.

This does not mean that our other Dominican saints were not contemplatives. Dominic was obviously a great contemplative. He is said to have always spoken either to God or of God. Considering his long nights in prayer and his total dedication to preaching, would he not be one of the great examples of a contemplative preacher?

It is also noteworthy that in his zeal for the holy preaching Dominic spent much of his time founding and nurturing convents of contemplative nuns.

Thomas Aquinas saw his commitment to study as a very important part of the contemplative life. Today he is being read as himself a great mystic.

Dominican contemplation has always been a search for God *in the world*. We do not close our eyes and contemplate God somewhere outside of ourselves and the universe we are part of. Eckhart and Catherine insist that we have to begin our search for God by looking deeply into *ourselves*. 'No one can know God,' writes Eckhart, 'who does not first know himself (herself)'.[1] Catherine too is very strong on this point.[2]

And then, as Paul Murray pointed out in his address, for Dominic, Eckhart and Catherine, *the neighbour*, especially those who suffer and are in need, 'formed part of their *contemplata*'. 'Reading through the early accounts of Dominic's prayer-life, what also immediately impresses,' according to Paul Murray, 'is the place accorded to others – to the afflicted and oppressed – within the act of contemplation itself'.[3] Catherine's deep love and respect for each individual person arises out of her contemplative vision of the beauty and dignity of the human soul.[4]

Albert the Great's keen interest in nature and *all of creation* was part of his contemplation of God. One can hardly imagine how excited he would have been by the new insights and observations about evolution and cosmology.

While all contemplation centres on God, the special Dominican focus is on the truth. Thomas refers frequently to our *contemplation of the truth*. This has two implications. In the first place, all truth should lead us to the reality and mystery of God.

---

1. Quoted in Bernard McGinn, *The Mystical Thought of Meister Eckhart: The Man from Whom God Hid Nothing*, 2001, New York, Crossroad, p. 44.
2. See especially the unpublished thesis of Patricia Fresen, *Self-Knowledge in the Writings of Catherine of Siena*, 1995, Pretoria, Unisa.
3. Acts, p. 274, and Paul Murray, *Preachers at Prayer*, 2003, Dublin, Dominican Publications, p. 29.
4. Acts, p. 271, and Paul Murray, p. 26.

And secondly, contemplation is primarily something of the mind rather than the will.

This was the famous contention of Thomas Aquinas that was rigorously opposed by many of his contemporaries, especially the great Franciscan theologian, Bonaventure who saw the contemplation of God as primarily a matter of love. Not that Thomas saw contemplation as nothing more than abstract intellectual thinking. When dealing with the gifts of the Spirit, especially wisdom, he speaks of another kind of knowing – a knowing by *connaturalitas,* which could be translated as 'by one's likeness to what one knows' (II II 45.2).

Today contemplation is described almost universally as a form of consciousness or awareness. It is not so much a matter of changing reality as a matter of becoming aware of what is already there. Contemplation is the experience of waking up to reality, developing a heightened awareness of what is happening around us and within us, and above all a deeper consciousness of the presence of God in everything.

Most people are hardly conscious at all. They are half asleep or living in a world of lies and illusions. Contemplation is a conscious attempt to dispel all the illusions we have about ourselves, about others and about the world. It is a search for the truth about ourselves, about others and about the universe we are part of, which is at the same time a search for God. Bernard McGinn, the renowned scholar of Christian spirituality and mysticism, defines mysticism as 'the transformation of consciousness through a direct encounter with God'.[5]

Consciousness is something more than conceptual knowledge. Being conscious of God's presence is different from the intellectual assertion that God is everywhere. Nor is it simply a

5. Fresen, op. cit., p. 35.

matter of feeling. We have learnt to become conscious of our feelings and to learn from them, but contemplation is more than that. It is sometimes described as 'unknowing' or recognising that we don't know. God is the great unknown. So that in the end we have to throw out all we thought we knew about God to make contact with the great mystery, not through our thoughts or feelings but through an experience of wordless wonder and awe.

This is not the place to elaborate on these matters. Our concern is with the impact a life dedicated to contemplation would have on our preaching today.

THE FRUITS OF OUR CONTEMPLATION

When we say that we preach our *contemplata,* the fruits of our contemplation, we are referring not only to the verbal content of our preaching but also to the message we communicate by who we are and what we are, by our attitudes and even by our body language. The fruits of contemplation include qualities like inner peace, freedom and fearlessness, a love for people, genuine humility, a spirit of hopefulness, gratitude and joy, and a profound sense of mystery. It is these fruits of our contemplative prayer that characterise and shape what I call contemplative preaching.

The list does not pretend to be comprehensive but let's take a closer look at these qualities.

Inner Peace

What people today are thirsting for, whether they are post-moderns or fundamentalists, is inner peace. Among those who hear our preaching are deeply troubled souls who long for a message that will bring them peace, a peace the world cannot give. Such people will be quick to recognise that the preacher is a man or woman of deep inner peace – or not.

Inner peace is, among other things, the fruit of years of silent meditation. With all the stresses and strains of life today our heads and hearts come to be cluttered with thoughts, plans, fears, resentments, desires and conflicts. The practice of silent meditation or centring prayer helps us to calm the storms within us.

However, something more than that is needed. The contemplative is someone who has spent a lot of time trying to get to know him/herself better. As we gradually come to face the truth about ourselves, we discover, among other things, that we are not free. We are chained like slaves to our comforts, our moods, our fears, our reputation, our achievements and successes, our health, our looks, our favourite devotions, our culture, our theological tradition and our names for God. These are our attachments, our chains. We say we need them and cannot do without them. They are not necessarily bad, and we don't necessarily have to give them up. But we do need to become detached from them, if we are ever to have inner peace.

Detachment, according to Eckhart, is more important than love because without detachment we do not have the inner freedom to love others.[6] John of the Cross calls it purgation and takes us through the long painful process of 'dark nights' on the way to freedom. Our paths may differ but it is only after years of struggle in prayer that the contemplative can enjoy the fruits of detachment and freedom.

It is this inner freedom that makes the contemplative preacher so fearless. No longer afraid of what people might think or say, the contemplative preacher is free to speak the truth regardless of the consequences.

Fearlessness and inner freedom are qualities we associate with

---

6. *Meister Eckhart: The Essential Sermons, Commentarioes, Treatises, and Defense,* 1981, New York, Paulist Press, pp. 285 ff.

prophets – those in every age who are bold enough to speak out when everyone else remains silent. And that is why contemplative preaching will become prophetic whenever the circumstances require.

Our freedom, fearlessness and inner peace, to the extent that we have them, will shine through in our preaching. They will speak louder than our words, just as they did so magnificently in the preaching of Dominic who was once described as 'stupifyingly free' (Acts p. 226). Was this not also one of the things that attracted people so powerfully to Jesus? He had no hang-ups, obsessions or compulsions. He was free and fearless, and so obviously at peace with himself and with God.

There is nothing that a post-modern audience would appreciate more than a preacher who shows himself/herself to be free and fearlessness – even when the post-modern listeners are not really free and fearless themselves.

A Love for People

The famous English Dominican, Vincent McNabb, is reputed to have said, 'If you don't love [people], don't preach to them – preach to yourself'.

Genuine contemplative prayer helps us to overcome our selfishness and self-centredness by making us more and more conscious of the unity of all things in God. Our separate individualised egos are illusions. The truth is that we all belong together, we are part of one another and part of the wonderful expanding universe that God is busy creating.

This kind of contemplative consciousness influences our preaching. We have from the start a deep sympathy and appreciation for the people we are preaching to. We feel with them in their struggles and their pain. We are able to forgive them in our hearts while we long to help them to change whatever may need to be changed.

In other words we don't begin by hating them. We don't hammer them and threaten them. We don't just condemn them and criticise them. We don't stand up there like self-righteous Pharisees who thank God that we are not like these sinful people. We love them and forgive them as Jesus did.

When our love for them is genuine and spontaneous, our post-modern listeners will recognise it and appreciate it. We are not playing games with them or venting our pent-up feelings on them. We are not trying to show them how learned we are and how well we can preach. We are not looking for praise and congratulations. We are not on some kind of ego-trip. We care for them as we care for our very selves.

It is from this position of loving care that the preacher is able to present, effectively and powerfully, the challenges of the gospel. No matter how demanding and difficult these challenges might appear to be, they will be heard and taken seriously.

Like Dominic, Catherine and Eckhart, among others, it is our contemplative prayer that will enable us to do this.

A Spirit of Hopefulness

In a way all our preaching should be a matter of giving an account of the hope that is in us (1 Peter 3:15). When we have no hope in us, when we have forgotten how to trust God and when the chaos of today's world has led us to despair and cynicism, then that is what will come through in our preaching even as we talk about the good news and the hope of resurrection.

It is no good pretending that we are hopeful when we are not. All we can do in that case is preach from the heart about the struggle we are experiencing with our feelings of hopelessness. Our listeners will appreciate that kind of honesty, especially if we then encourage them and ourselves to go back to our search for

God in prayer.

Hopefulness, as an attitude that imbues all we say and do, is one of the fruits of contemplation. Among other things it is the result of a life that is steeped in gratitude and thankfulness to God. In prayer we learn to thank God for the many, many good things in life, for nature, for the universe, for other people, for the wonder of human consciousness and for each new day. Eventually this positive attitude of gratefulness begins to transform our consciousness and gradually we come to shed our habitual negativity and pessimism.

Ronald Rolheiser sums up what many before him have said about gratitude: 'To be a saint is to be motivated by gratitude, nothing more and nothing less'.[7] In another place he sums up Gutierrez with the words: 'Only one kind of person transforms the world spiritually, someone with a grateful heart'.[8]

While all contemplatives experience times of painful dryness and darkness, in the end one of the outstanding fruits of our faithfulness to contemplative prayer will be joy. So many preachers are not only dull and boring but so obviously joyless. How can we stand up there and preach the good news without rejoicing in one way or another.

We cannot compensate for our joylessness by telling jokes or poking fun at people we don't like. True joy comes from a deep sense of the presence of God in all things. The people were able to recognise that joy in Jesus and they will be able to see at least something of it in the contemplative preacher today. Dominic was well-known for his cheerfulness and joy.

The contemplative preacher is someone who comes across as

7. *The Shattered Lantern: Rediscovering a Felt Knowledge of God,* revised edition 2001, New York, Crossroad, p. 180.
8. *The Holy Longing: The Search for a Christian Spirituality,* 1999, New York, Doubleday, p. 67.

a person who is full of hope, gratitude and joy.

A Sense of Mystery

All contemplatives have a deep sense of mystery – the mystery of God, the mystery of life, the mysteries of our faith. Contemplation leads to a recognition of the serious limitations of all human knowledge. Eventually we discover that we don't know God and what we thought we knew is, in fact, far off the mark. God becomes totally mysterious and we go through a process that has been called 'unknowing'. Ironically that brings us much closer to God. But we now experience the presence of God in a cloud or in the dark – in mystery.

Gradually we also begin to discover how mysterious we ourselves are and how mysterious all of God's creation is – not to speak of Jesus and what we call the mysteries of our faith. All is mystery, but that does not mean that all is lost. It means that everything is a marvel before which we can only stand in awe and wonder. Wonder is possibly the most profound form of consciousness.

The preaching of the contemplative will be imbued with this powerful sense of mystery and wonder. How different our sermons would be if they presented life as a mystery to be enjoyed rather than as nothing more than a series of problems to be solved.

But more importantly, living in the presence of the truly awesome mystery whom we call God, enables us to speak about God more authentically and from the heart. There are preachers today who avoid talking about God. They no longer know how to speak about God and when they do so, it is clear that God is nothing more than a abstract idea. What a difference when the preacher is speaking about his or her own experience of a mystery they have contemplated in wonder and awe for many years.

These are high ideals, but they are also gifts from God which will be given to us in some measure if we are seriously committed to a life of contemplative prayer.

Preaching and teaching, when it flows from an abundance of contemplation, would be powerful and effective at any time and in any place. In our post-modern world, today and tomorrow, it is especially true that only some kind of contemplative preaching will capture the minds and hearts of our listeners.

BIBLIOGRAPHY

Acts of the Elective General Chapter of the Friars of the Order of Preachers, Providence, Rhode Island 2001, English translation 2002, Dublin, Rollebon Press.

Berry, Thomas, *The Dream of the Earth,* 1988, San Francisco, Sierra Club Books.

Eckhart, Meister, *Meister Eckhart: The Essential Sermons, Commentaries, Treatises and Defense,* ed. E. Colledge and B.McGinn, 1981, New York, Paulist press.

Fresen, Patricia Anne, *Self-Knowledge in the Writings of Catherine of Siena,* 1995, unpublished doctorate thesis for Unisa, Pretoria, South Africa.

Kaufman, Gordon D., *In Face of Mystery: A Constructive Theology,* 1993, Cambridge, Harvard University Press.

Keating, Thomas, *Open Mind, Open heart: The Contemplative Dimension of the Gospel,* 1995, New York, Continuum.

McGinn, Bernard, *The Mystical Thought of Meister Eckhart: The Man From Whom God Hid Nothing,* 2001, New York, Crossroad.

Muray, Paul, *Preachers at Prayer,* 2003, Dublin, Dominican Publications.

Rolheiser, Ronald, *The Shattered Lantern: Rediscovering a Felt Presence of God,* revised edition 2001, New York, Crossroad.

Rolheiser, Ronald, *The Holy Longing: The Search for a Christian Spirituality,* 1999, New York, Doubleday.

Ruane, Edward M., 'The Spirituality of the Preacher', in *In the Company of Preachers,* Aquinas Institute of Theology Faculty, 1993, Collegeville, Liturgical Press.

Sheldrake, Philip, *Spirituality and Theology: Christian Living and the Doctrine of God,* 1998, London, Darton, Longman and Todd.

Swimme, Brian and Thomas Berry, *The Universe Story,* 1992, San Francisco, Harper.

Wessels, Cletus, *The Holy Webb: Church and the New Universe Story,* 2000, Maryknoll New York, Orbis.

Woods, Richard, *Mysticism and Prophecy: The Dominican Tradition,* 1998, London, Darton, Longman and Todd.

PREACHING AND MINISTRY IN A TIME OF EXPANSION

THOMAS F. O'MEARA, O.P.

Damian Byrne's Dominican life took him into various ministries and into ministry in different worlds reaching from Ireland to Mexico. Then he was elected to that service of Dominicans which is the enabling leadership of all the Friars Preachers, the Master of the Order of Preachers. At the time of his ordination to the priesthood he could not have foreseen how his preaching would assume various forms and reach people in so many countries.

This expansion of Byrne's personal preaching and ministry took place during a time of change in the Catholic Church, in a time that would expand and diversify the ministry itself. The work of the Church went beyond clerical states and lay apostolates as theology and society summoned forth a new awareness of the Pauline teaching of the corporate Christ where each Christian receives a charism intent on service. Pope Paul VI had written: 'At the Council, *the church is looking for itself*. It is trying, with great trust and with a great effort, to define itself more precisely and to understand what it is.' [1] In the postconciliar period the Church around the world sought to further rather than to flee pastoral diversity and vitality. Already in 1972, Hervé Legrand spoke [2] of new accents: the Church of God as the local Church; the Church of Christ as also the Church of the Spirit; collegiality between bishops and between Churches.

---

1. Cardinal Montini, 'Discorsi al Clero, 1957–1963' (Milan: Studi, 1963) cited in Yves Congar, 'Moving towards a Pilgrim Church,' in A. Stacpoole, ed., *Vatican II Revisited* (Minneapolis: Winston, 1986) p. 142.
2. Hervé Legrand, 'Revaluation of Local Churches: Some Theological Implications,' in E. Schillebeeckx, ed., *The Unifying Role of the Bishop, Concilium* (New York: Herder and Herder, 1972) pp. 60-62.

MINISTRIES EXPANDING

Only a few years after the end of Vatican II in 1965, ministry emerged in a startling new constellation. A new word for Catholics, the activities summed up in the biblically central word 'ministry' expanded: within a few years of the Council the ministry of the restored diaconate and the ministries of the baptized who were not priests became numerous. Karl Rahner observed how the conciliar document on the laity prepared for these unforeseen developments. The text 'leads into a many-sided problematic that includes more than just the issue of apostolates.'[3] He ascribed the growing self-consciousness of the laity to 'the unmistakable activity of the Holy Spirit; and further to the ecumenical and liturgical movements along with the lay movement in the broadest sense goes back to God.'[4] The goal of lay activity is not just personal sanctification or marginal assistance to the bishop but has to do with the sanctification and evangelization of peoples. In Europe lay ministry around World War I found an early rebirth in Catholic Action: it was a response to the de-Christianization of layers of European society; subsequently the liturgical and catechetical movements prepared for lay ecclesial ministry. In the Americas this impetus came from parish education, the pursuit of social justice, and liturgy.

In the 1970s, Yves Congar wrote that his pioneering work offering a theology of the laity, written fifteen years earlier, needed to be updated, to get beyond the model of a venerable single line dividing clergy and laity.

The Church of God is not built up solely by the actions of the official presbyteral ministry but by a multitude of diverse

---

3. Karl Rahner, Herbert Vorgrimler, 'Das Dekret über das Laienapostolat, "Apostolicam Actuositatem",' *Kleines Konzilskompendium* (Freiburg: Herder, 1966) p. 383.
4. Ibid., p. 383.

modes of service, stable or occasional, spontaneous or recognized, and, when the occasion arises consecrated, while falling
short of sacramental ordination. These modes of service do
exist … mothers at home, the person who coordinates liturgical celebrations or reads the sacred text, the woman visiting the
sick or prisoners, adult catechists … They exist now, but up to
now were not called by their true name, ministries, nor were
their place and status in ecclesiology recognized. [5]

Congar only sketched a model that would replace the bipolar
division of clergy and laity: a circle with bishop or pastor at the
centre (Christ's Spirit is ground and power animating ministries), ordained and other, in community. 'It is necessary to
substitute for the linear scheme a model where the community
appears as the enveloping reality *within which* the ministries,
eventually the instituted sacramental ministries, are placed as
modes of service of what the community is called to be and do.' [6]
Ten years later Congar wrote, 'The *responsibility* of witness and
service flows from the Christian quality as such: thus there is
mission in the broad sense, and this mission is equally incumbent
on every Christian. All the disciples received the Holy Spirit and
the gifts which render them responsible for God's cause.'
A burst of ministry followed upon the ecclesial event of
Vatican II and the social upheavals of the 1960s, and the patterns
of parish and diocesan ministry changed. They changed because
of the increase in the numbers of Catholics, and because the
ministries of education, liturgy, and social service emerged in a
new variety, and campus ministry and health care ministry
changed in their format and breadth; finally there was a develop-

5. Yves Congar, 'My Path-Findings in the Theology of Laity and Ministries,' *The Jurist* 32 (1972), pp, 169. 181.
6. Ibid., pp., 176, 178.

ment of diocesan offices directing ministries. The priests and the new permanent deacons were joined no longer only by principals and teachers in schools but by colleagues working in adult education, liturgy, family care and social action. The Sunday liturgies of deacons, lectors, cantors, and Communion-bearers illustrated the expansion of the ministry.

The early Church understood that the array of ministers active in the Eucharistic Liturgy were also ministries that nourished external, public help and evangelism. The venerable and central dual interplay of liturgy and public ministry returned: directors of different levels of education, ministers to families, to the aging or to the young, and permanent deacons. Diocese and parishes lived out of a pattern of concentric circles of ministry moving from the leaders to all full-time and professionally trained ministers and then out through levels of part-time ministers to all of the baptized. There are Christians who are in the ministry in quite limited and temporary ways – readers, occasional bearers of word and sacrament to sick and dying – and Christians in the ministry weekly for some hours from those in the ministry full-time and those ordained. Part-time ministries are also part of the global expansion of ministry and there is a wide spectrum of these. A model of staff or team around which work different degrees of involvements was the visible format for ministry in today's Churches. Some ministries and ordinations are less intense, of shorter duration, but these make a contribution. Ultimately, every Christian at times would be involved in such services. The pastor and the bishop are responsible for developing the theology of ministry and the identities of the ministers, and each ministry should include some preparation and some public commissioning.

In the model of team or staff around the leader rather than a

small pyramid of priests and religious, ministry expanded beyond the monoform framework of a single monastic and sacer-
dotal ministry, priesthood. The very model of ministry had
changed. The parishes had changed in their patterns – theological, ecclesiological and professional – of what was done and who
did it.

THE MINISTRY OF PREACHING

Preaching can certainly be look upon as one ministry but
would not all ministry, each proper ministry, involve preaching?
What greater way to serve the Gospel than to make it heard, to
give it expression, to preach it. The lists of ministries in the early
Church – educative, caritative, liturgical, or apostolic – did not so
much commission as presume preaching, preaching in various
forms. Baptism gives access to ministry and promises a pneu-
matic charism for some ministry. Initiation is an active orientation not a passive receptivity of ministry.

Paul welcomed all ecclesial gifts, refusing to be embarrassed
by or hostile to whatever was useful to the ministry of the Church.
He minimized sensational gifts and accented those that were
public services to the Gospel. Charisms empower the life of the
Church by growth for the ministries building up the community
through many activities (1 Cor 12:7; 3:7,16; Rom 12:4). A charism
is the contact between the life of the Spirit and an individual
personality. There can be many charisms ranging from momen-
tary inspirations to life-long services; at times in a Christian's life,
we suspect, invitations will be given to help the Church publicly.
The Pauline metaphor of the human body brought harmony to
the diversity of important ministries, as communal services aimed
at 'a unity in the work of service building up the body of Christ'
(Eph 4:13). Because the Christian community is a living organ-

ism, there is no inactive group and no spiritual elite.

Paul saw preaching as a ministry that was also a liturgy: 'The grace given me by God to be a minister of Christ Jesus to the Gentiles in the priestly service of the gospel of God, so that the offerings of the Gentiles may be acceptable, sanctified by the Holy Spirit' (Rom 15:16). In Philippians, the daily life of the Christian in its distinctive morality and hopeful faith in the future was depicted as a worship of God, a sacrifice not to be consumed in the present but enhanced and fulfilled in the future (2:17). Paul took terms from Greek or Jewish liturgies as he proclaimed that his mission to all the nations was public, a proclamation and invocation of the universal and eschatological event of God acting in Jesus Christ. In the early communities preaching, evangelization, and Christian life were sacrifice, liturgy, and priestly office.

The early Church knew distinctions between ministries but not radical ones between Christians. After the peace of Constantine, as the clergy came to mean those chosen for God's service, the corresponding laity soon found itself labelled with a religious existence that is secular, passive, removed. Yves Congar wrote: 'To look for a "spirituality of lay people" in the Scriptures makes no sense. There is no mention of laity. Certainly the word exists, but it exists outside the Christian vocabulary.'[7] In American usage a 'lay person' is someone who is ignorant of the area under discussion, someone who is removed from the field of action. As baptized Christians in large numbers undertake ministry in religious education, health-care, or evangelization or in services of leadership and preaching for communities where no ordained ministers are available, neither biblical theology nor contempo-

7. Yves Congar, 'Laïc et Laïcat,' *Dictionnaire de Spiritualité* 9 (Paris: Desclée, 1976) p. 79.

rary English meaning supports understanding the baptized as laity in an extrinsic, passive sense; nor should one limit preaching to priests. Direct access to God, a baptismal commissioning, the avoidance of a religious dualism, the basic equality of men and women in the Kingdom of God imply that ministries with their particular forms are many, varied, and active: according to the New Testament, they are founded upon a common faith and baptismal commissioning. In the writings of the first centuries, Christians seem to see Baptism as an orientation to preaching. Certainly the bishops are the central, enabling preachers, but it is likely that the 'prophets' are gifted preachers rather than fore-casters of the future, while 'teachers' proclaim the word in a more reflective, doctrinal way.

The central and order-giving preaching of the Eucharistic leader, bishop and presbyter, had its recognizable prominence but it was not in competition with other ministers; for instance, with apostles and prophets and teachers, whatever those forms mean in ministry. Orders arrange important ministries, but they are not the first principle of ministry. The first causative princi-ples of ministry are the Spirit, the person, and Baptism. The bishop coordinates and commissions ministry, but his ministry does not monopolize or contain all ministries.

Preaching and ministry go together. Preaching proclaims in human ideas and words the Spirit in the Gospel, while each ministry, after discerning how the Spirit might be present in this man or woman drawn to the Gospel, serves that presence of the Spirit personally or socially. It is likely that each ministry has a preaching component. Preaching would be analogous and would belong to the youth minister as well as to the deacon, to the theologian as to the bishop. The kinds, frequency, and impor-tance of these moments of preaching differ, but there would not

be public, educated, full-time ministers in the Church who had
no opportunity to preach.

FORMS OF PREACHING

As we saw, it seems likely that in the first centuries there was
a range of verbal expressions beyond basic instruction or the
example of a virtuous life. In medieval centuries ministry and
preaching were drastically reduced to one priestly order, but the
Holy Spirit found ways for their wider forms to exist in the
Church, in a few lay movements and in many religious orders.

Ministry and preaching go together. Ministry stimulates and
involves preaching, and preaching is the verbal aspect of ministry.

The writings of Damian Byrne are a postconciliar expansion
of preaching and ministry. He certainly saw them together in
Dominican life. His exposure to a variety of ministry, to ministry
in various countries, to the expansion of ministry prompted
observations about preaching. Yves Congar observed toward the
end of his life: 'The years after the Council are a global phenomenon with worldwide dimensions. A crisis would have come
anyway. The Council assisted changes entry into the Church by
ending the isolation of the Church, by giving a wider audience to
the Church, and by ending a monolithic institution protected by
fictions. The present time is linked to the gigantic changes
touching culture, the way of life in societies, and the shared
humanity of the world.' [8]

Much of Byrne's ministry in Latin America and Mexico took
place during and after Vatican II. His time as Master of the Order
of Friars Preachers took place during the later years of the vital
postconciliar era. At the end of his time at Santa Sabina he

8. Yves Congar, *Une passion. L'unité* (Paris: Cerf, 1974) p. 109.

experienced some bureaucratic meanness and repression but not yet the full reaction against the Council joined to a restoration of nineteenth century Baroque devotions and clerical Romanism, a change in papal direction that occasioned apathy and scandals in churches in countries whose legal tradition was Anglo-Saxon law.

NEW MINISTRIES

Damian Byrne's observations on preaching are linked to those on ministry. They are clearly stimulated by the peoples, nations, and cultures around him. He visited churches from San Francisco to Lagos where ministry and preaching were expanding. He had personally lived through the transition from a preaching that was abstract and universal, delivered apart from its audience and expressed in alien thought-forms, to a preaching seeking the existential, the personal, the social, the ecclesial (those four words indicate the development of theological alternatives in the mid-twentieth century to the reinstallation of neo-Aristotelianism from 1850 to 1950). His wide and frequent travels as Master of the Order led him to see the present time as one of many opportunities – declining numbers should not make a province insular. Then theology joined time to geography. 'We Dominicans should continue to seek to work in those countries which are beyond the borders of western culture ... Asia, Africa.'[9] Evangelization and preaching do not occur in a vacuum but in a vernacular – and this is equally important – in the thought-forms of a people. When we speak of 'culture,' 'age,' or 'epoch,' we mean a particular emphasis in a cluster of ways of thinking and living. Paul VI had spoken of African 'human values and cultural forms which can find their

9. Damian Byrne, 'The Challenge of Evangelization,' *A Pilgrimage of Faith* (Dublin: Dominican Publications, 1991) p. 13.

proper fulfilment, truly African': they could 'formulate Catholicism in terms absolutely appropriate to African culture.' [10]

At the centre of ministry and evangelism is 'the question of culture.' [11] Inculturation is a new awareness of a continuing challenge. Sensitivity to the culture of the other is its beginning; collaboration between provincial entities is the inevitable result of accepting cultural diversity. Byrne often spoke of how new models, stimulated by other cultures or by an analysis of modern society, await employment by the Church. Those ministries – of word and sacrament, of teaching and justice – involved journey and research into new cultures, places where the Church can unleash 'the hidden energy of the Good News.' [12] A theology of ministry explores what is culturally new even if, theologically, the contemporary renewal of ministry and the desire to expand preaching are traditional and go back to Christian origins.

To look at ministry in the local Church around the world is to be dismayed. So many people to serve, so many nations, so many regions. Many changes are occurring, and even simple ones alter the image and structure of human life. Gustav Thils observed the fact that the taking root of the Church in various cultures is happening simultaneously with an expansion of how the Church worships and serves. [13]

Byrne was critical of the past. 'There have been very few places where we have gone deeper…, two cultures living side by side … We are asked to develop and knowledge and an appreciation of the culture in which we work.' [14] Christians through the centu-

10. Cited in *La Documentation catholique* 66 (1969) p. 765.
11. 'The Challenge of Evangelization', p. 15.
12. 'The Challenge of Evangelization', p. 27.
13. Gustav Thils, *L'Après-Vatican II. Un nouvel âge de l'église?* (Louvain-la Neuve: Faculté de Théologie, 1985) pp. 81 ff.
14. Damian Byrne, 'The Role of Dominicans in the World Today,' *A Pilgrimage of Faith*, pp. 76f.

ries have done this, purifying culture and human religion even as they use their forms and seminal ideas.

Byrne's theology of ministry was not afraid to empower groups from whom charismatic power had in earlier centuries been removed: the poor, members of young Churches, the Dominican laity, particularly women. Today's exciting moment calls the Order to use its many members and charisms – they exist and flourish within a family of Dominicans – to further the Gospel mission 'in a world that has not yet discovered how women and men, lay and cleric, can join together in community as equals, respectful of differences, but united in faith.' [15]

The trajectory for the ministries of women in a general sense reaches from the New Testament to the present day, although, in terms of preaching, it passes through centuries of neglect and minimization. In the Dominican tradition, religious women had established in difficult circumstances all kinds of institutions, most of whose work corresponds to Pauline ministries. If we consider health care, religious education, the care of the poor, and retreat houses to be ministries, then one must conclude that in many countries over seventy percent of Catholic ministry during the twentieth century has been done by women.

The growing presence of laywomen in ministry followed after 1970 upon the large work of religious women. The opening of the Church's ministry beyond the Sunday Mass along with the dignity and mission of being baptized have led to theological questions, indeed to a further stage of women in ministry. Experience taught Byrne that sometimes 'those in the situations of greatest need proclaim the Gospel with the greatest power.' [16]

15. Damian Byrne, 'The Ministry of Preaching,' *A Pilgrimage of Faith*, p. 31.
16. 'The Ministry of Preaching,' *A Pilgrimage of Faith*, p. 31.

A WORLDWIDE MINISTRY

Byrne was elected to a kind of universal ministry as Master (*Magister*) of the Dominican Order. His ministry became 'a magisterial ministry', not in the sense that the Irish Dominican was an aloof academic or a condescending prelate but in that he had ideas about what it meant to head a worldwide religious group. He was obliged to visitate each province, each house, each friar, and this involved an enormous amount of preaching to all the members of the Dominican Family.

To serve those to whom he ministered and preached he brought about or continued changes in the ministry of the office, role, and service of the *Magister Ordinis*. There, he was a bridge-figure, continuing some initiatives of Vincent de Couesnongle and preparing for the further efforts of Timothy Radcliffe and Carlos Azpiroz Costa. [17] The ministry of those working for the Order at Santa Sabina on the Aventine in Rome, he saw, needed to move away from Roman stasis to global activity, to an atmosphere by the Master and his assistants of solidarity in presence with Dominicans everywhere in the world. This shift from a frozen geographical point administering what was frequently trivial to a service around the globe in great human struggles was not simply an administrative reorganization or a routine of travel. It drew on the shift from a monopolizing central authority to the local Church, the theology affirmed by Vatican II. At the same time, it recognized in the Order a new variety of ministries and ministers and a new variety of inculturated ministries.

Just as Church ministry after 1970 often came to resemble ecclesial life in the early Church, so the new approach of the

---

17. See the analysis of the milieu of Dominican preaching and ministry in terms of globalization composed by the General Elective Chapter of 2001: 'De Provocation-ibus Hodiernis ad Missionem Ordinis,' in *Acta Capituli Generalis Electivi Ordinis Praedicatorum Providentiae* (Rome: S. Sabina, 2001) pp. 31-52.

Master and his curia resembled earlier times in the Order when superiors travelled and chapters were frequent. Certainly it was a break with residing in Rome and waiting for an occasional request or canonical problem to arrive. There was a shift: (1) from Rome to numerous, culturally distinct provinces and vicariates; (2) from European provinces to provinces and regions around the world; (3) from fixed laws to new projects; (4) from residing in one place to an exhausting schedule of travelling; (5) from supervision to enabling; (6) from monoform administration to focused periods of conference and decision-making. That mode of leadership for Dominicans was able to further a certain globalization in the Order and to give on-the-spot direction for in regions and provinces. It moved from the limited fields of spiritual direction, organization, and canon law for provinces that were mainly European to the coordination of an array of services for fifty regions of the world.

Damian Byrne's teaching and preaching was a ministry but it was also about ministry. The service to the Order around the world whose form was a new realization of the Dominican office of Master and whose content was an inculturation of preaching. This was a typical project of the postconciliar age: new and yet traditional, full of energy; it was also a late modern enterprise in that it affirmed culture, sought out a variety of ministerial styles around the world, and pondered the sacramentality of God's grace not solely in texts or words but in movements and people.

If his work was a beginning, it was a rediscovery of the force present in every successful period in the Church's history. The expansion of ministry has taken place with extraordinary success; the expansion of preaching among the baptized has been blocked for the past fifteen years. Dominican men and women, illustrating the effect of Damian Byrne, have worked for the education, training, and empowerment of men and women, ordained and lay and religious, so that they might in this or that way, modest or significant, preach the Gospel that Jesus and Paul wanted to be preached everywhere.

Preaching empowers ministry, and ministry makes concrete the words of the Spirit at work in history. Cardinal Karl Lehmann speaks of the interplay of the ideal and the real in the texts and spirit of Vatican II. They ceaselessly nourish a process that deepens religious and spiritual foundations even as its opens Christians to the world. There is a need to preserve tradition but also a need to serve the presence of the always-greater God who seeks to lead the Church out of its sins of isolation and ambition toward a renewal made possible by the variety of charisms and cultures. [18] The expansion of ministry and preaching has been forcefully begun but its future is not well defined. All three worlds of preaching – the preacher, the individual and collective hearers, the language of cultural thought-forms – still invite reflection and expansion. The Spirit that inspired the Churches of the first century to reach different groups rapidly is today leading the Church out of the constrictions recent centuries placed upon its life into a newness that is both ancient and new.

18. Lehmann 'Vom Dialog als Form der Kommunikation und Wahrheitsfindung in der Kirche' cited in Gotthard Fuchs, 'Unterscheidung der Geister. Notizen zur konziliaren Hermeneutik,' in F. X. Kaufmann, *Vatikanum II und Modernisierung* (Paderborn: Schöningh, 1996) pp. 403 f.

PART 6

Preaching and Praxis

TEXT OR TOPIC? DOING OR BEING?
THE CHALLENGE OF
PREACHING ON MORAL ISSUES

CHARLES E. BOUCHARD, O.P.

WHAT I USED TO THINK ABOUT PREACHING
ON MORAL ISSUES

Some weeks after the Los Angeles riots in 1992, Archbishop John May of Saint Louis included the following in a regular communication to the priests of the archdiocese:

> Just recently, there have been many complaints that on Sunday, May 3, in many parishes, there was not even a mention of what happened in Los Angeles [i.e., the riots] the week before. [This] would seem to provide a real opportunity for relevant preaching on racial justice and not an excuse to avoid it.[1]

Years later, I remember a Sunday Mass at the height of the Monica Lewinsky affair. Long, detailed descriptions of the alleged sexual activity had already appeared in national newspapers. President Clinton maintained his innocence and made his famous statement about the meaning of 'is'. The mixture of sex, adultery, sexual harassment, lying and accountability – not to mention the relationship between personal morality and public office – made a potent brew of moral questions. The preacher that morning started out with a reference to the morning paper's article on the scandal, and I assumed that he was about to offer us some advice on how to make sense of it all. But almost as quickly as he had raised the issue, he dropped it, and went on to preach on a totally unrelated subject. At first I was just disappointed, since all of us were trying to sort out the questions and come up

---

1. Archbishop John May, 'Relevant Preaching,' *Notanda* (*'Blue Notes'*) XII, 2, May 15, 1992.

with some answers. Later, I felt resentful. The preacher missed an opportunity – a teachable moment – to talk about sex, lying or leadership. More than just an opportunity, he had a *responsibility* to bring the Gospel to bear on a topic that was totally preoccupying the country.

Even more recently, I have sat through many preaching events in which there were allusions to the destruction of the World Trade Centre in New York on September 11, 2001, or to the sexual abuse scandal that has shook the American Church in 2002. Most often, these issues were addressed marginally, if at all. I am sure that many preachers (myself included) were overwhelmed by the magnitude of September 11; we hardly knew where to start. As for the sexual abuse crisis, it touched so close to home that most of us felt anything we said would appear self-serving. And in all of the cases I have cited, there was the problem of texts. What are preachers to do when they are bound to a set of lectionary readings that do not appear to be relevant to the moral issue in the news that weekend? [2]

A CHANGE OF HEART

I last addressed the issue of preaching on moral issues in a book that was written by the faculty of Aquinas Institute. [3] In my essay, I urged preachers to identify moral issues they wanted to address, clarify the moral norms and the moral values behind those issues, and 'illuminate' those values with the scriptural word. My advice was based on the assumption that most of Catholic moral teaching comes from natural law, which is not really 'law,' but a process of reasoned reflection on human nature (experience) that

2. Gerard Sloyan addresses this tension in his article, 'Is Church Teaching Neglected When the Lectionary is Preached?' *Worship* 61 (1987) pp. 126-40.
3. 'Authentic Preaching on Moral Issues,' *In the Company of Preachers* (Collegeville, Liturgical Press, 1993) pp. 91-210.

leads us to draw conclusions about moral goods, that is, those things that are truly fulfilling to human persons. In this view, Scripture and revelation do not add anything new to our moral knowledge, but make these natural moral goods clearer and more appealing.

Finally, I urged preachers to plan ahead so that they could use Scriptural 'cues' from the lectionary readings that would allow them to segue into discussion of those issues. This would mean that the preacher could use Genesis to preach about ecology and the environment, the woman in caught in adultery to preach about marital fidelity, and the unjust steward to talk about business ethics.[4]

I still hold some of what I said then to be true. The goal of morality, for example, is not obedience to norms or law, but appropriation of the real, tangible moral values (or human goods) these norms are meant to protect. We refrain from lying, for example, not just because the Ten Commandments or the Pope tells us to, but because deceit breaks down the trust that enables us to live together. We promote peace not only because Jesus tells us to 'turn the other cheek,' but because we know that peace is essential if we are to pursue any other goal in life. In our tradition, morality is an intelligent search for choices that bring human persons happiness.[5] We believe that happiness is God's plan for us, and that this plan is refracted to us not only through Scripture

4. A good example of a similar method is found in Judith Hoch Wray, 'Preaching the Lectionary: The Religious is Political,' *The Living Pulpit* (April-June 1996) pp. 46-58. In this article she attempts to 'cross reference insights from the articles [on politics in the same issue of the *Living Pulpit*] with texts in the Revised Common Lectionary ... to reflect on the political implications mandated by faithful preaching of the Gospel.' I do not mean to disparage this method, as far as it goes.

5. See Thomas Aquinas, *Summa Theologiae* (*ST*) 1-2, q. 3, a. 1: 'In the first sense, [our] last end is the uncreated good, namely God, who alone in his infinite goodness can satisfy [our] will. But in the second way, [our] last end is something created ... the attainment or enjoyment of the last end. Now the last end is called happiness ... '

and revelation, but also through human experience and Church teaching. I also believe that much of Christian morality is human morality; that is, the bulk of what contributes to human fulfilment or happiness can be discovered through reason, and is thus available to any reasonable person, religious or not.[6]

What I no longer believe is that the preacher should use 'scriptural cues' as springboards to particular moral issues. This is not a viable approach, for several reasons. First of all, many important moral issues are simply not addressed in Scripture. Even though there are general passages that might be coaxed into shedding light on some of these, there is really no scriptural teaching on genetic engineering, cloning, nuclear weapons, civil rights of homosexuals, withdrawing hydration and nutrition, or medically indicated abortion.

Second, if there are passages that relate to specific issues in morality (e.g., David and Bathsheeba on adultery, Jesus casting the money-changers out of the temple on Church raffles, the destruction of Sodom and Gomorrah on homosexuality), using them in this way is a grave temptation to homiletic proof-texting in which the preacher first arrives at a conclusion and then finds texts to support it.[7]

---

6. See *ST* 1-2, q. 93, a. 2: Responding to the question, 'Whether the Eternal Law is known to all,' he says, 'Every rational creature knows [the eternal law] in its reflection, greater or less. For every knowledge of truth is a kind of reflection and *participation in the eternal law*, which is the unchangeable truth.' This suggests that as a function of reason or common sense, morality is not just obedience to law, and not necessarily religious. It is the process of discovering and appropriating God's plan in our lives.

7. St Jerome knew the dangers of proof-texting. Humbert of Romans quotes him as saying that some preachers 'disdain to find out what the prophets and apostles really meant. They fit texts to their own view which they do not really fit, forcing reluctant scriptures to serve their own purposes. They are like people who imagine that bells they hear chiming are saying whatever they themselves happen to be thinking of.' 'Treatise on the Formation of Preachers,' in *Early Dominicans*, Simon Tugwell, ed. (New York: Paulist, 1982) p. 208, n. 92.

The biggest problem with this approach is that it often misses the 'teachable moments' I referred to above. Congregations will benefit far more from the timely treatment of a moral issue that is forefront in their minds than from a long-range plan that will treat racism on the Eighteenteenth Sunday in Ordinary Time, no matter what is in the news.

I always begin my class, 'Preaching and Moral Issues', by asking how many students have heard a homily on a moral issue. Usually about half say they have. Then I ask them how many have heard a *good* homily on a moral issue. Usually only one or two say they have. Therefore, I will begin this chapter by describing some of the reasons preachers are reluctant to tackle moral issues.

I will then highlight some aspects of the Catholic theological tradition that produce a distinctive kind of moral preaching. I am convinced that both the frequency and the difference in styles of moral preaching from one Christian denomination to another are rooted in different theological presuppositions. I will try to show how the Catholic tradition, especially in its view of the relationship between nature and grace, produces moral preaching that has a method and a purpose that distinguish it from Pentecostal, Lutheran or Calvinist preaching.

Finally, I will propose a method for what I call 'contextual preaching', that is, preaching that allows the lectionary readings to address the real moral issues that occupy peoples' minds that day.

REASONS WHY PREACHERS FAIL
TO ADDRESS MORAL ISSUES

Perhaps the most important reason that we hesitate to preach on moral issues is that we fear to cause conflict or disagreement at the celebration of the Eucharist, which is supposed to be the apex of Christian unity. Issues like military intervention, abortion, taxes, and gay rights are certain to have passionate adherents on both sides of the fence. Although the preacher may fear confrontation by members of the parish, he also will not want to cause conflict *within* the congregation. He might also hesitate to enter into a discussion of an issue about which he actually knows very little, e.g., business, medical technology, or military strategy.[8]

Lack of familiarity with or understanding of moral teaching is also a problem. There are more than a few priests who could not explain the Church's position on contraception or *in vitro* fertilization if they had to. A priest may not be expected to know everything about business or medicine, but he *is* expected to be able to summarise the Church's teaching. In today's increasingly complex world, discernment about many moral issues will necessarily involve collaboration between those who know the theological tradition and those who know the day-to-day practices and technical aspects of the issue in question.

A second reason is the preacher's ambivalence about aspects of Church teaching, especially on matters of sexual morality. Priests know they are official spokespersons for the Church's teachings on moral matters, but many find it hard to give full assent. Teachings on contraception and divorce are particularly troublesome. They can deal with them privately in Confession or

8. One of the great frustrations of Catholic businesspersons is that preachers often naively condemn business or business leaders without really knowing much about either. 'Many of us really struggle with the moral implications of our business decisions,' one businessman told me, 'but our pastor just assumes he knows more than we do. We never get any credit for trying to bring the Gospel into the workplace.' An officer in the Air Force made a similar complaint: 'Whenever I hear the preacher start to talk about "peace," I close my eyes to wait it out. I know right off that it will be pie-in-the-sky pacifism. That simply isn't going to work in the real world.'

pastoral counselling, but they do not feel they can share their own doubts and questions from the pulpit. Since they cannot affirm the teachings one hundred per cent, they simply refrain from preaching on them.[9]

Another reason is that the complexity of many moral issues makes it impossible to deal adequately with them in the ten minutes or so that are allowed for Sunday homilies in Catholic churches. If, for example, the universal Church has not yet spoken univocally on the withdrawal of hydration and nutrition from some patients, and if various bishops have arrived at differing conclusions, some allowing and others disallowing the practice, how can a preacher clarify the matter in any useful way in a few minutes?[10] This also raises the question of adult catechesis, which in the United States is in a pitiful condition. We have at least two generations of Catholics who have had little or no effective catechesis on Church doctrine. It is unreasonable to expect that the preacher can remedy this in weekly homilies.

9. Some priests' fears are well founded. A novice master for a religious community in the United States was removed from weekend service at a parish and nearly had his faculties revoked because he urged the congregation to make 'inclusion' a priority when dealing with members who were divorced and remarried.

    In his recent book *Sacred Silence: Denial and Crisis in the Church* (Collegeville: Liturgical Press, 2001), Donald Cozzens cites the crisis of conscience occasioned by the publication of *Humanae Vitae* in 1968: 'The majority [of priests] chose to be obedient to their bishop who, no doubt, believed he was simply holding fast to his promise to be obedient to the Bishop of Rome. Many did so in good conscience; I suspect many others did so with a very troubled conscience' (p. 46). Describing factors that contributed to the sexual abuse crisis in 2002, journalist Laurie Goodstein cites conflict priests felt about sexual morality: 'Amid surging use of the birth control pill [in the 1960s] many priests say it fell on them to promulgate a teaching they could not agree with.' ('Train of Pain in Church Crisis Leads to Nearly Every Diocese,' *New York Times*, January 12, 2003, A21).

10. Noted social justice advocate Msgr George Higgins said thirty years ago: 'The pulpit, as a general rule, is not the proper forum in which to pontificate on complicated and highly controversial political and socioeconomic issues' ('The Problems in Preaching: Politics/What Place in Church?' *Origins*, September 21, 1972, p. 213).

Yet another reason for the lack of good preaching on moral issues is confusion about the purpose of moral preaching. Is the preacher's role merely to raise questions? To provide information? To articulate teaching, especially conclusions? To pass judgment on real or presumed behaviour? To form conscience and facilitate good judgement?[11] To enforce specific behaviours? To shape moral character? To stimulate the moral imagination by the use of metaphor?[12] To catechise?[13] Depending on how the preacher understands her task, the outcome will differ.

The final impediment to moral preaching is the preacher's own moral weaknesses or vulnerability. All preachers know that they 'preach first to themselves,' out of their own weakness and need for forgiveness; but still, none of us wants to 'cast the first stone'.

Although the problem is in high relief today because of the enormous publicity surrounding clergy misconduct and sexual abuse, it is not new. Humbert of Romans raises it in his thirteenth century *Treatise on the Formation of Preachers*, when he notes that being 'afraid of the kinds of sins which inevitably occur in the life

11. The great American Jesuit preacher Walter Burghardt says conscience formation is primary: 'If I dare not dogmatize, I may still raise the issues, lay them out, even tell a congregation where I stand and why. Not to impose my convictions as gospel, but to *quicken their Christian conscience*, spur them to personal and communal reflection' ('Preaching Politics?' *The Living Pulpit* 5[1996] pp. 4-51).

12. Philip Keane notes the importance of imagination in the moral life: 'Genuine imagination, even when it deals with fiction, clearly surpasses idle fancy. It seems to be productive; it seeks to open us to the truth. ... The experience of metaphor helps clarify the difference between true imagination and mere fancy. Metaphors strike us as incongruous at first ... But in the end, our ability to imagine enables the metaphor to open up fresh and more adequate insights into truth.' *Christian Ethics and Imagination* (New York: Paulist, 1984) p. 83.

13. Cardinal John O'Connor of New York created a controversy when he urged that the Catechism should be 'preached' from the pulpit. Pressure to make preaching more catechetical led the United States Conference of Catholic Bishops (USCCB) to produce 'Preaching the Truth of Christ: A Resource for Catholic Preachers that Correlates the Catechism of the Catholic Church with the Sunday Readings in the Lectionary for Mass' (available online at www.usccb.org/dpp/advent.htm).

of a preacher,' can cause preachers to neglect mention of those sins.[14]

In a marvellous article entitled 'Words to Match,' Fr Michael Heher describes how preachers can subtly distance themselves from their own sinfulness and their own experience:

> Putting God in the spotlight was supposed to have the added attraction of keeping me a few steps away, safely in the shadows, but it didn't. I wanted my insights and my loves to be known, of course, and I was still young enough to imagine my virtues were worthy of emulation. But I also knew the light to be bright enough to expose my doubts and vices, and when they were revealed, well, then the jig would be up. Who would be convinced by a preacher who does not believe enough of what he professes or puts into practice only part of what he preaches?
>
> To protect myself from the prying eyes of my parishioners, and them from the scandal of my weaknesses, I unconsciously began changing the way I preached. While I continue to be unambiguous about my message of God's presence and love, the methods I used to present it left me more and more out of the picture. My preaching voice developed a timbre quite distinct from the inflection I used with my family and friends. Pious, objective and tinged with the distant ring of authority, I loved the way it sounded. I thought it resonated with the depth of eternity …
>
> But this change in my preaching style had an unexpected result: my parishioners missed me.[15]

14. Humbert also cites length of preparation, nervousness, laziness, unreal lack of confidence, false humility, corruption found among the leaders of the Church, and preference for the tranquility of contemplation as 'trivial reasons which deter people from preaching' (*Treatise,* n. 94).

15. Michael Maher, 'Words to Match,' *Image: A Journal of the Arts and Religion* (Summer 1999) pp. 95-109, at 106.

Once while travelling in Europe, I saw a huge baroque pulpit with a winding staircase leading up to it. Under each step there was a scripture quotation about sinfulness or humility. No doubt many a preacher ascended those steps with fear and trepidation, but they ascended nonetheless. Many of the most persuasive homilies are those in which a prudent amount of self-revelation shows the congregation that the preacher himself struggles to acquire virtue. As 'broken vessels' and 'wounded healers', all preachers must have the courage and humility to hold up moral values even if they have not fully achieved them in their own lives.

DISTINCTIVE ASPECTS OF CATHOLIC THEOLOGY
THAT AFFECT OUR PREACHING

Mary Catherine Hilkert has done a great service by describing fundamental differences in theology, especially Christian anthropology and the relationship between nature and grace, that shape different kinds of moral preaching among Catholics and Protestants. In her book, *Naming Grace*, she outlines the difference between two different Christian spiritualities: one based on the dialectical imagination and the another based on the sacramental (or analogical) imagination:

> The *dialectical imagination* stresses the distance between God and humanity, the hiddenness and absence of God, the sinfulness of human beings, the paradox of the cross, the need for grace as redemption and reconciliation, the limits and necessity for critique of any human project or institution including the Church, and the not-yet character of the promised reign of God. The *sacramental imagination* (or what Tracy calls the analogical imagination) emphasizes the presence of the God who is self-communicated love, the creation of human beings

in the image of God (restless hearts seeking the divine), the mystery of the incarnation, grace as divinizing as well as forgiving, the mediating role of the church as sacrament of salvation in the world, and the 'foretaste' of the reign of God that is present in human community wherever God's reign of justice, peace, and love is fostered. [16]

Although Hilkert notes that these approaches cannot be 'identified simply as Protestant and Catholic,' they do reflect the distinctive theological emphases of those two traditions. This distinction is rooted in the fact that while Protestants tend to see human nature as mostly, if not totally, corrupted by sin, Catholics, admitting that human ability has been weakened by original sin, insist that it still is capable of knowing something of God's will.

This comes as a surprise to Catholics who have been led to believe in something called 'Catholic guilt.' But in fact, guilt for Catholics is only skin deep. Far from seeing humans as fundamentally sinful, we retain a firm belief that creation is 'good enough' to bear the weight of, and even be transformed by, grace. As one professor described the difference between Catholics and Lutherans: 'Lutherans believe in Sin, but Catholics believe in *sins*.' This means that Catholic preachers don't just use the Gospel to call to judgment or despair and total reliance on God's grace, but to 'name grace' already present in the human condition. [17] It

16. Mary Catherine Hilkert, *Naming Grace: Preaching and the Sacramental Imagination* (New York, Continuum, 1997) p. 15. Aquinas describes the sacramentality of preaching when he asks 'Whether any gratuitous grace attaches to words?' He replies that it does in several ways, including when one speaks in order to sway hearers. 'In order to effect this, the Holy Ghost makes use of the human tongue as of an instrument; Even as by a miracle God sometimes works in a more excellent way those things which nature can also work, so too the Holy Ghost effects more excellently by the grace of words that which art can effect in a less efficient manner' (ST 2-2, q. 177, a.1).

17. This perspective is reflected in an article by Aquinas Institute student Randall

also means that the goal of moral preaching is not to replace our humanity, but to fully realize it as God intended it.[18]

The Catholic emphasis on the relative compatibility of nature and grace allows us to root morality in acquisition of virtue rather than obedience to a law. Virtues may be described as 'moral skills' that train our natural abilities of knowing, willing, desiring and fearing so that they work together harmoniously in service of our overall good, both temporal and eternal. When this happens, we also become radically open to grace, which perfects and 'elevates' these natural virtues. We are thus able to strive for human perfection, but also for supernatural perfection, which is the specific destiny of human persons. The 'knowledge' of this destiny is planted in us as deeply as instincts for mating and nurturance of their young are planted in animals.[19] Thus for Catholics, moral preaching is not so much imposing a foreign order on the moral life, but eliciting the 'natural' yearning for

---

Rosenberg. He notes that as a high school teacher, he has found 'that young people sometimes have a difficult time seeing how the sacred relates to their ordinary experience. The realm of the holy, for many, lies outside their everyday conscious horizon. Would it not be helpful then to point out the grace that erupts from within one's own conscience … ?' ('The Religious Dimensions of Life: Can We Discover the Extraordinary in the Quotidian?' *America* [December 9, 2002] p. 7-9, at p. 8).

18. Thomas Merton describes how becoming holy is not becoming someone else, but becoming who God has planned for us to be: 'The seeds that are planted in my liberty at every moment, by God's will are the seeds of my own identity, my own reality, my own happiness, my own sanctity. For me to be a saint means to be myself … Therefore the problem of sanctity and salvation is in fact the problem of finding out who I am and discovering my true self … Therefore, there is only one problem on which all my existence, my peace and my happiness depend: to discover myself in discovering God …' (O'Meara, *Thomas Aquinas, Theologian* [Notre Dame, 1996] p. 206; quoting Thomas Merton, *Seeds of Contemplation* (New York, 1949) pp. 25f.

19. Aquinas notes this destiny: 'It is not suitable that God provide more for creatures being led by divine love to a natural good than for those creatures to whom that love offers a supernatural good. For natural creatures, God provides generously … Even more for those moved to reach an eternal, supernatural good, he infuses certain forms of qualities of the supernatural order according to which easily and enthusiastically they are moved to attain that good which is eternal.' (ST 1-2, q. 110, a. 2, 'Whether grace is a quality of the soul?')

human wholeness and for divine transcendence.

NON-RATIONAL MORAL KNOWING
AND THE GIFTS OF THE HOLY SPIRIT

Our tradition is sometimes criticised for being too rational and deductive, but there is another aspect of the Catholic moral tradition that emphasises 'non-rational' knowing, instinct, or intuition. This is closely related to 'connatural knowledge,' which is not just knowing *about,* but *having.* The gifts of the Holy Spirit represent this kind of moral knowing. Even though discussion of them has been largely absent from Catholic moral theology in recent times, they are divine 'instincts' that enable us to 'taste' and orient ourselves to our divine destiny.[20] They complement, but do not replace, our more rational attempts to know God's will in our lives. They round out the human person and save us from being mathematical in our moral searching. They are a powerful link between morality and spirituality, and are a distinctive characteristic of Dominican moral theology. Aquinas insists that these gifts are available even to children, but I am convinced that learning to profit from them is the sign of a truly mature, adult moral life.[21] Effective moral preaching in the Catholic tradition must not only help people *think* clearly, but help them develop the sensitivity to *feel* these promptings of the Spirit.

20. Thomas O'Meara quotes Aquinas on this point: 'It is suitable that there be in the human being higher perfections according to which a person is disposed to being moved by God. And these perfections are called gifts … An easy and prompt response to divine inspiration, a meeting between the divine and the human at an instinctual level, the gift is a less deliberative mode of living. Here the struggle of virtue has reached what Aquinas named a *connatural* contact with the realm of God' (ST 1-2, q. 68, a.1, 2). See O'Meara's *Virtues in the Theology of Aquinas, Theological Studies* 58 (1997) p. 269

21. For a fuller description of the Gifts and their role in the moral life, see my article, 'Recovering the Gifts of the Holy Spirit in Moral Theology,' *Theological Studies* (September 2002).

THE COMMON GOOD: BEYOND 'JESUS AND ME'

There is a strong strain of individualism in modern Christianity, especially in American Protestantism. This accounts both for an individualistic piety and for elements in our 'cultural code' that resist sacramentality and the common good.[22] Because Catholic moral theology is deeply rooted in the tradition of the common good, our preaching must avoid excessive preoccupation with individual perfection and holiness that neglects the social reality of the human person.

The *Catechism of the Catholic Church* defines the common good as 'the sum total of social conditions which allow people, either as groups or as individuals, to reach their fulfilment more fully and more easily.' It requires respect for the person as such, the social well-being and development of the group itself, and peace, or the stability and security of a just order.[23] This means that when the preacher addresses social issues, her vision must include not only the congregation before her, but the larger society of which the faithful are a part. Achievement of the common good requires the cooperative efforts of all citizens, not just believers.

WHAT DO WE MEAN BY 'CONTEXTUAL PREACHING' ON MORAL ISSUES?

I suggested at the beginning of this chapter that I had rejected

22. American sociologist Robert Bellah notes the individualism that arises from the 'exclusive [Protestant] focus on the relationship between Jesus and the individual, where accepting Jesus Christ as one's personal lord and savior becomes almost the whole of piety.' ('Religion and the Shape of National Culture' *America* [July 31, 1999] pp. 9-14, at p. 12). He also notes that this radical religious individualism becomes particularly problematic when 'joined with a notion of economic freedom that holds that the unrestrained free market can solve all problems.' He says this view is 'virtually inarticulate about the common good' but that it can be helped by the Catholic tradition which gives greater salience to the sacramental life and especially to the Eucharist (p. 13).

23. *Catechism of the Catholic Church*, nn. 1906-9.

'textual cues' in favour of responding to the moral issues that are actually in the news and on people's minds. Doing so takes advantage of natural receptivity on the part of the congregation.

My change of heart resulted from a lecture by a colleague who suggested that the 'text or topic' question was a false dilemma. He said that because of the richness of Scripture, any set of readings could yield a moral message on any particular moral situation. I was skeptical, but intrigued. I decided to test this theory out.

During a summer preaching institute, in which about sixty-five students were enrolled, I used the following exercise.

I created five 'moral contexts' that reflected common moral questions: (1) a city in which a highly controversial criminal execution is about to take place; (2) a 'human rights' ordinance that would extend rights to housing and employment to gays and lesbians; (3) the possibility of a more liberal abortion law, which has polarized 'pro-life' and 'pro-choice' forces; (4) the death of a young black man shot by a white policeman after a chase; (5) the case of a young woman critically injured in a car accident who has been in an unresponsive coma for several years. Her parents now want to discontinue artificial hydration and nutrition, but the local bishop opposes it.

I divided students into five groups, giving each group a description of one of the contexts described above. I told them to prepare a homily outline using everything they knew about good preaching, including thorough exegesis. I instructed them to preach on the moral issue their context reflected. The only catch was that they all had to preach on the *same set of Sunday readings* (which happened to be the Fifteenth Sunday in Year C of Ordinary Time, Deuteronomy 30:10-14; Psalm 69; Colossians 1:15-20, and Luke 10:25-37, the Good Samaritan).

I was astounded by the results. There were at least three or four distinct approaches for each moral context. Some were obvious connections: Seeing the condemned prisoner as the injured traveller whom the Samaritan helps. But others were far more creative: 'What if we saw the homosexual as today's Samaritan?' 'The priest and Levite who passed by were afraid. Perhaps we too are afraid to confront the injustice of capital punishment.' 'What must we do to make "the road to Jericho" safe so that murder and capital punishment become a thing of the past?'

I have done this exercise several times since, and each time the results have been equally impressive: students were able to preach faithfully from the readings in a wide variety of 'moral contexts'. This suggests that the Word is, indeed, richer than I had ever imagined.

PERSONAL MORALITY IS NOT THE SAME
AS PUBLIC POLICY

Even though I believe this method applies both to questions of personal morality and to social questions that involve civil law, there is an important distinction that the preacher must bear in mind. Many people believe that the difference between morality and law is rooted in faith: *viz.*, I believe certain things about morality because of my faith; in a pluralistic society, however, I refrain from 'imposing my religious beliefs' on others. This is the most common argument invoked by politicians who favour 'the right to choose' in abortion even though they themselves are 'personally opposed to it'.

There are two problems with this approach. The first is that faith and religious convictions *do* have a place in public discussions. In the United States, we frequently invoke the 'separation of Church and state' in order to marginalise religious belief, but in fact religion is a deeply interwoven part of our culture. In a country founded on religious freedom we do not suppress religions, but treat each one equally. Therefore, even religiously based convictions have a rightful place in public discourse.[24] The second problem is that morality is not necessarily faith-based: even non-religious persons can and do pursue moral goodness. Therefore, we must find a way to define 'moral' that is not exclusively religious.

Charles Curran draws a helpful distinction between morality and public policy rather than between religion and politics. He says that morality, whether religious or not, has 'personal perfection' as its goal. Personal perfection is an internal reality that involves my identity and character.[25] Because it is internal, it can be influenced but not enforced by external events or demands. Law can, for example, compel me to perform an act of restitution, but it cannot make me a just person.

Public policy or civil law has a more modest goal. It aims only to preserve public order for the sake of the common good. Good laws are those that preserve freedom as much as possible, and only curtail it when necessary for public order. Laws that curtail freedom in order to 'make people moral' inevitably fail. (Prohibition in the United States is a perfect example. Not only did it fail

24. See Ronald Thiemann, *Religion in Public Life: A Dilemma for Democracy* (Washington: Georgetown, 1996): 'Public religion presents a dilemma for American democracy. The reasons why some would encourage a religious voice in our public life can easily be identified. Given the pervasiveness and importance of religious convictions within the American populace, it would indeed be odd to deny such profound sentiments any role in public life' (p. 3); Kenneth and Michael Himes, *Fullness of Faith: The Public Significance of Theology* (New York: Paulist, 1993): 'Public theology wants to bring the wisdom of the Christian tradition to public conversation to contribute to the well-being of the society. But public theology also aims at rending an account of Christian belief that articulates what it means to be a member of the Church;' Christopher Mooney, *Public Virtue: Law and the Social Character of Religion* (Notre Dame, 1986), especially Chapter 1, 'Religion in the Public Sphere.'

25. Charles E. Curran, 'The Difference Between Morality and Public Policy' in *Toward An American Catholic Moral Theology* (Notre Dame, 1987) pp. 194-201.

to instill the virtue of temperance, it gave birth to organised crime.) You can prevent people from doing destructive things, but you cannot 'legislate morality' with a view to making people morally good. That comes from within.

Practically, this means that while some actions might risk scandal or may be immoral, that is, incompatible with personal perfection and holiness, they may be tolerated by civil law in the interest of public order or public health. Abortion, needle exchange programmes for drug users, education about 'safe sex' practices, civil rights for homosexuals, and non-criminalisation of homosexual or other kinds of extramarital sex, are examples of these kinds of behaviour. We may find them morally repugnant on religious or other grounds, but it may be imprudent for legislators to attempt to ban them through legislation.[26] In some cases, we may have to tolerate permissive laws while working to persuade the wider public to embrace moral values more fully. We may also have to acknowledge that two persons of good will may both find an action (e.g., abortion) to be immoral, but disagree on the specific strategy to eliminate it.

Preachers should not advise, nor even appear to advise, congregations to vote for one candidate or another. Nor should they attempt to deliver specific conclusions to public policy issues that

26. Thomas Aquinas recognized the difference between morality and civil law. He asks 'Whether it belongs to law to repress all vice?' and responds: 'Human law is framed for a number of human beings, the majority of whom are not perfect in virtue. Wherefore human laws do not forbid all vices, from which the virtuous abstain, but only the more grievous vices, from which it is possible for the majority to abstain; the purpose of human law is to lead us to virtue, not suddenly, but gradually. Wherefore it does not lay upon the multitude of imperfect citizens the burdens of those who are already virtuous, viz., that they should abstain from all evil. Otherwise, these imperfect ones, being unable to bear such precepts, would break out into yet greater evils (*ST* 1-2, q. 96, a. 2). Elsewhere, he asks 'Whether the rites of unbelievers ought to be tolerated?' Although he assumes these rites are sinful, he says they may be tolerated by law on account of some good that might occur, or to avoid scandal or disturbance (*ST* 2-2, q. 10, a. 11).

have a moral dimension. Rather, they should help congregations clearly articulate the question or questions posed by these issues, and put these questions in the context of Catholic social teaching about the common good, justice, subsidiarity and solidarity. In the end, each voter will have to make his or her own choice. American social ethicist Bryan Hehir provides an excellent description of the task of the preacher on public policy issues:

> The Church enters the political arena not because it has specifically political gifts but because decisions taken in the political, economic, and legal sectors of society have direct bearing on the dignity of the human person. There is no division between a deeply personalist conception of the Church's ministry and its public engagement on secular questions.
>
> The Church makes its way in the public arena on the basis of its moral authority, its capacity to persuade, to convince and to create coalitions in support of changes in law and policy. The emphasis is on an approach that works through the informed conscience of the citizenry. The public ministry seeks to change society with an emphasis on working from the bottom up.
>
> *The potential of this method of public ministry lies in its capacity to draw the community of the church and the wider civil community into a dialogue about the moral content of public policy.* In a time when the moral content of issues is the link between religious and politics, the church most effectively exercises its public ministry by *creating space in the public argument for explicit moral analysis* [italics my own].[27]

Behind this approach is an assumption about how the Church

27. 'Preaching and Public Policy: The Parish and the Pastorals.' *Church* (Fall 1985) pp. 3-7, at p. 5 and p. 6.

'stands in the world'. Faith communities can relate to the world around them in a number of ways. They can, like the Amish or other sectarian groups, see the world as a threat to the integrity of their religious faith and the holiness of their community, and simply withdraw, keeping society at an arm's length. They can, on the other hand, try to make society resemble a Christian community by imposing their religious beliefs on those around them. This is often the case with Christian fundamentalism which would, if it could, create a Christian society through aggressive legislative activity. Another approach would be accommodationism, in which believers see faith as essentially a private matter than has no place in public discourse (this is prevalent in the United States).

The Catholic understanding of this relationship sometimes resembles all of these, but is best described as 'persuasive collaboration.' This means that, because of our concern for the common good and human dignity, we do not retreat from the world; nor do we see faith as private and therefore irrelevant to public life. Because we respect religious freedom and believe that God's grace is mediated through means other than the Church, we also do not try to create a theocracy. Rather, we bring our values and beliefs – whether in explicitly religious language or in more accessible 'natural law' language – into the public dialogue. We try to 'persuade' the wider public of the truth of these claims, but we are also willing to 'collaborate' with those who might not fully share these views. The danger of collaboration is compromise, especially if we cannot achieve one hundred percent; but we are willing to accept that, at least as a transitional stage, if it contributes in some way to the common good, which we see as a manifestation of 'grace-in-the-world'.

PREACHING ON PERSONAL MORALITY

Preaching on personal issues of morality – or urging the pursuit of personal perfection – is difficult because the preacher can't see into the hearts of his hearers and therefore cannot know whether or to what extent his hearers have achieved this perfection. There is the risk of 'preaching to the choir,' on the one hand, or of laying excessive burdens on those who are not as far along in their moral journey. In addition, there is the question of purpose: what does the preacher intend to do? Enforce or proscribe specific behaviours, hold up high ideals that are impractical, or help shape conscience and form moral character?

I believe the preacher's task in preaching on personal morality must focus on conscience formation and character. Moral preaching cannot aim at 'What ought I to *do?*' because there are too many differing circumstances, contingencies, and subjective factors that affect specific decisions. In morality, one size does not fit all.[28] Discernment of specific moral choices must take place in spiritual direction, pastoral counselling or the Sacrament of Reconciliation, but not from the pulpit. Preaching on questions of personal morality must aim, not at what I ought to do, but at 'what kind of person I ought to be'. It should address questions of personal morality directly, but give people the tools to make good decisions rather than making the decisions for them.

28. See Aquinas, 'Whether the natural law is the same in all?' He responds that in some sense it is, but in matters pertaining to the human behavior, 'although there is necessity in the general principles, the more we descend to matters of detail, the more frequently we encounter defects. In matters of action, truth or practical rectitude is not the same for all, as to matters of detail, but only as to the general principles, and where there is the same rectitude in matters of detail, it is not equally known to all.' (ST 1-2, q. 94, a. 4). It is important to note that Aquinas is not talking about epikeia, which is the prudent *dispensation* from law, but about the nature of moral law itself, since moral law shapes itself according to reality rather than the other way around.

VIRTUES AND THE MORAL LIFE

I have already noted that virtues are 'moral skills' or habits. Much like athletic or musical skills, they are acquired over a period of time and eventually make good moral choices second nature. Just as the musician can play a beautiful sonata with no apparent effort, so the virtuous person can produce beautiful moral acts out of habitual or connatural knowledge that requires little or no reflection.

Preachers must also avoid the trap of 'filling the empty pitcher,' that is, assuming that their listeners are empty vessels waiting to be filled with moral knowledge.[29] The vast majority of persons to whom we preach have already had a lot of experience, some good and some bad. This experience has shaped them as moral agents. Rather than simply filling a void, the preacher must help persons (especially adults) tap this experience and critically reflect upon it. This is especially important in our tradition where God's plan for us is discovered not only through revelation and Scripture, but by growing awareness of what leads us to happiness and fulfilment, and what does not.

One author referred to this process as 'striking the responsive chord.' He says the challenge is 'not to get stimuli across, or even to package stimuli so they can be understood and absorbed. Rather [the communicator] must understand the kinds of information and experiences stored in the audience ... The point is not to deposit your message in the other person's mind, but to somehow activate the layers of meaning already deposited there ...'[30]

29. Humbert of Romans notes, however, that preachers should allow themselves to be filled: 'There are other [preachers] who have not yet received the fullness of those heavenly blessings they must have before they can pour them out upon others. If you are sensible, make yourself into a bowl, not a pipe. A pipe receives and pours out almost simultaneously, but a bowl waits till it is full' (*Treatise*, n. 167).

30. Jay Rosen, 'Playing the Primary Chords' (*Harpers* March 1992) p. 23. Professor Rosen was speaking about how the media can effectively communicate in a political campaign, but his ideas have important implications for preaching, too. It is

In moral preaching, our goal is to tap experiences of moral goodness and nurture them. Instead of striking a responsive chord of fear or hatred, we should strike a chord of virtue and wholeness.

There are innumerable virtues, or moral qualities of persons, that can be acquired. Our tradition generally groups these around four 'hinge' or 'cardinal' virtues: temperance, fortitude, justice and prudence. From these, many others flow. Temperance and fortitude are both considered 'affective' virtues in the sense that they relate to emotions rather than our intellects.

Temperance moderates desires, especially 'desires of touch'. Intemperance is the root of many personal sins because the satisfactions of touch, particularly food, drink, and sex, are very powerful. But temperance also has social and even political implications. Gossip, for example, is an intemperate desire for knowledge we do not need or have a right to; anger is satisfaction of a desire for revenge. Clemency, not justice, is the main moral question in capital punishment. Even if a criminal 'deserves to die', the important issue is whether citizens will grow in virtue by imposing such a sentence. Will an exercise of vengeance hurt us as a society more than the criminal?

Fortitude, on the other hand, has to do with fear rather than desire. We need to have the skill of courage in order to persist in our pursuit of the good, even when faced with adversity. Though we often think of courage as the 'virtue of heroes,' it is also very much an everyday virtue. It involves the determination just to stick with our commitments, even when they are difficult and burdensome.

Justice is a thoroughly social virtue, aimed at achieving a 'web

---

important to recall, however, that there is a fine line between 'activating layers of meaning' and manipulating.

of right relationships'. Intimately bound up with the common good, justice is highly eschatological. We work at it through our lives, constantly adjusting rights and obligations so that everyone has what they need; in the end, however, we never get it quite right in this world, and have to hope that in God's reign it will finally all come together.

Prudence may well be 'the queen of the virtues'. It is partly practical and partly intellectual because it involves the skill of 'knowing what ought to be done'. It is essential for all the other virtues, and is manifest in wisdom and in those persons to whom we would go for advice on a very troublesome and complicated moral problem.

Preaching virtue is far more effective than preaching 'rules,' because virtues admit of degree; if we preach obedience to a rule, there are only two answers: right or wrong. With virtue, we can judge growth and progress, and there is always room for improvement. After all, the goal of morality is not obedience to the norm, but real appropriation of the moral good or value that the norm protects.

CONCLUSION

In this article, I have tried to articulate some of the reasons why good preaching on moral issues is rare, and how basic Catholic doctrines shape the way we approach moral preaching. It is more focused on 'why' than on 'how,' so those who sought a step-by-step guide to preaching on moral questions may be disappointed. I am convinced, however, that our tradition has all the tools to recreate a rich and vital practice of moral preaching. I invite my homiletic colleagues to test and critique what I have outlined here.

PREACHING GENEROSITY – LESSONS FROM THE FATHERS

RICHARD FINN, O.P.

St Augustine, in Book Two of the *City of God*, issued a challenge to the pagans: where did their gods assemble people so as to instruct them in avoiding the vices of greed, ambition, and extravagance? For Christians could point to churches established for that purpose wherever the faith had spread throughout the empire (*City of God*, 2.6). Temples, unlike churches, were not built to house a congregation; their priests did not expound sacred texts from any pulpit. Augustine appealed to what educated pagans and Christians held in common, a traditional reprehension of those vices which were thought endemic to, and corrupting of, Roman political life. This enabled him to capitalise on distinctive features of Christian worship. He presented the Church as a school of virtue, where the assembled faithful were taught both through readings from Scripture and the preaching which accompanied the readings. At church, Christians heard: 'how virtuously they should live in this present world in order to merit, when this life is over, eternal life in bliss. Sacred Scripture and instruction in justice, given out from a raised pulpit in everyone's sight, reverberate through the Church, where those who put it into practice hear something to their advantage and those who do not bring judgment on themselves' (*City of God*, 2.28).[1] Preaching, understood as the teaching of morality, is advanced as a measure of Christianity's status as a superior religion.

St Augustine's account raises three questions about preaching in Late Antiquity, and a related question about preaching in contemporary society. The historian can ask how far preaching

1. All translations are my own unless otherwise stated.

in the fourth and early fifth centuries functioned in accordance
with the bishop's idealised and abstract account of Christian
ethical teaching, but also what means preachers used to convey
their teaching, and to what effect. We can try to see what their
discourse achieved. We can then ask what value Late Antique
preaching might have for our current practice. This article
attempts to answer these questions by looking in detail at one
element in Christian moral preaching: the call to almsgiving.[2]

It might be objected at the outset that Augustine's account is
highly misleading, because preaching may not have been frequent and may have reached only a few in the Christian community. Preachers certainly complained that Church attendance
was patchy. St Basil attacked the low attendance at a penitential
service held at Caesarea when food shortages threatened in the
late 360s (*In Time of Hunger*, 3). There were often more women
and children than men in the congregation: Augustine imagined
a bearded man being mocked for his Church attendance, described by the mockers as 'going where the widows and old ladies
go' (*Sermon* 306B.6 [3]). This might reflect an imbalance between
the sexes in Church membership, but is more likely to reflect
different patterns of worship. Yet both men and women often
crowded the Carthaginian churches: Bishop Aurelius had moved
to segregate the sexes, who were to enter through different doors
into different areas of the church (Augustine, *Sermon* 359B.5). At
Augustine's own basilica in Hippo the congregation swelled for
the Nativity, Easter and the Ascension. Augustine remarked

---

2. This article draws on my wider study, *Almsgiving in the later Roman Empire:
   Christian Promotion and Practice (313-450)* (Oxford University Press, forthcoming
   2006). I have omitted here, for simplicity's sake, the references to critical editions of
   the primary texts in Latin and Greek.

3. Augustine's sermons are referred to here by the numbers adopted in Augustine,
   Sermons, ed. John Rotelle, O.S.A., trans. Edmund Hill O.P., 1990-, New York,
   New City Press.

there on the Sunday after Easter how 'everyone' was at church for
the solemnity (*Sermon* 259.6).

Evidence for patchy attendance does not in any case lessen the
importance of preaching as the only vehicle for instructing the
many who were wholly or partially illiterate, and so had no access
to texts which promoted almsgiving, such as popular *Lives* of the
saints or the apocryphal *Acts* of various apostles. If some people
did not attend often, what they heard when they did attend was
crucial to their understanding of Christianity. Those who did
regularly hear sermons belonged to groups significant for the
wider formation of opinion concerning almsgiving: candidates
for baptism (the *competentes*) in Lent and neophytes at Easter,
when attendance was compulsory and sermons were a main
vehicle of Christian initiation; enrolled widows and virgins,
monks and clerics, all of whom had either entitlements to Church
alms or duties of almsgiving.

It is sometimes argued that the destitute themselves were
absent from Church, as they were rarely addressed by preachers;
but this failure of preachers to address the very poor may say
more about their low status than their absence from the congregation. The *Apostolic Constitutions*, a late-fourth century 'Church
order' which describes the ideal form and practice for an urban
church in the Greek-speaking East, instruct the deacons to find
a place in the church for a 'beggar or low-born man or stranger',
while the deaconess is to greet the women in the same way,
whether they were 'rich or poor' (*Apostolic Constitutions* II.58.6).
One sermon by Augustine, dated to around 420, talks of how 'all
the beggars, the sore-infested, the cripples, the rejects' identify
with Lazarus on hearing the story of Dives and Lazarus in
church. It imagines one such man's thoughts, 'a poor man in
need, with scarcely enough to fend for himself or perhaps a
beggar' on hearing the Gospel read in his presence and the

thoughts of a well-dressed rich man (*Sermon* 20A.9).

What place within this preaching did almsgiving occupy? It is beyond the scope of this article to study more than a small sample of extant sermons from Late Antiquity. I shall take Augustine's extant *corpus* to ask in how many of his sermons almsgiving figures as either the sole theme or as a major theme, how often it is briefly promoted in passing, as it were, its whereabouts in those sermons, and when such sermons may have been preached in the liturgical year.

Some caution is required. Later copyists frequently excised material from individual sermons and created new sermons from a catena of passages extracted from a number of longer originals, each of which may well have been preached at different times of the year. We should not assume that Augustine's *corpus* represents a typical sample of Late Antique sermons. We may presume that sermons on controversial doctrinal matters were more often kept and copied than sermons on less contentious moral teachings, due to the former's utility in combating per-ceived recurrences of earlier heresies. The *corpus* may be further biased in favour of sermons on saints, whose universal or widely celebrated feasts provided an additional incentive for preserva-tion. It is also possible that the role of monks in the transmission of sermons may have acted to save a disproportionate number of sermons promoting asceticism. On these grounds the extant *corpus* probably under-represents the almsgiving promoted by preachers, but, as will be shown, this is not to say that almsgiving is rarely promoted in the *corpus*.

Counting Augustine's extant sermons is an art in itself and one still subject to new discoveries. In 1997 John Rotelle counted 546 sermons, to which he added twenty-one from the thirty sermons newly edited by Francois Dolbeau, making a total of 567. Promo-tion of almsgiving is found to a greater or lesser extent in 113 of these 567. Ten sermons are primarily devoted to the promotion of almsgiving, though one of these may be a cut-down version of another, and a further two are of doubtful authenticity.[4] Almsgiving features in ten sermons as the right use of wealth in an extended treatment of riches and poverty,[5] and features in another forty-five as one important topic among others.[6] In sixteen sermons almsgiving is promoted in conclusion to a text otherwise on different topics,[7] and in thirty-two, almsgiving features only briefly and in passing.[8] Many of these sermons cannot be dated with any accuracy to a given date or liturgical season. But, according to the notes drawn up by Edmund Hill, O.P., to accompany his translations of all Augustine's sermons, thirteen of our 113 were apparently given in Lent,[9] a further five at Easter.[10] Eleven appear to have been delivered during the winter.[11] Nine probably originate in the period from May to June, three of these at least in the period between Ascension and Pentecost.[12] Ten were delivered on saints' days at different times in the year.[13] A further three can be placed in September.[14] A number were given on Sundays.[15]

What may be gleaned from this information? First, the high

---

4. *Sermons* 61, 86, 113, 164A, 350B, 350C, 367, 388, 389, and 390.
5. *Sermons* 14, 36, 39, 41, 42, 50, 60, 85, 107A and 177.
6. *Sermons* 11, 18, 25, 25A, 32, 37, 53, 53A, 56, 58, 93, 103, 104, 105A, 113B, 114A, 114B, 149, 164, 172, 178, 198, 205, 206, 207, 208, 209, 210, 211A, 217, 236, 239, 259, 299E, 302, 305A, 335C, 338, 339, 345, 352, 356, 358A, 359A, 399.
7. *Sermons* 9, 47, 66, 91, 95, 99, 102, 114, 122, 123, 125A, 142, 261, 337, 357 and 376A.
8. *Sermons* 15, 15A, 16A, 16B, 21, 22, 38, 45, 62, 72, 83, 87, 88, 90, 113A, 163B, 174, 204A, 229Z, 296, 299A, 299D, 311, 313C, 313E, 346, 346A, 350A, 355, 359B, 360B, and 362.
9. *Sermons* 11, 45, 56, 58, 205, 206, 207, 208, 209, 210, 211A and 352, 390.
10. *Sermons* 229Z, 236, 239, 259, and 376A.
11. *Sermons* 18, 53, 83, 86, 95, 114B, 125A, 204A, 346A, 359B, 362.
12. *Sermons* 14, 15, 60, 85, 177, 261, 296, 299A, 360B. To these may be added *Sermon* 114 (delivered April to July?).
13. *Sermons* 37 and 296, 299A, 299E, 302 and 305A, 311, 313C, 313E, 359B.
14. *Sermons* 15A, 113A, 163B.
15. *Sermons* 14, 113A.

level of promotion, present to a greater or lesser degree in one fifth of the sermons, makes the theme at least as prominent as, and arguably more prominent than, Augustine's promotion of asceticism in sermons and certainly more prominent than promotion of virginity and monastic life. Second, this promotion was a conventional feature of his winter and Lenten preaching, though not found in every winter or Lenten sermon, and a feature of sermons which he preached at designated times of fasting, such as the ember days around Pentecost. Such winter and Lenten exhortation to give alms coincided with a time of likely food shortages and high prices before the new harvest brought cheaper supplies onto the market.[16] Third, promotion reached the *competentes* and neophytes during Lent and Easter. Fourth, it was not limited at other times of the year to the faithful who attended regularly on weekdays.

So, the analysis of Augustine's sermons offers one measure of how frequently and when almsgiving was promoted in Late Antiquity. We can look next at sermons by Augustine and others to ask what manner this promotion took. Sermons, not surprisingly, were the works in which explicit exhortation to almsgiving was most often found, and this explicit exhortation took many forms, both *with* quotation of clearly supporting biblical verses (e.g., Augustine, *Sermon* 198.3) and *without* such quotation (e.g., Augustine, *Sermon* 208). It was often couched in scriptural language, or alluded to Scripture, relying on an accepted interpretation of certain passages: Chrysostom's call to 'buy oil' at the close of one sermon is an exhortation to almsgiving dependent on a particular reading of the parable of the foolish virgins (Chrysostom, *Homilies on Matthew*, 20.6). The faithful were exhorted in circumlocutions or technical terms to 'works of mercy' (*'opera*

16. Peter Garnsey, *Famine and Food Supply in the Graeco-Roman World,* 1988, Cambridge, Cambridge University Press, p. 24 and p. 54.

misericordiae' or '*opera iustitiae*') where these were understood to consist in, or include, almsgiving (e.g., Chromatius, *Sermons* 24.3, 28.2, and 35.2).

Deliberate promotion commonly took the form of favourable presentation and praise of almsgivers in the Scriptures or those in the Bible who practised hospitality, figures such as Abraham, Job, the widow of Zarephath, Zacchaeus, Cornelius and (less frequently) Tabitha (e.g., Chrysostom, *Homilies on Matthew*, 83.4); the inclusion of almsgiving among the traits of the good or just individual (e.g., Augustine, *Sermon* 15.9); inclusion of almsgiving and care of the poor among the virtues characteristic of monks (e.g., Chrysostom, *Homilies on Matthew*, 68.3 and 72.4); stories in which almsgiving highlights the sanctity of the protagonist or his conversion (Augustine, *Sermon* 178.8); the assertion that almsgiving ensured that prayers would be answered swiftly by giving them wings (Chrysostom, *Homilies on Matthew*, 77.6); and the portrayal of heaven as a place where, unlike here, almsgiving is no longer needed (Augustine, *Sermon* 299D.7).

To this may be added the explicit condemnation of those who fail to give alms, both biblical figures such as Dives and others (Chrysostom, *Homilies on Matthew*, 27.4). Condemnation, too, might be couched in the language of Scripture, or allude to Scripture, with a corresponding dependence on accepted readings: Chrysostom reproached his congregation for being unmoved at the sight of Christ as a naked stranger, for giving him at most a morsel of bread, a reference to almsgiving dependent on an accepted reading of Matthew 25:35-42 (*Homilies on Matthew*, 7.5).

Chrysostom recognized the value of indirect promotion. His *Homily on 2 Corinthians* 16 explained how St Paul avoids direct and immediate exhortation to give alms, but 'says this first, not what he wants, but something else instead, to reach the topic by a different route, so as not to reveal his true intention' (*Homilies on 2 Corinthians*, 16.2). He noted how Paul praises what had already been achieved, to prepare the ground for exhortation and how the apostle sought to provoke 'emulation' in describing the almsgiving already demonstrated in the Macedonian churches. In the following homily he observed how Paul humours the Corinthians and avoids giving offence (*Homilies on 2 Corinthians*, 17.1). Elsewhere, he distinguished between the three different types of good example or persuasion in almsgiving to which St Paul appeals in the letter: the example of other Christians, the earlier example of the Corinthians themselves, and the example of Christ himself in making himself poor to enrich others by his incarnation (*Homilies on 2 Corinthians*, 19.1). Examples promote good practice 'because man is an emulous creature'. The preacher observed that the apostle advances both spiritual and temporal considerations in exhortation (*Homilies on 2 Corinthians*, 20.1). He noted the importance of Paul's metaphor of 'seed' in suggesting the great reward which almsgiving brought for a small or modest outlay. We should expect a similar artfulness in Chrysostom's preaching and perhaps more widely among his contemporaries.

The most important element in the promotion by preachers was obviously the use and interpretation of biblical texts, which, as God's word, carried an irrefutable authority. Elizabeth Clark gave as the aim of her book *Reading Renunciation* 'not to focus on specific genres, but to illustrate how across the whole gamut of Greek and Latin patristic literature, Biblical verses could be pressed to promote an ascetic form of Christianity.'[17] She identified a number of exegetical strategies used in the texts she

17. Elizabeth A. Clark, *Reading Renunciation: Asceticism and Scripture in Early Christianity*, 1999, Princeton, Princeton University Press, p. 11.

examined and which may be summarized as follows: (1) the
highlighting of favourable biblical texts; (2) the use of translations which favoured ascetic interpretations of the preachers or
authors; (3) close reading of passages which otherwise threatened
their promotion of asceticism; (4) inter-textual exegesis, where
texts were to be reconciled and used to interpret each other; (5)
'talking back' – the use of biblical citations to refute readings of
other texts or to trump those texts; (6) 'textual implosion' – where
texts about other topics are read as being, despite appearances,
about asceticism; (7) changes in the context in which the biblical
texts had meaning, in, for example, a re-interpretation of Israelite
ritual law for a Christian community which did not practise that
law; (8) changes in the target audience, so that texts originally
directed at one individual or group were applied to others; this
included (9) changing the sex of the target group, so that a text
originally referring to one sex was read as referring to the other;
(10) establishing what Clark termed a 'hierarchy of voice', deter-
mining the authority of who says what in such a way as to favour
the cause of asceticism; and (11) resolving difficulties by reference
to the difference in times between the Old and New Testaments.
It is worth asking which of these strategies were also widely
employed to promote almsgiving.

Promoters had frequent recourse to favourable biblical texts,
though each promoter did not necessarily use the same texts, or
did not use particular texts as frequently as others, or did not use
them in the same combination as others did. Augustine, for
example, made frequent reference to Isaiah 58.7 'Break your
bread to the hungry ... clothe the naked' (Augustine, *Sermons*,
47.25, 56.11, 58.10, 62.18, 217.5, 299D.7, 339.6).

Almsgiving, unlike certain forms of asceticism, in particular
the exaltation of virginity for women as a higher state than
marriage, did not run contrary to particular biblical passages, but

there were, nonetheless, problematic passages to be explained through close reading and what Clark has termed 'talking back'.

The insistence that in almsgiving one was giving to Christ in the person of the destitute, secured by Christ's words at Matthew 25:40 ('whatever you do to the least of these you do to me'), had to be maintained despite his words at Matthew 26:11 ('the poor you have always with you, but you do not always have me'). In the latter passage Jesus distinguished between himself and the poor to defend a woman who had spent on perfume for his feet money that might have been given in alms. Chrysostom moved to distinguish between what Christ held good in the woman's case and what holds true as a general law: 'if someone were to ask him, had the woman not done this, he would not have given this answer' (*Homily on Matthew's Gospel* 80).

Giving alms to those who had no gainful employment appeared contrary to St Paul's injunction that 'if any would not work, neither should he eat' (2 Thess 3:10). Chrysostom opposed to this the injunction a few verses later at verse 13 ('do not tire of doing what is right'), which he interpreted as a command to prompt almsgiving, and then sought to reconcile the apparent contradiction (*Homilies on Matthew*, 35.4). He differentiated between the audiences to which each verse was addressed, so that the first injunction was aimed at the poor healthy enough to work, while the second was directed at potential benefactors.

The high number of biblical texts promoting almsgiving obviated the need for much 'textual implosion', but it was common to read the parable of the wise and foolish virgins of Matthew 25:1-12 so that the oil possessed by the wise was the alms they had given. In Chrysostom's preaching this implied the greater value of almsgiving over virginity, a meaning certainly not intended by the original text (*Homilies on Matthew*, 47.4 and 50.4).

Alongside the appeal to biblical texts were other aids in promotion. Compassion was excited through graphic portrayal of the miseries of the poor, especially in winter: 'the temperature drops below freezing and the poor man lies prostrate on the pavement in his rags, all but dead from the cold, his teeth chattering. How he looks, how he is dressed, should exhort you' (Chrysostom, *Homilies on Hebrews*, 11.3). Preachers responded to what they presented as the excuses advanced by those who refused to give: the need to secure the well-being of one's children was answered by provision for their eternal happiness; the charge that beggars were fraudulent shirkers met with the response that no one would endure the humiliation of begging unless driven by necessity. Fear of impoverishment met with a reminder that wealth did not bring happiness and could not be secured. The faithful might be called upon to give alms as an expression of their supposedly distinctive Christian identity *vis-à-vis* their pagan neighbours: Augustine urged his congregation at Hippo Regius not to take part in the pagan festivities for New Year, but to maintain a distinctive identity through a different set of Christian practices: 'They give good luck presents; see to it that you give alms' (*Sermon* 198.2-3).

Preachers, of course, advanced theological reasons why their congregations should give alms. The most common arguments advanced by Latin preachers were admirably described with a wealth of detailed reference some twenty years ago by the Dominican scholar Boniface Ramsey: the identification of Christ and the poor; the merit of almsgiving in atoning for post-baptismal sins; and the value of alms in securing the intercession of the poor.[18]

---

18. Boniface Ramsey O.P., 'Almsgiving in the Latin Church: the Late Fourth and Early Fifth centuries', *Theological Studies* 43 (1982), pp. 226-59.

Greek preachers used the same stratagems and arguments. Susan Holman has noted, for example, that with respect to St Basil, St Gregory of Nyssa, and St Gregory Nazianzen, the 'metaphor of Matthew 25, in which ministering to the poor is ministering to Christ, is a dominant theme throughout all three Cappadocians' writings on poverty relief.'[19] Promotion of almsgiving as an exchange of valued gifts, the prayers offered in return for alms, facilitated a multiple re-description of the destitute. Michael De Vinne has detailed how Augustine and Chrysostom in particular redescribed the poor as gladiators, athletes, and actors who offered the wealthy a didactic spectacle in which the feminising evils of wealth are opposed to the masculine virtues of a Christ-like poverty nobly endured.[20] The destitute became active subjects rather than passive objects of pity. Chrysostom, for example, portrayed the poor as surgeons whose outstretched hands excised scars and healed wounds (*Homilies on 1 Corinthians*, 30.7).

As Job's alms made him a father to the poor, Christian discourse presented donor and recipient as parent and offspring. Basil convicted the rich young man of Matthew 19:21 of failing to love his neighbour: had he clothed the naked and acted as a father to the orphans, he would not still retain considerable riches (*On the Wealthy*, 1). Elsewhere, Basil sought to persuade the rich man to almsgiving by holding out the praise of being addressed as the 'father to countless children' on account of his alms (*I Will Knock Down My Barns*, 3). Ambrose, drawing on Basil's sermons in the *On Naboth*, made the same point to present the donor as the

19. Susan Holman, 'The Entitled Poor: Human Rights Language in the Cappadocians', *Pro Ecclesia* 9 (2000), pp. 476-89, at p. 483.
20. Michael De Vinne, *The Advocacy of Empty Bellies: Episcopal Representation of the Poor in the Late Roman Empire*, unpublished Ph.D. thesis, 1995, Stanford, pp. 48-83.

'father of orphaned children' (*On Naboth*, 7.36). Bishops in particular were presented as fathers of those to whom they gave alms. Gregory Nazianzen presented Athanasius as the father of the orphans at Alexandria (*Oration* 21.10).

All these forms of redescription aided the campaign by clerics to remove the contempt frequently shown to recipients in classical society in an attempted remodelling of the donor's attitudes and character as well as practice. Almsgiving was promoted in the context of a character trait or virtue held central to Christianity, that of being 'a lover of the destitute' (*philoptôchos*). The Greek adjective and its corresponding abstract noun are rarely attested in classical usage. In the *Apostolic Constitutions*, when a bishop investigates the characters of disputants who appear before him, this is one of the traits which is to identify the virtuous Christian (*Apostolic Constitutions*, II.50.1). It was one of the principal virtues which Cyril of Alexandria urged the faithful to show in Lenten almsgiving (*Paschal Homilies* 15, 16, 25 and 30).

The meaning of almsgiving as an exchange of gifts, and the relationships of paternal or fraternal charity both acknowledged in and established through almsgiving, meant that almsgiving could be advocated as expressing the virtue of mutual love or *philallêlia* (Cyril of Alexandria, *Paschal Homilies,* 17, 18 and 25). In particular, almsgiving was promoted as an expression of justice and generosity. Preachers frequently cited Psalm 111 (112):9: 'He has given funds; he gave to the poor; his righteousness remains' (Basil, *I Will Knock Down My Barns*, 3, and *On the Wealthy*, 2; Chrysostom, *Homilies on 2 Corinthians*, 19.3). Most important of all was the understanding of almsgiving as an act of generosity, in a redefinition by Christians of the classical virtues of *liberalitas* and *humanitas*.

It has been said that in John Chrysostom's *Commentary on Matthew* the words *philanthropos* and *philanthropia* appear 'dans la plupart des passages où il est question de l'aumône et de la charité à l'égard des pauvres.'[21] Other terms from this constellation of related virtues appear in his homilies on the Gospel. In describing Jesus' entry into Jerusalem, Chrysostom compared the warmth and enthusiasm of the crowds who greeted him with the half-hearted or grudging actions of his congregation in almsgiving, when they saw Christ naked. Were they, he asked, so generous – *philotimoi* – (*Homilies on Matthew*, 66.3)? He threatened that he would stop preaching on almsgiving, because of their poor response, giving something, but 'not with an open hand' (ibid.). In another sermon he reminded them that what they thought of as their own possessions were only what God had entrusted to them to give generously to the needy (*Homilies on Matthew*, 77.5). Elsewhere Chrysostom glossed almsgiving as 'philanthropy, generosity towards the needy' (*Commentary on the Psalms*, 49.4).

Christian discourse promoted this form of generosity by claiming it was already practised by holy men and women. Gregory Nazianzen's funeral oration for his sister Gorgonia and the oration for his father, the local bishop, both present copious almsgiving as part of *megalopsuchia* or 'magnanimity'. Of Gorgonia he asked the rhetorical question 'Who was more open-handed to the needy?' (*Oration* 8). While wishing to stress his relatives' excellence in this respect, he nonetheless suggests that such generosity was not uncommon: 'When it comes to magnificence with money, someone may have no difficulty in finding among other cases, both many where money is wasted on civic and public ambitions, and many where it is loaned to God via the poor, these being the only ones that store up savings for the spenders. But we do not readily find anyone who passes up the

21. Hélène Pétré, *Caritas, Étude sur le vocabulaire latin de la charité chrétienne*, 1948, Louvain, Spicilegium Sacrum Lovaniense, p. 211.

glory attached to it' (*Oration* 18.21).

Gregory Nazianzen presented Basil's poor-relief at Caesarea as expressing *philanthropia* and *megalopsuchia*: 'He did not treat the city in this way, but treat the surrounding country and foreign parts differently. No, when it came to the exercise of philanthropy and magnificence towards the poor, he set a contest for the leaders of the people that was open to all.' (*Oration* 43.63). He defined *philanthropia* both as a general readiness to assist the weak and a particular devotion to almsgiving: 'Philanthropy is a noble undertaking, both feeding the destitute and coming to the aid of human weakness.' The characterisation of the virtuous donor was accompanied by a corresponding representation of the gift as a benefaction which in some cases was approximated to classical, civic benefactions (e.g. Basil, *In Time of Famine*, 2). Chrysostom urged his congregation to win many who had enjoyed their benefactions of alms (*Homilies on 1 Corinthians*, 10.4). Basil promised his hearers that the almsgiver would enjoy at the Judgment the honourable titles of 'provider and benefactor' together with all the other names belonging to charity (*I Will Knock Down My Barns*, 3).

Finally, listeners to sermons were invited to see generous donors as exercising a form of leadership or patronage of those whom they aided by alms. The phrase 'the leadership of the needy' was a formula used by certain promoters of almsgiving (e.g., Chrysostom, *Homilies On Prayer*, 2.1). Gregory Nazianzen portrayed Athanasius not only as a father of the orphans, but as *prostates* of the widows, their protector or patron: 'Widows will, I think, praise him as their champion, orphans as their father and beggars as one who loved beggars' (*Oration* 21.10). Chrysostom urged his congregation to exercise their *prostasia* in helping their needy neighbours, and promised them that others would praise them for saving the recipients of alms through their *prostasia*

(*Homilies on Matthew*, 78.3).

What, then, were the changes in social relations brought about by this adapted generosity as it interacted with the re-description of the poor as intercessors and of their donors as benefactors and leaders? Inscriptions show that generous and assiduous alms-giving on a large scale or over a long period conferred honour on its practitioners. An epitaph in one of the Milanese basilicas remembers the virtues of a woman from the senatorial elite, Manlia Daedalia, plausibly identified as a sister or daughter of Flavius Manlius Theodorus, the consul of 399. This consecrated virgin is proudly described as a 'mother' to the needy, presumably because of her provision of the alms on which they lived (*CIL* V 6240).

As a source of honour and the social prominence and leader-ship which honour conferred, almsgiving featured in the con-struction and negotiation of spiritual authority in the Christian communities, especially that exercised by the bishop. Uranius described Paulinus of Nola as being as generous ('*munificus*') as Melchisedech (*Life of Paulinus*, 8). He told how at his obsequies Christians, pagans and Jews 'all bewailed the patron, defender, and guardian snatched from them ... Spurning no one, he gave to all, he bestowed on all ... He defined gold and silver and the rest in such a way that his liberality claimed them for giving away, not his cupidity for hoarding them' (ibid., 9). Uranius, in a metaphor that recalls Christ's impoverishment for humanity's enrichment, stated that Paulinus, in his 'concern for wretched, [and] compassion for the weak ... alone was a beggar so that he might overflow for all.' There is a conflation here of different types of euergetism (the benefactions which the wealthy tradi-tionally gave to their native cities and fellow citizens in return for the honour in which they were held), civic patronage, almsgiving, and the foundation of churches. But these coalesce in exalting the status of the bishop.

Spiritual authority built up through almsgiving brought popular support which might help a bishop to retain his see, whether because recipients of alms might prove loyal agents and defenders of the bishop who provided for them, or because it served to legitimate the bishop's rule over his entire congregation. According to Sozomen, the fifth century Church historian at Constantinople, the initial failure to remove Gerontion from the see at Nicomedia in 398 was due to successful popular opposition, and it is significant that those who spoke in Gerontion's favour praised this former Milanese deacon for his use of medical knowledge on behalf of both rich and poor (Sozomen, *Ecclesiastical History* 8.6). A reputation for almsgiving might also help a candidate to become bishop. Sokrates (another early Church historian from the fifth century, not be confused with the more famous ancient philosopher) related that Sisinnios was chosen to become bishop of Constantinople in late 425 or early 426 with the backing of lay supporters impressed 'above all because he devoted himself to comforting the destitute beyond his means' (Sokrates, *Ecclesiastical History*, 7.26).

Hilary of Arles described the hospitality and almsgiving practised by Honoratus and his brother on their family estate in the late-fourth century as episcopal in style: 'even then a form of unofficial episcopacy was to be seen at work in their conduct'. It was a lesson to bishops (Hilary, *Life of Honoratus*, 9). This suggests that almsgiving was so closely associated with the exercise of episcopal authority by the turn of the century that some forms or practices could become in other hands a means to rival or criticise individual bishops. This is confirmed by other *Lives*: in an urban setting the honourable virtues of monastic almsgiving, exercised in organising distributions in time of famine or the running of hostels, might amount to, and fuel, competition with the local bishop. Callinicus wrote in the mid-fifth century a *Life of Hypatios*, the head of a monastic community at Rouphinianes near Chalcedon. He shows him exercising a typically episcopal form of almsgiving, when he stores food to distribute in a period of scarcity (*Life of Hypatios, 31.3-4)*. Monks were often discouraged from storing alms. Hypatios himself rebuked a monk who tried to store clothes which he should have re-distributed at once (ibid., 34.4-6). The regular feeding of a great crowd from stores was a bishop's responsibility, and Hypatios was a noted opponent of his own bishop on doctrinal grounds. The detail serves, so to speak, to steal the bishop's clothes.

Competition sharpened through almsgiving could involve others than monks. At the Council of Chalcedon, Bassianos, bishop of Ephesus, described how as a young man 'I devoted my life to the destitute and created a hostel for them' which he had furnished with seventy beds for the care of the sick and injured. This, however, had excited the envy of Memnon, the then local bishop, on account of the popularity Bassianos enjoyed as a result of his almsgiving. Memnon sought to neutralise a rival and remove him from the city in forcibly consecrating him as bishop of another city. When that failed to work, Memnon had him assaulted.[22] Almsgiving had a primary role in the leadership exercised by the bishop over the widows and other recipients of alms, and a significant, but not necessarily a primary, role in the exercise of wider leadership in the Christian community, where the bishop's care for the poor was symbolic of his good government and orthodoxy.

---

22. Eduard Schwartz, ed., *Acta Conciliorum Oecumenicorum*, 4 vols, 1914-74, Berlin, vol. II.i.3.46 [405].

Almsgiving exercised by lay men and women enhanced their claim to honour in the Christian community, and justified, in the eyes of most but not all, their continuing possession of great wealth, while it offered one reason for the respect which they received from Church leaders and writers; but any contribution of almsgiving to the exercise of lay leadership proves much harder to characterise. The language of *prostasia* which was directed at (potential) lay donors may work otherwise than as the description of a new and particular form of leadership or patronage available to them. It should be seen in the context of the varied forms of *prostasia* already exercised by lay figures in the civic community, often to the disadvantage of the poor. The Egyptian monk Isidore of Pelusium insisted to a local bishop, Leontius, in a letter dated by his modern editor to c.420, that bishops must not form alliances with those who used their *prostasia* of the people to fleece the poor.[23] Promoters of almsgiving presented it as an expression of an existing leadership in order to encourage its practice by those leaders and thereby to mitigate the deleterious effects on the poor of that pre-existing exercise of power.

We have now reviewed the place of almsgiving in Late Antique sermons, the manner in which preachers sought to communicate Christian moral teachings, and suggested some of the effects brought about by this preaching. What lessons may the contemporary preacher find here across the profound cultural divide which separates then from now? Things once related and inter-connected in a discourse which gave particular significance to almsgiving now lie fragmented and separated: moral teachings and the virtues, the gifts of the wealthy and the prayers of the poor, the public care of the poor and the authority of Church leaders. It is not clear how much could or should be re-assembled.

---

23. Isidore of Pelusium, *Ep.* 888.

One approach, much in evidence over the past thirty years, is to plunder the past for isolated treasures. Selected passages from the Church Fathers are published in 'readers' and cited in support of modern statements of Church teaching on social justice. But in this process of extraction we have neglected the extent to which the Fathers engaged with the language of success to re-define the power and the glory in which those who heard their sermons were invited to share through their conduct towards the poor.

PREACHING ON THE WIDER WORLD

JOHN ORME MILLS, O.P.

GOING BEYOND OUR OWN CONCERNS

About, for example, sex, it is extraordinarily easy to preach. Rather, it is extraordinarily easy to preach about sex badly. The congregation will take it for granted that it knows exactly what the preacher is going to say and that it probably knows far more about the subject than the preacher does. On the other hand, it will assume that the preacher is only doing what powerful Church authorities expect preachers to do and so should be heard out fairly patiently. It is, then, easy to preach on sex but very difficult to open minds and hearts regarding the subject – the problems are too familiar.

Profoundly different are the problems that face the preacher who decides that the moment has come to speak on the great fundamental issues confronting the world of our time, and especially its politicians: on justice, peace, and the preserving of the environment. These are issues that the congregation will know about almost solely from the mass media, issues hardly touching directly on the private lives of most of them and often difficult to understand. Furthermore, they are likely to be profoundly unpopular topics to preach on in some places. All the same, if what was said in Britain in September 2002 at the National Conference of Priests is at all representative, it would seem that a fairly high percentage of Roman Catholic clergy and informed laity in the Western world now consider that at least occasionally we ought in our preaching to remind our congregations of the earth we live in.

What this boils down to is that at least occasionally we ought to remind our congregations that our lives as Christians are bound up not only with our inner hopes, fears and temptations, and not only with the people around us, but also with those huge global issues. It is not enough to confine such issues to petitions in the Prayer of the Faithful.

Although it was Protestants in Europe and the US who pioneered in the nineteenth century the movement called 'the Social Gospel', more recently it has been the Catholic Church which has been speaking most powerfully about those particular global issues. Ever since Pope Leo XIII published *Rerum Novarum* in 1891, the first of many 'social encyclicals', popes have been drawing attention to the fact that the basic rights and living conditions of human beings, and the impact of modern wars on millions of people, and also, now, the damage we are doing to our world and its climate, are not just problems for the politicians but matters of grave Christian concern.

Yet even though those issues clearly are issues of life and death, how can we possibly preach on them to the average congregation without seeing before us in all directions eyes becoming glazed and ill-concealed yawns, or even looks of profound irritation and hostility?

Let us, as always, whatever our topics may be, start by thinking about the people we are preaching to.

R.E.C. Browne, in *The Ministry of the Word* (1976, London, SCM, p. 77), observed that great preaching, like great poetry, deals with love and death, with life and birth, with hatred and treachery. As every good preacher well knows, in people's private lives there is in fact all too often quite a lot of tragedy – quite a lot of injustice and violence and loss – and if preaching consistently avoids these disturbing themes the preachers will entertain, amuse or comfort the hearers, but will not touch on the deepest concerns of many of them. In fact, the preaching will not be conveying to them the message of Jesus Christ (see, for example,

Mt 11:28, 12:20, Lk 4:18). So it is part of the task of preachers to say something, at least at times, about the tragic side of the human condition. Play that down and the victory of Christ will seem something remote from people's lives.

Surely, though, as Christian preachers we should not confine ourselves just to these particular painful issues, in other words the painful issues in people's individual lives? After all, no preaching, if it is to be authentic Christian preaching, can concentrate solely on our own private condition. The famous mystic and preacher Meister Eckhart, who was constantly being asked to pray for people, could say seven centuries ago, at the end of one of his sermons: 'Dear children, I will tell you how I think of people: I try to forget myself and everyone and merge myself, for them, in unity.' (sermon 64, tr. M.O'C.Walshe, 1987, Shaftesbury UK, Element, sermon 78). Eckhart was saying here that by putting people as individuals out of his mind, he entered on behalf of all people into that divine unity which is all good. No present-day preacher could speak quite like that to a congregation. Nevertheless, in today's culture as much as in Eckhart's time, Christian preaching should always lead us beyond ourselves.

The question is: how far can preachers expect to lead their hearers beyond the confinements of their own concerns? John Burke, O.P., when Executive Director of the Word of God Institute in Washington DC, stated in his book *Gospel Power: Toward the Revitalization of Preaching* (1978, New York, Alba House) that the greatest and most significant idea in the world can be irrelevant to a Church congregation unless it bears upon their life situation (p. 84). The tragedy in the private lives of so many people – the lack of justice or peace or security, and quite frequently the lack of all three of these – may remarkably resemble the plight of our world, tormented by those three great global issues which we hear so much about these days, justice, peace and preservation of the earth. But is realising that going to make more tolerable the sufferings of individuals? Or are the sufferings of individuals going to make those individuals more open to the great global issues? Only extremely rarely, it would seem.

On the other hand, as people become more aware of the injustices and violence and instability in the world immediately surrounding them, or that is affecting the lives of people close to them, they can sometimes become more sensitive to the troubles of the wider world. Repeat: sometimes. They are equally likely to become even more inward-looking than ever, more anxious than ever to close the shutters and lock the doors. How they respond will depend, at least to some extent, on the preacher.

THE EARTH IS THE LORD'S

The preacher who is preaching on the wider world has, then, to start by trying to discern what are the felt needs and perceptions of the members of the congregation. The preparation of a sermon of this sort begins long before the day of its delivery, in fact long before the preacher had even thought of delivering it. A parish priest has the advantage of getting to know the people to be preached to many months, and even years, before delivering a difficult sermon like this one. All those little chats over coffee that are so much a part of parish life help to teach the preacher what to say, whereas a visiting preacher has to depend on knowledge of human nature culled elsewhere, often in very different places.

Possibly even more important is the need for pastors to create in the local Church itself a milieu that is going to make the people sensitive to God's calls to them – and, in this particular case, what we are thinking of is, of course, sensitivity to God's calls to them to see their world as if with new eyes. As we have all been told over and over again, preaching is something that is not just done with words, and this is especially true if one is preaching on a theme. If the preacher announces to a totally unprepared congregation something like 'This morning we are going to reflect on what the Church has to say to us about the big issues facing the world today', he will have already effectively killed the topic off.

One of the things that makes it hard to preach convincingly on justice, peace and the environment is that people's presuppositions about the wider world have become profoundly materialistic. For a start, then, the preacher has to try to make his hearers aware that concern for these global issues is an integral part of the Christian life, in other words of their own lives. In fact, that without this dimension there will only be limited progress at the personal level.

Saying this is not saying something at all novel. All the preacher will be doing is reminding people of a great tradition with its roots in the Bible and the teaching of the Church. 'The Lord's is the earth and its fullness ... Who shall climb the mountain of the Lord? Who shall stand in his holy place? The man with clean hands and pure heart.' So said the Psalmist (23/24, Grail translation). And, some 750 years ago, we can find St Albert the Great, the teacher of St Thomas Aquinas, telling people that it was wrong to think (as many did) that the world was a place unfit for any good Christian to be in, for the world was God's world and wherever you looked in it you could trace there God's presence.

Here is a way of thinking and of seeing things that not only deepens our sense of the sacredness of our world – in other words, of our need to care for our environment. It also deepens our sense of the sacredness of all the people in that world, in other words of our need to promote justice and peace. We should in our preaching help our hearers to integrate these concerns into the living-out of their Christianity, both at the practical level and also in their prayer-life. In modern times one of the first writers to draw attention to the connection between love of our neighbour and loving the order of the world was the French Jewish thinker Simone Weil, who, in her essay 'Forms of the Implicit Love of God', written a year before her death in 1943, said:

> The love of the order and beauty of the world is ... the complement of the love of our neighbour ... By loving our neighbour we imitate the divine love which created us and all our fellows. By loving the order of the world we imitate the divine love which created this universe of which we are a part. (*Attente de Dieu*, 1950, English translation, *Waiting on God*, 1977, London, Collins Fountain, pp. 113f.)

ROME'S WORDS ON THE SUBJECT

So far, however, this essay has confined itself to generalities of the broadest kind, in spite of the fact that it has quoted with approval Father John Burke's remark: 'the greatest and most significant idea in the world can be irrelevant to a church congregation unless it bears upon their life situation.' Basically, we have so far been concentrating on how to prepare a parish community to listen and respond to a sermon on the relationship between the wider world and us. However, before saying something rather more practical about how a sermon of this sort ought to be preached we must consider briefly what the Roman Catholic Church has been teaching in recent times on social justice, world peace and care of the environment, for many Catholics are still unaware that not solely political theorists and idealists but also a number of popes have confronted these issues.

We are living in what looks like an increasingly dangerous world. The gap between the rich and poor widens. The likelihood of war grows and now the world's annual expenditure on arms (more than $4,000bn) is twice as much as the combined foreign debt of all developing countries in the world. The environmental problems worsen. Yet there appears to be a growing conviction among the majority of people in the West that these are things that they themselves can do nothing about. On the other hand, popes have been delivering a wide range of teachings and statements on these matters – both general statements of principle and pronouncements on particular problems.

For example, they have been saying that human beings, being sons and daughters of God, have basic rights. Pope John XXIII said in his famous encyclical of 1963 *Pacem in Terris* (Peace on Earth) that human beings have

> the right to live ... and a right to the means necessary for maintaining a decent standard of living... a natural right to be respected ... to freedom of speech ... and to be accurately informed about public events ... the natural right to share in the benefits of culture ... to be able to worship God in accordance with the right dictates of their own conscience ... the right to choose for themselves the kind of life which appeals to them ... the right to own private property ... and to form associations with their fellow human beings ... the right to freedom of movement ... the right to take an active part in public life ... and to legal protection of their rights (nn.11-27).

Furthermore, Pope John strongly emphasised that it was not society that gave them these rights, but their dignity as sons and daughters created by God, and this teaching was further developed in 1967 in Pope Paul VI's *Populorum Progressio*, and then by Pope John Paul II in his encyclical of 1987, *Sollicitudo Rei Socialis*. In our culture it is widely taken for granted that we are very much a product of our world, and what these popes have been doing is trying to remind people that, on the contrary, deep down all they are and all the strength they have they owe to God, and it is to God that they owe their freedom.

Vatican II, in its Pastoral Constitution of 1965, *Gaudium et Spes*, on the Church in the modern world, also made the point that 'everybody should look upon his or her neighbour (without any exception) as another self.' (n. 27) The fears, prejudices and attitudes of pride and selfishness which make impossible the building up of truly fraternal societies cannot be done away with by legislation, but only through that love that discovers in every person a neighbour – a brother or a sister. We are living in a world that alienates, which is dominated by 'structures of sin' (in crude language, greed and the thirst for power) that tend to make us see the human beings around us as objects. We have no chance of creating a more humane world without a change of heart.

In n. 38 of *Sollicitudo Rei Socialis* Pope John Paul II writes about the interdependence of relationships in the contemporary world, and the need to respond to this fact by a sense of solidarity, 'a firm and persevering determination to commit oneself to the common good, that is to say, to the good of all and of each individual, because we are all really responsible for all.' The Pope roots what he is saying in Jesus' teaching to his disciples: 'whoever wishes to be great among you must be your servant' (Mk 10:43).

At the same time as repeating again and again these basic statements of principle we find the Church making over and over again concrete statements directed particularly at the world's governments about specific matters of social justice. The Church has been drawing attention above all to the lack of basic human rights in many countries (including, of course, of the right to life), to racism, to the needs of refugees, and to the effects of grinding poverty of millions who are living in the so-called developing countries – particularly in their sprawling megalopolises. In these countries 30 per cent of the population are still without clean water (the cause of four-fifths of their illnesses) and 800 million people still suffer from hunger. In the 1960s it was widely believed that economic development on its own would solve many of the world's problems. In fact even as early as 1967 Pope Paul VI, in his encyclical *Populorum Progressio*, was emphasising the difference between 'having' and 'being', and now hardly any well-informed person in the world believes economic development on its own is the answer to all our troubles.

Of course, social justice is not the only issue of worldwide concern that modern popes have spoken on. All the popes since 1914 (at least, all those who have reigned for more than 33 days) have spoken strongly on the need to safeguard peace. Peace, however, 'is not merely the absence of war', as the *Catechism of the Catholic Church* says (*CCC*, 2304). Peace cannot be attained in this world without safeguarding people's goods, without free communication and without respect for human dignity. Human dignity is not being respected so long as on average every hour of every day one human being is maimed or killed by an anti-personnel landmine.

As *Gaudium et Spes* says in n. 79, 'governments cannot be denied the right of lawful self-defense, once all peaceful efforts have failed', so the Church has certainly not abandoned the doctrine of 'the just war'. All the same, in line with the teachings of Popes Pius XII, John XXIII and Paul VI, *Gaudium et Spes* states in n. 80: 'Every act of war directed to the indiscriminate destruction of whole cities or vast areas with their inhabitants is a crime against God and humanity.' In fact, one is morally bound to resist orders that command genocide (*CCC*, 2313).

The third issue of world-wide concern – the preservation of the environment (or, as Church documents would seem to prefer to call it, 'respect for the integrity of creation') – is, of course, by far the newest of the three basic issues that we are focussing on, and so the number of official Church documents on it is very much smaller.

In any case, sacred texts had not so amply prepared the way for them. It does not take us long to discover that in the Bible there are numerous summons to us to be caring and compassionate to our fellow human beings (even our enemies), and also some commands to us to promote peace in the world. However, there is nothing in the Bible on whether we should preserve our world or even our fellow humans from the potentially disastrous consequences of global warming and global pollution and deforestation. What we read in Genesis chapter 1 is:

> God said: 'Let us make humankind in our image, according to our likeness; and let them have dominion over the fish of the sea, and over the birds of the air, and over the cattle, and over all the wild animals of the earth, and over every creeping thing that creeps upon the earth.'

Christians took it for granted that the natural world was something inferior to human beings, to be controlled and used by them, and eventually to be transcended by them; in fact, human beings should ultimately be apart from the world. So, for example, St Thomas Aquinas wrote:

> In nature the less perfect serve the more perfect: plants feed on

> the earth, animals on plants, and men on both plants and animals ... So the subordination of animals to man is natural ... Man was master of other things to the measure that he was master of himself. (*Summa Theologiae* 1a. 96, 1-2)

This kind of thinking inevitably shaped the Church's teaching on the relationship between human beings and the rest of creation.

A significant shift in papal teaching on this relationship does not really appear until the reign of Pope John Paul II. It is to be found in n. 34 of *Sollicitudo Rei Socialis*, in nn. 37-38 of *Centesimus Annus* (the encyclical of 1991 commemorating the centenary of *Rerum Novarum*), and in nn. 2415-6 of the *Catechism of the Catholic Church* (part of the Catechism's treatment of the seventh commandment). In these texts we are told that the seventh commandment ('You shall not steal') reminds us that our dominion over other created beings, animate and inanimate, is not absolute, being limited both by respect for the quality of life of our fellow human beings (including future generations) and also by respect for the fact that in creation all beings are in one way or another interrelated in an ordered system, in other words are part of what the Greeks called a 'cosmos'.

The Pope has surrounded his statements with cautious qualifications, but it is obvious that he considers rampant development of the kind that is so swiftly making a terrifyingly large chunk of our world a dead and desolate mess is utterly contrary to the will of God and is eventually going to be the ruin of us all, spiritually as well as materially.

The former Master of the Dominican Order, Father Timothy Radcliffe, recently said: 'Now the "preferential option for the poor" and a commitment to human rights are no longer the cry of a minority but part of the ordinary teaching of the Church, even if not always implemented in practice.' (*Justice, Peace and Dominicans 1216-2001*, 2001, Dublin, Dominican Publications, p.11.) More, however, is at stake than the need to be generous to the disadvantaged people of the world, extremely important though this is. These issues that the Church has been speaking on and that we have summarised here do, to a greater or lesser extent, touch the lives of us all.

TURNING SOBER STATEMENTS INTO SERMONS

How, though, are we to go about preaching on these massive and complicated issues?

It would be only too easy for our sermons on them to turn into lectures. And that, every preacher knows, would be disastrous. It is not the job of preachers to give what are in effect lectures on topics much more pithily and arrestingly covered in the media.

Neither should we take off in these sermons with quotes from papal encyclicals, however admirable. No, we should take off with a story, and that here is the same thing as saying we should take off from lively words of Scripture. Probably the most suitable of these would be one or two of those sayings of Jesus or those remarks in letters of the apostles in which the popes have rooted these encyclicals.

Sollicitudo Rei Socialis, for example, is rooted in Mark 10:43, in Jesus' teaching to his disciples, 'whoever wishes to be great among you must be your servant' (Sunday 29, Cycle B), and in Matthew 10:40, in Jesus' instructions when he sends out the disciples, 'Whoever welcomes you welcomes me, and whoever welcomes me welcomes the one who sent me' (Sunday 13, Cycle A). Here arguably is the core of Pope John Paul's teaching on how human beings should understand their relationship to others, and never should forget what is the true source of human dignity, human rights.

In the same encyclical, in n. 13, where he warns us that we cannot pretend that world-wide want and suffering have nothing to do with us, he cites Matthew 25:31-46 (the Gospel reading for the Feast of Christ the King in Cycle A). And, in n. 46, where he says 'The freedom with which Christ has set us free encourages us to become the servants of all', he cites Galatians 5:1, the words with which St Paul launches into the toughest passage in his letter: 'For freedom Christ has set us free' (Sunday 13, Cycle C).

In *Populorum Progressio*, where Pope Paul pointed out that economic development alone can promote human selfishness rather than reduce it, we find that startling text James 4:1-2 being cited: 'What causes wars, and what causes fightings among you? Is it not your passions that are at war in your members? You desire and do not have.' And in *Pacem in Terris* (n. 170) Pope John quotes from the parting words of Jesus to his disciples in John 14.27: 'Peace I leave with you: my peace I give unto you' (words read on the Sixth Sunday of Easter in Cycle C). One of the central ideas in that much-discussed encyclical was that it was Christ who brought us true peace, who bequeathed it to us.

By now it will be obvious what our thinking is on how best to preach on justice, peace and the environment. The best way of introducing these topics to a congregation is not by devoting a Sunday or a series of Sundays to the subject but by, first of all, introducing some of the key themes, linked to well-known teachings in the Bible, and doing this in the course of the Church's liturgical year, as an integral part of the parish's worship-activity. Something like, for example, Pope John Paul's idea of 'solidarity' in relationships in the wider community can, in fact, be returned to a number of times, in all sorts of different contexts. Discussion groups in the parish will, in the meantime, be encouraged to focus on one or more of the worldwide issues.

And then (and only then) one or more of these can be the main theme of a Sunday Mass.

GOING FURTHER

The three great issues that we have been focussing on are profoundly volatile. In July 2001 there was published the book on justice and peace matters mentioned above, edited by this author. It contained no mention of the close connection of justice and peace issues with ecological issues, and no mention of the threat of terrorism which since that year's September 11 has so severely undermined hopes of world peace. We do not know what those worldwide issues are going to be like even in five years, let alone in twenty-fifty. It is, then, difficult to predict what exactly the Church will, in the fairly near future, have to preach on these matters, and how.

All we can fairly safely anticipate is that the issues are likely to become more urgent and so more prominent, and that the one thing that will not change will be the Church's fundamental teaching regarding these issues. What Rome has had to say on them has been one of the best things it has done during the last half-century.

Catholics could, then, become more willing to listen to what the Church has to say on the wider world. So preaching on the wider world could become quite a frequent occurrence in Catholic churches.

Nevertheless, almost certainly what I said earlier on in this essay will continue to hold true – what I said about the preacher having to be aware of the hearers' felt needs and of the confinements that hearers' concerns and presuppositions impose on their perceptions. Finding out what the Church has to say about the wider world will not absorb a lot of the preacher's time. What will take up a preacher's time if he or she is not already a hardened campaigner will be learning more refined skills, skills that preaching on all sorts of subjects today require, not just this one.

But this should not depress the new preacher. It is, in fact, an immensely exciting challenge to try to arrest a congregation's attention and win its sympathy when what you are preaching about is something that nearly everybody assumes at the very start must be a terribly remote and depressing subject. To do it well you have to have something of the sensitivity of a good cartoonist. It is much more exciting than preaching at a Christmas Midnight Mass.

PREACHING BIBLICAL JUSTICE

BARBARA E. REID, O.P.

There has been a marked increase in the use of the term 'justice' in public discourse in the days and months that have followed the tragic events of September 11, 2001 in the U.S.A. In reaction to the horror of the lives lost and to a sense of vulnerability, people have called for 'justice' to be done. When the retaliatory strikes against the Al-Qaeda in Afghanistan began on October 7, 2001, the campaign was first named 'Operation Infinite Justice,' an alarming title. It was quickly changed to 'Operation Enduring Freedom'. There are many other such recent instances in which 'justice' is used when what is clearly intended is retaliation or vengeance. This is far from the biblical meaning of the term.

In this essay I will first examine the various terms for 'justice' and their meanings in the Scriptures. Then I will offer reflections on five contemporary areas of concern for which a biblical perspective on justice can aid preachers. I will then offer a method of biblical interpretation and a mode of preaching toward justice drawn from the parables.

At the outset it must be clarified that one does not preach justice; what we preach is the gospel, which announces God's desire and promise for justice, that is, for all to be in right relation, with God, self, others, and the whole of the cosmos. We preach Christ crucified and living, and God's power at work in us through the Spirit, drawing all into right relation. Thus, in the face of grave injustices, a preacher of the just word speaks a word of truth and hope, one that brings comfort to those who are victimised by injustice and that challenges those who benefit from unjust structures.

BIBLICAL JUSTICE: TERMINOLOGY

In the Scriptures justice is a quality of God that is manifest in divine dealings with creation, and which enables God's creatures to act uprightly. In the Hebrew Scriptures there are three terms for 'justice.' While there is much overlap of meaning, each highlights a slightly different aspect. These words all have their roots in legal language: one is 'justified' when proven right or innocent before the law.

Moral Rectitude: sëdäqâ

The noun *sëdäqâ*, 'to be straight, true, righteous, just,' emphasizes the aspect of moral rectitude.[1] God is extolled for this: 'Your power and your righteousness (*sëdäqâ*), O God, reach the high heavens' (Ps 71:19). Some human beings, also maintain right relation, like Noah, who was said to be 'a righteous (*saddîq*) man, blameless in his generation' (Gen 6:9). Judah declares that Tamar acts more uprightly (*sëdäqâ*) than he when she takes extraordinary means to ensure the continuance of the line of David (Gen 38:6). The word *sëdäqâ* is used to describe the process of weighing the evidence in a case and deciding equitably. For example, after all his sufferings and protestations of his innocence, when Job makes a final summary of his cause to God, he asserts that calamity befalls those who are unrighteous, not those who walk in the way of goodness. He pleads, 'Let me be weighed in a just (*sedeq*) balance and let God know my integrity!' (Job 31:6).[2] Job

1. There is also a masculine form of this noun: *sedeq*; the verb is *sädëq;* the adjectival form is *saddîq.* See F. Brown, S. R. Driver, C. A. Briggs, eds., *Enhanced Brown-Driver-Briggs Hebrew and English Lexicon* (Boston: Houghton, Mifflin & Co., 1907; reprinted by Associated Publishers and Authors, Inc., 1981) pp. 841-43; Ludwig Koehler, Walter Baumgartner, eds., *Lexicon in Veteris Testamenti Libros* (Leiden: Brill, 1958) pp. 794-95; Gregory J. Polan, 'Justice,' in *Collegeville Pastoral Dictionary of Biblical Theology* (ed. Carroll Stuhlmueller; Collegeville, MN: The Liturgical Press, 1996) pp. 510-12.

2. Quotations of Scripture are taken from the *New Revised Standard Version* (N.Y.: Oxford University Press, 1990), unless otherwise indicated.

is sure of his own moral uprightness and that the scales of justice would demonstrate this. But here we have a prime example of how biblical justice does not mean that people get what they deserve. Job has been sorely afflicted, but it is not because he is unjust.

Visible Deeds and Execution of Judgment: mispat

The noun *mispat* [3] appears over four hundred times in the Hebrew Scriptures, and emphasises visible deeds of justice and the execution of judgment. In speaking of God's attributes, *mispat* is often used in tandem with *sëdäqâ*, as in Jeremiah 9:23, where God says, 'I act with steadfast love, justice (*mispat*), and righteousness (*sëdäqâ*) in the earth.' *Mispat* occurs frequently in the prophetic literature. Micah, for example, tells Israel that what God requires is to 'do justice' (*mispat*, 6:8). An interesting example is found in 1 Samuel 24, where the verb *saphat* is used to refer both to the visible evidence of David's righteous deeds and to God's judgement and declaration of him as just. Saul is pursuing David in the desert near Engedi. He enters a cave to 'ease nature,' not knowing that David and his men are in the inmost recesses of the cave. David creeps forward, undetected by Saul, and cuts off a piece of Saul's mantle, while restraining his men from harming Saul. When they both emerge from the cave, David calls out, 'May the Lord therefore be judge, and give sentence (*saphat*) between me and you ... and vindicate me (*u'yisp'tënî*, from *saphat*) against you' (1 Sam 24:15). He shows Saul the evidence that he has not sinned against the king even though Saul is seeking his life. Saul replies to David, 'You are more righteous (*saddîq*) than I; for you have repaid me good, whereas I have repaid you evil' (1 Sam 24:16-17).

---

3. The verb is *saphat*. See further Brown-Driver-Briggs, *Lexicon*, pp. 1047-49; Koehler-Baumgartner, *Lexicon*, pp. 1002-03.

Truthfulness, Consistency, Strength: 'emûnâ

The feminine noun *'emûnâ* [4] emphasises the notion of consistency and strength, truthfulness – being what you appear to be. When used of God, it is often paired with *hesed*, 'merciful love,' as in Psalm 92:2, 'I will declare your steadfast love (*esed*) in the morning, and your faithfulness (*'emûnâ*) by night.' Moses tells the Israelites, 'Know therefore that the LORD your God is God, the faithful (*hanne'emûn*) God, who maintains covenant loyalty ... to a thousand generations' (Deut 7:9). This word is also used of individual Israelites. Moses is said to be God's 'trusted' (*ne'emän*) servant (Num 12:7), as is David (1 Sam 22:14); and 'all Israel from Dan to Beer-sheba knew that Samuel was a trustworthy (*ne'emän*) prophet' (1 Sam 3:20).

This same term appears also in the New Testament, translated as 'truly' or transliterated as 'Amen.' It occurs most frequently in the Gospel of John, where Jesus begins key revelatory assertions with 'Amen, Amen, I say to you' (1:51; 3:3, etc.).

The three Hebrew nouns, *sëdäqâ*, *mispat*, and *'emûnâ*, emphasize different aspects of justice: moral rectitude, public judgment and visible fulfilment of what is right, trustworthiness, consistency, and strength. All these are attributes of the divine, occurring together at Deut 32:4, where Moses says all God's ways are 'just (*mispat*), a faithful (*'emûnâ*) God, without deceit, just (*saddîq*) and upright.' As human beings exercise justice, it is rooted in the mind and heart, can be counted on in people's actions, and converges in public declaration.

COVENANT FIDELITY

In the Hebrew Scriptures, justice is always understood in terms of covenant faithfulness. God's justice is manifest in saving

---

4. There is also a masculine form of the noun, *'emeth*; the verb is. *'ämën*. See further Brown-Driver-Briggs, *Lexicon*, pp. 52-54; Koehler-Baumgartner, *Lexicon*, p. 60.

deeds toward Israel in faithfulness to the covenant; human justice is expressed by keeping God's commands. There is a great difference, however, in the ability of the two partners to maintain right relation. While God is always faithful, human beings are not able to be just of their own accord. The Psalmist captures this well when praying, 'Do not enter into judgment (*mispat*) with your servant, for before you no living person is just (*saddîq*) (Ps 143:2). The prophets portray this vividly, depicting God as bringing charges of infidelity in a lawsuit against Israel (e.g., Is 43:25-26; Jer 12:1). God's justice always results in a guilty verdict against Israel, but it is always followed by acquittal.

ESCHATOLOGICAL HOPE

There is one other important aspect of God's saving justice. In the context of the exile, right relation is spoken of not as a present reality, but as an eschatological hope. Isaiah, for example, speaking for God, tells about the future when 'a teaching will go out from me, and my justice (*mispat*) for a light to the peoples' (Is 51:4). The expectation is that, once again, it will become evident that 'There is no just (*saddîq*) and saving God'[5] but the God of Israel (Is 45:21).

This same dimension of eschatological fulfilment of justice is also expressed in the New Testament. In the explanation of the parable of the weeds and the wheat, for example, Jesus speaks of how at the end of the age 'the righteous will shine like the sun in the kingdom of their Father' (Mt 13:43). Paul also speaks of right relation as both a present reality and one yet to reach fulfilment: 'through the Spirit, by faith, we eagerly wait for the hope of righteousness' (Gal 5:5).

---

5. Translation of the revised *New American Bible* (1986).

JUSTIFICATION

In the New Testament, the term *dikaiosynë*, 'justification,' carries many of the same connotations as do the three Hebrew terms.[6] In the New Testament, however, it is Christ through whom right relation is accomplished. Paul's famous formulation in the Letter to the Romans sums up the meaning of *dikaiosynë* most completely: it is right relation that is a gift of God, already accomplished through Christ, in which the believer participates through faith (Rom 3:21-26). As in the Hebrew Scriptures, justification is not something a person can achieve by human striving; it is a gift of God (Rom 3:20; Gal 3:11). In the Letter to Titus justification is linked with baptism, which comes by 'the goodness and loving kindness of God ... not because of any works of righteousness that we had done' (3:4-5). The justification effected by Christ brings freedom from sin and death (Rom 5:12-21), from the 'old self' (6:1-23), and from the Law (Rom 7:1-25), through the power of the Spirit (Rom 8:1-39). It is offered to all and makes irrelevant differences of race, ethnicity, gender, and socio-economic status: 'There is no longer Jew or Greek, there is no longer slave or free, there is no longer male and female; for all of you are one in Christ Jesus' (Gal 3:28).

Justification refers both to God's action in Christ, and to human conduct that strives for right relation. While Paul insists

6. It is difficult to find a word in English that adequately expresses all that *dikaiosynë* conveys. At times it is translated 'justice,' but for many English-speakers this word connotes something more akin to retribution, or everyone getting what they deserve. Sometimes it is translated 'righteousness;' other times, 'justification.' A problem with both these terms is that they often call to mind '*self*-righteousness,' or '*self*-justification,' which is not the meaning of *dikaiosynë*. Another translation is 'uprightness.' None of these English renditions quite captures the biblical nuances. In this computer age, however, 'justification' may say it best, as when one uses 'full justification' for the margins of a document, all is lined up in perfect relation. See further Barbara E. Reid, 'Justification,' in *Collegeville Pastoral Dictionary of Biblical Theology* (ed. Carroll Stuhlmueller; Collegeville, MN: The Liturgical Press, 1996) pp. 520-22.

that justification comes through faith and not through works of
the Law, he clarifies that faith is not simply intellectual assent, but
works itself out through love (Gal 5:6; similarly Jas 2:21-26). In
the Gospel of Matthew Jesus teaches his disciples to strive for
God's reign and righteousness (6:33). He urges them to hunger
and thirst for justice (Mt 5:6), while blessing those that are
persecuted for the sake of justice (Mt 5:10). He instructs his
disciples that their righteousness must surpass that of the scribes
and Pharisees (Mt 5:20). At the same time, however, they must
take care not to perform righteous deeds [7] in order that people
may see them (Mt 6:1).

In the Lucan writings Jesus is presented as justice incarnate. In
the crucifixion scene, Luke modifies the words of the centurion
who sees Jesus die, so that instead of declaring 'Truly, this was the
Son of God' (Mk 15:39), he proclaims, 'Truly, this man was just'
(*dikaios*, Lk 23:47).[8] Luke also emphasizes Jesus' righteousness in
Acts of the Apostles, where in three key speeches, Jesus is said to
be *ho dikaios*, 'the Just One' (Acts 3:14; 7:52; 22:14).

In this cursory sketch, we have a sampling of the various
nuances of 'justice' in the Scriptures. It is not a topic of biblical
reflection, *per se*, but it is something that permeates the whole of
the Scriptures: the entire biblical narrative speaks of God's action
and of human response toward right relation with God, self,
others, and all of creation. I offer now reflections on five contemporary areas of concern for which a biblical perspective on justice
can aid preachers: Justice and Forgiveness, Economic Justice,
Ecological Justice, Jubilee Justice, and Justice for Women. Each
is interrelated and cannot be easily separated from the other.

---

7. The expression *dikaiosynë ... poiein*, translated by *NRSV* as 'practising piety,'
   literally means 'do justice.'
8. Some translations, as *NRSV*, here render *dikaios* as 'innocent'.

JUSTICE AND FORGIVENESS

In our age of globalization, where the interconnectedness of peoples all over the world is the reality, the difficulties of living in right relation with one another are greater than ever before. At a time where we have witnessed genocide, terrorism, ethnic cleansing, holocausts, and violence of unimaginable proportions, one of the most serious challenges is to undertake the biblical mandate of forgiveness in relation to achieving justice.

It has become an oft-repeated refrain that there is no peace without justice. In recent years Pope John Paul II has augmented this dictum by adding 'no justice without forgiveness'. In his homily on the feast of the Solemnity of Mary, Mother of God and the Thirty-fifth World Day of Peace (January 1, 2002), he elaborated: 'Justice and forgiveness: these are the two "pillars" of peace, and I wanted to draw attention to them both. Between justice and forgiveness there is not opposition but complementarity, because both are essential for promoting peace.' This is a crucial insight – that forgiveness is not an alternative to justice, but is a necessary and constitutive element in peacemaking and the restoration of right relation.

In a number of biblical texts justice and forgiveness are linked. [9] When God is revealed to Moses on Mount Sinai, it is as 'a God merciful and gracious, slow to anger, and abounding in steadfast love (*hesed*) and faithfulness (or 'justice','*emeth*), keeping steadfast love for the thousandth generation, forgiving iniquity and transgression and sin' (Ex 34:6-7). Frequently in the Hebrew Scriptures an intercessor, such as Moses (Ex 34:9), or one of the prophets (e.g., Amos 7:2), pleads with God on behalf of Israel to forgive their sins so that right relation may be restored. In some

---

9. See John Käselman, James H. Charlsworth, Gary S. Shogren, 'Forgiveness,' in *Anchor Bible Dictionary* (6 vols.; ed. David Noel Freedman; Garden City: Doubleday, 1992) 2.831-38.

instances the righteousness of a few persons effects forgiveness
for many, as when Abraham bargains with God to spare Sodom
if he can find a few just ones there (Gen 18:22-31; similarly Jer
5:1).

In the New Testament this righteous one who effects forgiveness for all is Jesus (Mt 26:38; see also Heb 9:22; 10:12-18). Paul
links justification with expiation of sin in Romans 3:24-26. The
Gospels recount several episodes in which Jesus restores people to
right relation through forgiveness: a man who is lame (Mk 2:1-
12; Mt 9:2-8; Lk 5:17-26); a woman who was caught in adultery
(Jn 8:2-11); and a woman who anoints Jesus' feet (Lk 7:36-50).

Jesus teaches his disciples to continue his mission of forgiveness. He instructs them to pray, 'forgive us our sins, as we
ourselves forgive everyone indebted to us' (Lk 11:4 // Mt 6:12).[10]
A parable from the Gospel of Matthew (18:23-35) illustrates how
forgiveness is not earned; it restores right relation in a way that
contradicts the notion that justice is about people getting what
they deserve. The parable is set in the context of instructing the
community on the steps they are to take in bringing an offender
to repentance and reconciliation (Mt 18:15-20).

It tells of a servant who has been released from an unpayable
debt, but then refuses to forgive another. When this is reported
to his master, the latter rescinds his forgiveness, angrily denounc-
ing the servant for not having forgiven his fellow servant as he
had been forgiven. The parable concludes, 'So my heavenly
Father will also do to every one of you, if you do not forgive your
brother or sister from your heart' (v. 35). It depicts in stark terms
that the only possible response to the limitless forgiveness that
human beings receive from God in Christ, is forgiveness toward

---

10. Lk 6:37 also underscores the reciprocity of forgiveness: 'Forgive and you will be
    forgiven.' See also Mark 11:25. Forgiveness is a ministry entrusted to the whole
    community, empowered by the Spirit (Jn 20:23; cf. Mt 18:18).

another. Jesus' reply to Peter's query about how often he must forgive someone who sins against him – 'seventy-seven times' – indicates that the need to engage in processes of forgiveness and reconciliation is ceaseless (Mt 18:22; see also Lk 17:3-4).

Repentance

Forgiveness, however, does not consist in overlooking offences or in ignoring injustice. It is a step in the process of reconciliation, which must be accompanied by repentance on the part of the offender, in order for right relation to be restored. Jesus' persistent practice was to name and confront unrighteousness, to invite people to repentance (Mk 1:15), leading to restoration of right relation. This process usually begins with the willingness on the part of the one wronged to offer forgiveness. [11] As the parable in Matthew 18:23-35 illustrates, the reason why Christians are willing to extend forgiveness to another is because they themselves have first experienced it. [12] If the offender accepts forgiveness, repents, and makes whatever restoration is possible, then justice, right relation, is restored. Both healing for the victim and restoration of the humanity of the offender are necessary for reconciliation. [13] But if repeated efforts at confrontation do not

11. It does not often happen that the one who has committed the offence takes the initiative in asking for forgiveness, although Jesus advises one who remembers that a member of the community has something against them, to go and seek reconciliation before offering their gift at the altar (Mt 5:21-26).

12. The conclusion of the 'love your enemies' passage in Mt 5:38-48 expresses this similarly. God makes the sun rise and the rain fall on all alike, whether they act with righteousness or not (Mt 5:45). As children of God, Jesus tells his disciples they must imitate God's treatment of the those who act unjustly. See the analysis of Walter Wink (*Engaging the Powers* [Minneapolis: Fortress, 1992] pp. 175-93), who interprets the passage not as advocating passivity in the face of oppression, but as giving creative examples of how a victimized person can take nonviolent action toward an aggressor in order to destabilise the situation and open up a new possibility for forgiveness, repentance, and reconciliation.

13. See Robert J. Schreiter, *Reconciliation. Mission and Ministry in A Changing Social Order* (The Boston Theological Institute Series 3; Maryknoll: Orbis, 1992); *The Ministry of Reconciliation. Spirituality and Strategies* (Maryknoll: Orbis, 1998).

bring an offender to repentance, the aggrieved party hands over to God the responsibility to complete the process of forgiveness and reconciliation.[14] The most dramatic enactment of this is when the crucified Jesus prays for his tormenters, 'Father, forgive them, for they do not know what they are doing' (Lk 23:34). At this moment the one who has been unjustly executed embodies true justice.[15]

This way of 'bringing to justice' evildoers presents an enormous challenge in contemporary conflicts. Yet, as Paul says, this ministry of reconciliation is now entrusted to Christ's followers so that 'we might become the righteousness (*dikaiosynë*) of God' (2 Cor 5:21).

ECONOMIC JUSTICE

As the economic disparities of our world become ever more alarming, a sense of biblical justice confronts us with different practices than those of capitalist economies. One parable from the Gospel of Matthew (20:1-16) features a vineyard owner who goes out to the village square at five different times of the day to hire workers. With each he agrees on a wage of one denarius, the usual subsistence wage for day labourers. At the end of the day each receives this same amount, despite the difference in the number of hours they have worked. The first hired, who thought they would receive more, complain to the owner, 'you have made them equal to us' (v. 12). He sends them away, insisting, 'I am doing you no injustice' (v. 13), and reminds them of their agreement. The parable concludes with the owner saying, 'I choose to give to this last the same as I give to you. Am I not allowed to do

---

14. See further Troy Martin and Avis Clendenen, *Forgiveness* (New York: Crossroad, 2002).
15. As recognized by the centurion, who declares Jesus *dikaios*, 'just,' or 'innocent,' Lk 23:47.

what I choose with what belongs to me? Or are you envious because I am generous?' (vv. 14-15). This last phrase, which says literally, 'Is your eye evil because I am good?' is an accusation of evil-eye envy, the force most destructive of community. The ironic truth expressed in the workers' complaint, is that, if the vineyard owner is a figure for God, then all the workers are, indeed, equal, no matter the length of time they have worked. Matthew's community likely heard this as an image of the justification offered to Gentiles, the newcomers, who were now equally saved, and the 'injustice' felt by Jewish Christians, who had been toiling in God's 'vineyard' far longer.

From the perspective of the first hired, the owner seems terribly unjust. But when one takes the stance of the sick, the elderly, those with disabilities, the weakest ones, who would have been left standing all day in the marketplace, until hired as a last resort, then it becomes easier to see that a wage of any less than a denarius would be worthless. Workers could not feed their families on anything less. Those who worked longer have the satisfaction of knowing all day that they will be able to feed their children. Those who waited anxiously all day have their fears relieved. In God's justice all deserve to eat at the end of the day, regardless of the amount of time they have worked.

Another aspect of economic justice through a biblical lens involves the forgiveness of debt and jubilee practices. The Book of Leviticus details how every fiftieth year the Israelites were to release others from debt and servitude, return to their own land, and care for those who fell into need, without gaining any advantage for themselves (Lev 25:8-55). They are to do this because this is how God cared for Israel in bringing them out of Egypt and giving them the land of Canaan (v. 38).

As Jesus begins his public ministry he frames his mission in terms of jubilee justice, bringing release for all who are bound (Lk 4:18). And as Christians pray the prayer he taught, 'forgive us our debts, as we have also forgiven our debtors' (Mt 6:12), it is important to know that *ta opheilēmata,* 'debts' refers not only to sins, but to economic debts. Neither in human relations nor in economic dealings do the Scriptures portray justice as people getting just what they earn. Reflection on patterns of consumption, greed, exploitation, and embracing transformative action toward levelling the economic playing field for all peoples needs to be part of Christian practice not only in a rare jubilee year, such as the turn of the millennium, but throughout ordinary time, as well.

ECOLOGICAL JUSTICE

While people of the biblical world would not have expressed concern for eco-justice in the same way as we do today, there is in the Bible reflection on how right relation encompasses all of creation. The accounts of creation in Genesis 1–2 underscore how God's intent for creation was for all to be in harmonious relation. This is very good in God's eyes (Gen 1:31). When human beings sin, the repercussions involve not only their relationship with God and with one another, but with the rest of the created universe. Relations with the earth, plants, animals, and among human beings, become adversarial, rather than harmonious (Gen 3:14-19). As interconnectedness is ruptured; domination, pain, and suffering, enters in.

The Deuteronomist also recognizes the interconnectedness of human action and productivity of the earth. When Israel is faithful to the divine commands, then God gives rain for the land in its season, and Israel gathers in grain, wine, and oil. There is grass in the fields for their livestock, and people can eat their fill.

But when Israel is unfaithful, then God shuts up the heavens, and there is no rain, and the earth yields no fruit, and human beings perish (Deut 11:13-17).

In the New Testament, Paul speaks about how the redeeming work of Christ is not only for human beings, but all creation will be freed from its bondage to decay, and will obtain the glorious freedom of the children of God (Rom 8:18-25). The biblical authors recognize that the web of all life is interconnected; ecological sustainability and justice for human beings are not alternatives.[16]

JUBILEE JUSTICE: SABBATH AND WORK

One other dimension of living justly involves a balanced rhythm of work and rest. In industrialised countries people who are upwardly mobile struggle with overwork, burnout, and sleep deprivation, responding to demands of the global marketplace, which wants them available 24 hours a day, 7 days a week, 365 days of the year. For the poor, when work is available, the reality is that they often hold multiple jobs, working overlong hours, seven days a week, in order to try to make ends meet.

Biblical admonitions to observe Sabbath rest offer an alternate way toward right relation. In the Hebrew Scriptures there are two versions of the commandment to observe the Sabbath, and two different reasons are given. In Exodus 20:8-11 Sabbath rest is grounded in the creative work of God: no one is to do work on the Sabbath 'for in six days the LORD made heaven and earth, the sea, and all that is in them, and rested the seventh day; therefore the LORD blessed the Sabbath day and hallowed it.' Sabbath rest

16. See further Dianne Bergant, *The Earth is the Lord's. The Bible, Ecology, and Worship* (American Essays in Liturgy; Collegeville, MN: The Liturgical Press, 1998); Ivone Gebara, *Longing for Running Water. Ecofeminism and Liberation* (Minneapolis: Fortress, 1999); Rosemary Radford Ruether, *Women Healing Earth: Third World Women on Ecology, Feminism, and Religion* (Maryknoll: Orbis, 1996).

is not so that God can recoup energy to continue working; rather, one might say that the whole reason for creation is for God to delight in all that was made; it is the crown of all creation.[17] Human beings share in this divine joy when they observe the Sabbath. Observance of Sabbath creates space for a holy people to worship together, an indispensable aspect of expressing right relation.

The second account of the decalogue, in Deuteronomy 5, gives a different reason for observing Sabbath: 'Remember that you were a servant in the land of Egypt, and the LORD your God brought you out from there with a mighty hand and an outstretched arm; therefore the LORD your God commanded you to keep the Sabbath day' (Deut 5:15). In this version, Sabbath is to make present again God's liberation of the oppressed. One of the ways in which Sabbath does this is by it being a great equaliser: no one, whether Israelite, foreigner, servant, or free, nor any animal, is to work on the Sabbath. Moreover, cessation of work for one day allows for a hiatus in the exploitation of the poor by the rich. The prophet Amos spoke of this when he denounced unjust merchants who made a mockery of the Sabbath, trampling on the needy, chomping at the bit for the end of Sabbath so they might resume cheating the poor (Amos 8:4-6).

Sabbath observance, then, is a an indispensable constituent of justice. It both expresses and enables right relation with God, self, others, and all creation, as it fosters worship, trust in divine providence, freedom from compulsive consumption and overwork, abatement in exploitation of the poor, and reverence for all creation.

---

17. See Ellen Davis, 'Sabbath: The Culmination of Creation,' in *The Living Pulpit* 7/2 (April–June 1998) 6-7; Abraham Joshua Heschel, *The Sabbath. Its Meaning for Modern Man* (New York: Farrar, Straus and Giroux, 1951).

JUSTICE FOR WOMEN

While there have been many advances toward justice and equality for women in recent decades, much remains to be done. It is still a fact that no country treats its women as well as its men in terms of income, education, and life expectancy.[18] Governance and exercise of decision-making power reside primarily in the hands of men. Sexism, while denounced by the US bishops in their attempted pastoral on women, *Partners in the Mystery of Redemption*, is still very much alive in the Church.

The Bible can be an important aid in the struggle for justice for women. The accounts of creation clearly assert that women and men are equally created in God's image (Gen 1:27). Examples of godly women, such as Miriam, Deborah, Huldah, Judith, Mary Magdalene, Susanna, and Joanna, who exercise ministries of prophet, judge, liberator, preacher, evangelist, and leader, abound in both Testaments. The gospels are replete with stories of Jesus treating women with dignity equal to that of men. Paul's letters name important female co-workers, teachers, heads of house Churches, deacons, and apostles, such as Phoebe, Prisca, Nympha, and Junia. Many fine efforts have been made to mine these traditions in ways that promote justice for women.[19]

One of the critical aspects that yet needs to be more fully appropriated by preachers is female language and imagery for God. Significant examples are found in both testaments. In Deuteronomy 32:18 and Isaiah 42:14 God is portrayed as a

18. See the report of the United Nations Commission on the Status of Women and information on the Committee for the Advancement of Women at: http://www.un.org/womenwatch/daw/cedaw/

19. See the ground-breaking works by Elisabeth Schüssler Fiorenza, *In Memory of Her: A Feminist Theological Reconstruction of Christian Origins* (New York: Crossroad, 1983), Rosemary Radford Ruether, *Sexism and God-Talk: Toward a Feminist Theology* (Boston: Beacon, 1983); Mary Rose D'Angelo and Ross S. Kraemer, *Women and Christian Origins* (New York: Oxford University Press, 1999); Sandra Schneiders, *Women and the Word* (New York: Paulist, 1986).

mother giving birth. Isaiah speaks of God's tenderness as that of a mother consoling her child (Is 49:15; 66:13). Isaiah 66:9 and Psalm 22:10-11 portray God as a midwife, drawing Israel forth from the womb. The Psalmist talks of God's care for humans like that of a mother eagle for her brood (Ps 91:4).

Jesus uses this same image in Luke 13:34 to express his care for Jerusalem. He also tells parables about a woman mixing dough (Luke 13:20-21 // Mt 13:33) and of a woman searching for a lost coin (Lk 15:8-10) to speak about the divine activity in the realm of God.[20] These metaphors are equally apt for speaking of God as is 'father.'

Exclusive use of male, patriarchal language and imagery for God feeds injustice toward women and blinds us to the reality that women and men are equally created in God's image. Preachers of biblical justice must be skilled not only in using gender-inclusive language and imagery for people, but also female language and imagery for God.

BIBLICAL INTERPRETATION TOWARD JUSTICE

In their study of the biblical text, preachers know that different methods of biblical interpretation yield different results. Historical-critical, literary, rhetorical, and social-scientific methods, all hold certain hermeneutical keys. For preaching toward justice, one indispensable method is a liberation approach,[21]

---

20. See further Sallie McFague, *Models of God. Theology for an Ecological, Nuclear Age* (Philadelphia: Fortress, 1987); Elizabeth Johnson, *She Who Is. The Mystery of God in Feminist Theological Discourse* (New York: Crossroad, 1992); Rosemary Radford Ruether, *Sexism and God-Talk* (Boston: Beacon, 1983); Gail Ramshaw, *God Beyond Gender* (Minneapolis: Fortress, 1995).

21. See Christopher Rowland and Mark Corner, *Liberating Exegesis. The Challenge of Liberation Theology to Biblical Studies* (Louisville: Westminster/John Knox, 1989); Clodovis Boff and Jorge Pixley, *The Bible, the Church, and the Poor* (Theology and Liberation Series; Maryknoll: Orbis, 1989); Carlos Mesters, *Defenseless Flower. A New Reading of the Bible* (Maryknoll: Orbis, 1989).

which begins with the experience of the poor, brings it into dialogue with social analysis and critical reflection on the text, and leads to transformative action.

I will give one example of how use of a feminist liberationist method with the parable of the widow and the judge in Luke 18:1-8 yields a message that prompts action toward justice – a very different interpretation than is usually derived. The most common approach is to focus on the unjust judge, seeing him as a negative image, portraying what God is not.[22] This, however, creates a theological difficulty in which the parable can be read as encouraging believers to badger God in prayer until their request is granted – a very poor theology of prayer! Luke's redactional spin (vv. 1, 6-8), further reinforces this, as he tries to tame a very unconventional portrait of a justice-seeking widow into one more akin to the non-threatening Anna, who spent all her days praying in the temple (Lk 2:36-38).[23]

Using a feminist liberationist method,[24] which begins by identifying not with the powerful male in the parable, but with women who struggle against multiple structures of oppression, as embodied by the widow, one can see that it is she who characterises the divine. With her unrelenting confrontation of an unjust leader, doggedly working until justice is accomplished, she is the one who is most like God who always, in biblical narratives, takes the side of the poor and oppressed and works to set all in right relation. Like the widow who gives her whole life to the Temple (Lk 21:1-4), and the women of Galilee who pour themselves out in service to Jesus and his mission (Lk 8:3), this

22. E.g., Joseph A. Fitzmyer, *The Gospel according to Luke* (AB28A; Garden City, N.Y.: Doubleday, 1981) pp. 1175-78).
23. For further detail, see Barbara E. Reid, *Parables for Preachers. Year C* (Collegeville, MN: The Liturgical Press, 2000) pp. 227-36.
24. Elisabeth Schüssler Fiorenza, *Wisdom Ways* (Maryknoll: Orbis, 2001).

woman is the Christ-like figure in the parable. The parable encourages believers to persist in action to confront injustice, and not to give up until each small victory is accomplished. One who feels powerless against those who wield authority can find, with this widow, the courage to emulate Christ, who, in seeking justice, becomes vulnerable to the point of crucifixion, paradoxically exhibiting most forcefully the power of God (1 Cor 1:23-25; Phil 2:6-11).

Preachers who use a liberationist method also recognise how their social, cultural, and religious location shape their experience with the text, as they critically evaluate the oppressive tendencies and the liberating possibilities of the text. They bring a hermeneutics of suspicion to both the text and to commentaries on it, recognizing that most of these have been written by élite males of the dominant culture, privileging their experience, and serving their interests. Using a hermeneutics of remembrance and reconstruction, they attempt to make the marginalised visible, the silent audible, placing the forgotten at the centre. All of their creative imagination is engaged in imagining a world of justice and well-being for all as they articulate from the text a vision for a new humanity, global ecology, and religious community which impels believers to transformative action for change, creating oases of hope in a needy world.

PREACHING JUSTICE PARABOLICALLY [25]

A preacher not only needs an understanding of biblical justice and methodological skills for interpreting the text, but, most importantly, must become conformed to the One who was justice incarnate. The gospel parables offer one model for us to emulate

25. See further Barbara Reid, *Parables for Preachers* (3 vols.; Collegeville, MN: The Liturgical Press, 1999, 2000, 2001); Walter J. Burkhardt, *Preaching the Just Word* (New Haven: Yale University, 1996).

Jesus' manner of preaching justice.

First, in telling parables, Jesus drew on the every-day experience of his hearers, helping them reflect on all kinds of life-situations in relation to God's realm. As with liberation hermeneutics, the experience of those who are most marginalised is the stance into which he invites his audience. When he is addressing matters of injustice, his use of story is often able to draw even the most hostile listener into the narrative. In this way, he hooks them into the process, as with Simon, the Pharisee, who insists that Jesus is not a prophet and that the woman who has been forgiven remains a sinner (Lk 7:40-43). He tells a simple parable about two debtors being forgiven. He ends it with a question about which loves the generous creditor more. The point is easy to see in the story; discerning its meaning and its demand for action in real life is then the challenge.

Often, Jesus catches his listeners off-guard with a radical twist to the tale, or an ending that is unexpected and unfinished. He does not give the moral of the story, but leaves an open ending with which the hearer must wrestle. What does it mean? What does it demand? He does not answer these questions for his hearers,[26] but he has clearly directed them how to respond in a way that leads to right relation.

Preaching justice parabolically does not provide pat answers, but invites communities of faith to seek together those solutions that invite conversion to the Teller of the parables and to transformative change toward the equal good of all.

---

26. The only parables that have an explanation in the gospels are that of the sower, explained at Mt 13:18-23 (// Mk 4:13-20 // Lk 8:11-15), the parable of the weeds and the wheat interpreted at Mt 13:36-43, and the explanation of defilement from within at Mt 15:15-20 (// Mk 7:17-23). Most scholars believe these to be creations of the early Church and not from the lips of Jesus.

CONCLUSION

Biblical justice is not people getting what they deserve. In fact, in the New Testament, if there is any sense of retaliatory action in relation to establishing right relation, it is expressed as forgiveness of others in turn for having been forgiven, releasing others from debt because one has been freed, loving others because one has been loved by God. God is just and God's justice is manifest in saving deeds toward humankind, culminating with the earthly ministry, death and resurrection of Christ. This free gift, which sets all in right relation, rests as a quality of mind and heart in believers, and is visible in their words and actions toward transformative change. We taste it imperfectly now, while yet awaiting its fulfilment. Preachers of the just word are drawn ever more into the mystery of the One who was justice incarnate, while inviting their hearers more deeply into this journey of hope.

A HOMILETIC OF MERCY

EDWARD VAN MERRIENBOER, O.P.

Christianity has made many contributions to the development of civilisation in the areas of art, law and culture. One of its greatest gifts has been to awaken and promote an expectation within humanity that their quality of life can improve. Catholicism, at its best, has kept the relationship between human history and eternal life connected. In a sense, faith in Jesus Christ has given people permission to expect more from life than what they have in the present moment. The revelation of eternal life has changed the human perspective and given the Christian community a mission to build the Reign of God with different theologies of society in history. People in all the Christian centuries have explored and discovered new ways to live with the hope that their lives will be better than that those who have come before them.

We must acknowledge that Christians have not always been effective agents of human progress. In fact, some of these limitations have been rooted in a partial understanding of the Gospel's demand to be at the service of humanity. In particular, preaching at the service of a just society does not seem to be enough to motivate communities of nations to act morally. Discussions of obligations to one another are rich in documentation but are often weak in applications. Too many people, often well-intentioned, have not moved beyond awareness of social challenges, or have proposed solutions that have not resulted in a better life of the masses of people who demand that their human dignity be acknowledge in concrete ways. In some cases, situations have worsened because of programmes that have not accepted all the dimensions of God's reign when working for a just society.

My purpose is to reflect upon efforts by religious movements for justice, and to argue that to set the agenda solely for justice without taking into consideration the virtue of mercy can often produce conditions that are harsh, and, possibly, create new forms of alienation. I want to demonstrate that justice with mercy offers humanity a broader pathway to an experience of being more human than may have previously been thought by social ministers. To make this argument, I believe that it is important to first to provide a panoramic history of the efforts at social change during the last half of the twentieth century.

THE QUEST FOR JUSTICE AND
THE PROMOTION OF HUMAN RIGHTS

One of the hallmarks of the second half of the twentieth century was the growing, active concern for human rights within the context of social justice. This concern had its roots in a number of historical events which required social and theological reflection. With the defeat of the Axis powers at the end of World War II, the world became aware of the great human atrocities that had occurred in the concentration camps and during the occupations of many nations. This awareness resulted in a global discussion of the meaning of human rights. The Nuremberg trials articulated principles that clarified the role of individual responsibility in the context of political authority. The Charter of the United Nations and its Human Rights Declaration attempted to codify these principles for the global community of nations. While they clearly were influenced by a Western philosophical and legal understanding of the human person, they did offer the world community a direction for the future.

This global awareness of the dignity of nations led to dismantling the European colonial system. The transition to national independence was guided by concepts of justice that would enable these new nations to take their place in the international community. Often, independence was followed by civil strife and new forms of oppression for these post-colonial nations. The bipolar dynamics between the former Soviet Union and the United States of America, with their allies, created new dimensions of global injustice. Poor nations were forced to choose between the two political-economic systems in order to survive in the bipolar political culture.

Development was the central concept used by the international community to guide the evolution of society to a just ordering of rights and duties. International institutions established by the Brentwood Agreements became major influences in poor nations' efforts for development. The actual thrust of development became the desire to become industrial societies that could provide work for the masses, consumer goods for a new emerging working class, and a political order that would allow for greater participation by a more educated population.

In fact, political rights have been too often subjected to the goals of economic prosperity. Asia, Africa and Latin America have had numerous cycles of military governments that control any radical actions taken by the poor masses whose life expectations have increased. The dimensions of the atrocities committed by these regimes have been discovered after their removal from power. Few of those responsible for these atrocities have been brought to justice, thus creating a new sense of injustice for the victims and their relatives who survived the ordeal.

The suppression of the free exchange of ideas and the central control of political freedoms within the former Soviet Union and its Eastern European allies only delayed conflicts that had deep historical roots. The wars in Croatia and Bosnia are two examples of how conflicts along ethic lines turned into genocidal massacres. The death toll among civil populations had many characteristics with the great atrocities of the Nazi regime during the Second World War. For a long period of time, the world community seemed frozen and unable to take effective action, and even now it struggles to find ways to bring those who perpetrated these acts to legal justice. Part of the inability of the world community to address the crisis was the need to locate blame and to establish within the public mind who had the right to take revenge. The crisis of Croatia and Bosnia illustrated the shift in the international legal system from a process to re-establish justice to the task of placing blame. Once blame was located, those who suffered as a result of the actions of others were given a sense of their righteous need to get even.

No situation in the world illustrates this emerging 'mentality of revenge' more than the conflict between the state of Israel and the people of Palestine. An escalation of violence flowing from both parties mutually fosters acts of aggression that will be repaid with even greater acts of violence. Each new attack, whether it is an organized response of the state or a surprise attack by a militant group, is never seen as the ultimate action that behooves trying an approach other than violence. Acts of terror that have taken place throughout the world as part of the Middle East crisis are an essential part of the logic of the escalation of revenge, due to injustice. We are at a point that any action is acceptable as a response to injustice.

This mentality is not exclusively located on the level of inter-national relationship. We see this acted out on the interpersonal level as well. Those who have suffered because of their national, racial, gender, or culture often feel that they can say or do anything to members of the group that enjoys privilege at their expense. Human conversation is often devoid of simple manners or civility. For example, some women can insult any man because of real and perceived gender discrimination. This behaviour is justified as part of one's right to get revenge. On the other hand, in response to this type of vengeful insult, some men will dismiss all the legitimate demands of women to take their just place in the world. Another example of this type of interpersonal behaviour of revenge can be witnessed by public figures who defame the good name of those they oppose on issues by questioning the person's character.

It is not difficult to see that very often programmes which start from the idea of justice, when put into practice suffer from distortions. It is not the quest for justice that is the core of the problem but rather negative forces of spite and revenge have overtaken the desire for true justice. The desire to hurt or even annihilate the enemy becomes the fundamental motive for action. Revenge can be contrasted with justice in that it has no desire for equality and harmony between parities in conflict. This distorted understanding of justice is an abuse of the very essence of justice.

People's experience of world conflicts for the last half of the twentieth century and beyond has demonstrated that justice is not enough. My intention is not to detract from the urgency of justice in our world rather my purpose is to show that when individuals and groups seek only justice they are vulnerable to the distortion of vengeance. I believe that when justice combines with mercy, actions to correct wrongs take on a more human face. In mercy there is a deeper promise for lasting social change.

A SOCIO-POLITICAL ISSUE AND MORE

In the parable of the unforgiving servant (Mt 18:23-35), Jesus points to the fundamental issue that is under discussion here. The story traces the behaviour of a person who forgot how much he was dependent on his king for forgiving this debt and does not learn from his forgiving experience when dealing with others.

There are at least two levels of theological reflection contained in this parable. On the level of faith, we are challenged to recognize that we are blessed by God's redemptive love through the saving action of Jesus. This reality moderates our demands on others because we are humbled by the loving action of Christ through his passion, death and resurrection (Rom 5:12-21).

This New Testament story in many ways captures the theology that we find in the books of Exodus and Deuteronomy which defines social relations in liberated Israel (see Ex 22:20-26; Deut 24:5-22). It was in recalling God's saving action of liberating the Jews from slavery in Egypt that the community was transformed into a more human society. Aliens, widows and orphans – three classes of dependent people – were given new dignity. They become the living memory of God's justice and mercy through the Exodus, and a concrete opportunity for Israel to participate in God's life of justice and mercy. On the human level, this parable illustrates that when persons and nations lose touch with their social history and forget how many mistakes they have made on their journey, they become cruel and arrogant in their dealings with others. Too often, people and social groups forget they too are social products and much of their achievements have resulted from the generous help of others. In its essence, the Exodus is the critical memory of God's mercy.

Elsewhere, Jesus reminds us in his challenge to his listeners that a revenge ethic expressed in the words: 'An eye for an eye and a tooth for a tooth' (Mt 5:38) is a corruption of the true justice that seeks forgiveness. The ethic of forgiveness offers a future hope for better relationships between persons and nations. Guided by these principles, the Catholic moral tradition has taught that there are times when it is better to accept an injury without punishing the offender, because human relationships will only worsen in the process of trying to correct the injustice. The desire to punish every offence leads to the corruption of a society into hostile camps because it is part of the human reality that we do offend each other throughout life.

In the United States of America, we have developed a culture of litigation. Court action can be taken against anyone for real or perceived injury. Even if the legal action is without substance, the person who is the object of the allegations must defend himself or herself. This process is often long and painful, resulting in a loss of property and one's good name, no matter the legal outcome. The core of this litigation culture is that vengeance is a proper response because it is legal. The result is that in the home and work-place, many people function in a context of fear because any action might be interpreted as an offence. Lost to United States culture is the fact that people are not perfect, mistakes are made without the intention to hurt and the proper response is to forgive.

THE OIL OF MERCY

In the preaching of Jesus to the crowds and in private to his disciples, he exhorts all to take another path, the way of mercy. He reminds us that those who seek forgiveness must be granted it. The actual practice of mercy will become the criterion for obtaining mercy. In the beatitudes he declares, 'Blessed are the merciful, they shall have mercy shown to them' (Mt 5:7). And, when instructing the disciples in the Lord's Prayer, the criterion of forgiveness becomes a petition of the faithful (Mt 6:12, see Mt 7:1-5). This bold request puts every disciple on notice that they are the behavioural reference that they wish to be measured by at the time of judgment.

An honest evaluation of one's life would give some reserve in making this petition because we know that we are capable of being harsh at times. This truth can lead us to another petition in prayer: the cry for mercy. This cry requires that we adjust our behaviour and, where needed, go back to those we have treated harshly and put the oil of mercy on the wound we inflicted. This sacred balm has the ability to transform the offended and the offender.

The preaching of Jesus offers a number of challenges to contemporary preachers of mercy. The preacher will stand against a strong cultural current of revenge. When the word of mercy is proclaimed, the preacher should expect some negative reactions. This should not deter the preacher from speaking boldly of God's desire that we make an integral connection between the quest for justice and expressions of mercy. Preachers can at times avoid speaking about topics that cause conflicts in the community because they don't always understand that when people get angry about a homily it is a sign of disagreement but it is also an indication that they care about their faith to such a degree to get emotionally involved. The preacher has an opportunity to challenge that 'angry caring' into a deeper understanding of discipleship. Once they make the connections between their life in Christ and the practice of mercy, they have the possibility of discovering a renewed inner peace. To live one's life within the rubric of revenge takes a great amount of negative energy that detracts from inner wholeness. When a person extends mercy to an offender, they reclaim their dignity as disciples and have an opportunity to reclaim some of what was lost or injured by the other person.

To pursue this further, the content of the homily must be theological and not a type of sentimental devotion. Most of the current writing on mercy is done within the context of the devotion of Divine Mercy and the visionary comments of St Faustina Kowalska.[1] The words of the preacher cannot be sweet to the point of being out of contact with reality. To suggest that just by being nice all will be fine, will not convince a community or individual that has experienced injury. True mercy confronts the harm done and deals with it in the context of the love of Christ. Mercy never denies the evil done or the need for repentance. The Christian life acknowledges that sinful malice does exist in the world and that human beings are capable of such actions. In this context it does set limits on repentance with the hope of a better life for oneself and for the community.

Astonishingly, there is little theology on mercy available in recent Catholic writings.[2] Julia Upton, R.S.M., comments on the biblical meaning of mercy, noting:

> 'Mercy' is used as the translation of three Hebrew words the most common one being *hesed,* which has a broad range of meaning. It is the covenanted love between Abraham and Sarah (Gen 20:13), David and Jonathan (1 Sam 20:8), and Yahweh and the people (Exod 20:6). It is mutual and enduring, implying action on both parts. *Rahamim,* the plural form of 'womb' is also translated as 'mercy'. God's mercy is a nurturing womb, implying a physical response and demonstrating that mercy is felt in the centre of one's body. This dimension of mercy also requires action. Also translated 'mercy' is the

---

1. Sister M. Faustina Kowalska. *Divine Mercy in My Soul.* 1987. Stockbridge, Massachusetts: Marian Press.
2. The author found that the most frequently quoted source was the encyclical *Dives in Misericordia.* John Paul II, 1980.

Hebrew *hen/hanan*, meaning 'grace' or 'favour.' Unlike the other terms, this is a free gift with no mutuality either implied or expected. Not necessarily enduring, this quality is dependent solely on the giver and usually occurs between unequals.[3]

The threefold meaning of mercy in Hebrew offers preaching rich channels of thought to be developed. *Hesed* lends itself to applications and illustration within interpersonal relationship. To approach marriage and family life through the lens of mercy could lead to new and rich insights for daily living. To think of mercy as our 'womb' that has the potential to birth new ways of thinking and acting within the Body of Christ, is another rich image that gives the preacher a creative opportunity. We find the womb in the very centre of a woman; we can find a spiritual core in our being that is mercy. Finally, the Hebrew understanding of mercy points us to the great gifts we have from God. We who are nothing have become the 'crown of creation' because of divine favour. Out of love we are invited to participate in the very life of God.

This rich Jewish understanding of mercy finds its perfect expression in the life of Jesus, both in his words and actions. The core or 'womb' of his ministry is to reveal to us and convince us that we have been saved by divine mercy. His public ministry is a constant revelation that God does not want humanity to suffer, but rather has a divine design for our happiness. This happiness is a pure gift to all who believe.

The preacher is challenged to provide images and models that are meaningful for the faith community. Christian history offers us images of mercy in the lives of holy men and women who have gone before us. Images highlight moments in their lives when

---

3. Michael Downey, ed., 'Mercy', in *The New Dictionary of Catholic Spirituality*. 1993. Collegeville: The Liturgical Press.

God's favour was expressed in word and deed. But images can be distant and even vague at times; the modern Christian hunger is for models. Models differ from images in that they are concrete in our immediate reality. Mercy is not limited to something that happened in another century, in a far away place, in a radically different culture. Rather, models give us daily experiences of people who incarnate God's mercy. We find these models among parents who nurture their children, in teachers who take that extra moment to instruct their students in the loving wisdom of God even when the students struggle, and in public persons who take on grand projects that make us all more human.

We have learned from Eastern spirituality that icons have a great power to remind us of grace in our lives; the West stresses the importance of practical models to complement our spiritual journey. We need real people in our daily lives to point the way, make our values concrete, and encourage us to live deeper realities.

DAMIAN BYRNE, O.P. AS A PREACHER OF MERCY

Before I was assigned to the general offices of the Dominican Order to be one of Damian Byrne's assistants, I had met him only once, during a General Chapter in Germany. We had only one serious conversation, about how I had organised a planning process in my home province. From a distance in the assembly hall, I was able to observe him as a man of convictions who took care to respect those who held other perspectives about the issues at hand.

When I took up residence in Santa Sabina at Rome, my first days were busy trying to get settled into my new quarters. I had shipped many boxes of books to Italy and was delighted that all had arrived safely, and I was working into the night trying to sort

them on the shelves of my office when I hear a knock at the door.
It was Damian Byrne, Master of the Order and successor of Saint
Dominic. I immediately thought that there must be some urgent
business that would bring him to my office at such a late hour.
No, it was not urgent by my standards but, nevertheless, a very
important meeting for me. He said that he saw my light and was
concerned that maybe I was unable to sleep. We spoke for a while
and he concluded the visit with this comment, 'We can all sleep
well in this house if we are faithful to God and Dominic.' I share
this story because I think it tells us much about Damian Byrne as
a spiritual person. He did not enjoy public occasions and would
only share his deepest thoughts and feelings with a few in private.
He was personally shy.

Over the years that followed, it became apparent to me that a
core value to his leadership was the virtue of mercy. When news
came that one of the friars had committed a serious failure in
regard to chastity, he would remark, 'He must have been very
lonely to do such a thing.' On one such occasion when one of his
assistants recommend a harsh response to correct a brother,
Damian responded by noting: 'Jesus only asks us to forgive each
other, but when he forgave us he made excuses for us. "Forgive
them, Father, for they know not what they are doing".' (Lk 23:24)

On another occasion, when one friar accused another of steal-
ing his research and publishing it under his name, they both
prepared large dossiers to document their case. These documents
arrived about one month before the two friars were to come to
Rome to air their positions. When they walked into Damian
Byrne's office, one saw both documents on the desk and commented, 'I see you have our documents; I hope they were helpful.'
Damian replied, 'I haven't read either of them, I am not interested in the past. We are here today to find a way that we can live

together as brothers.' This comment changed the dynamic of the meeting and it concluded with these two rather proud men being reconciled. This was only possible when they were able to reflect on how much they both needed the mercy of God and the Dominican Order. Once that was re-established in their hearts, all other issues seemed rather unimportant.

Next day, when I complimented him on how he had resolved such a difficult situation, Damian's response was to quote his predecessor, Vincent de Couesnongle: 'To live the Gospel means first of all to have a merciful heart. Take away what the Gospel says about mercy, and not a line will be left.'[4] He went on to say that he believed this to be at the heart of the renewal set in motion by the Second Vatican Council. This, he said, was not always the case in his approach to ministry. Earlier when Damian was in Trinidad, Father Bernard Häring come to give lectures on moral theology. The law of love became a fresh way to understand preaching. Preaching, in its essence, was to point to the ultimate good which is love, and only when necessary to speak of evil. He recalled a joke he heard once: 'Preachers spent so much time talking about sin that the devil did not have to advertise.'

The contemporary task of the preacher, for Damian Byrne, was to name the blessing of God in our lives.[5] The truth is that we are not capable of knowing anything about God, but in mercy God has spoken to us. Throughout salvation history we hear, through God's preachers, 'that I love you, I forgive you, I want you to be happy, I understand and have mercy.' The greatest challenge, I believe, facing preachers today is to make these divine revelations real within each faith community. It is some-what ironic that Damian Byrne died while trying to discover a

---

4. *Confidence for the Future.* (Dublin: Dominican Publications, 1982.) p.23.
5. 'A Vision for Our Times,' in *A Pilgrimage of Faith.* (Dublin: Dominican Publica-tions, 1991. pp. 81-91.

merciful response to the victims of clergy child abuse and for the clergy who had done these horrific things. It was noted during his funeral that the kindest and most sane voice in the midst of this scandal is now silent. But this can only remain true if there are no other preachers to speak of mercy.

Preaching is at the heart of the mystery of salvation. It is a story of cycles: as one voice becomes silent others fills the void with the good news that we have been saved not by our just lives but by the mercy of God. As a Church, we are slowly becoming aware that our baptism requires us to proclaim the mystery of God's saving love within the context of each of our vocations. There are many in our world who promote revenge as a way of life, often with the assistance of the media which celebrates conflicts. At times, the media can even provoke revenge for the sake of a story.

The preacher stands in the midst of revenge, to model, by word and action, the alternative of mercy. The preached word breaks down false walls between faith and human events, to point to the light of God's salvation revealed by Jesus Christ. It is in places where the violent evil of revenge has most taken root, that the preacher finds the pulpit to proclaim that history has been turned upside down forever by the merciful redemption of God. With this faith truth, the preacher calls for the unfolding in time of the age of love, forgiveness, and mercy.

CONTRIBUTORS

Vivian Boland OP, a member of the Irish province, is master of students at Blackfriars, Oxford, where he is also a lecturer and tutor in theology. Senior lecturer in theology at St Mary's College, Strawberry Hill, London, he contributes frequently to theological and pastoral journals. He is editor of *Watchmen Raise Their Voices: A Tallaght Book of Theology* (Dominican Publications, 2006).

Charles E. Bouchard OP, of the St Albert Province, is associate professor of systematic (moral) theology at the Aquinas Institute, St Louis, Missouri, and has been President of the Institute since 1989.

Rolando V. de la Rosa OP obtained his Doctorate in Sacred Theology at the Katholieke Universiteit Leuven, Belgium. He teaches Church History and Hermeneutics at the University of Santo Tomas, Manila, Philippines.

James P. Donleavy OP, of the Irish Province, has for over forty years been committed to a ministry of preaching missions and retreats in Ireland and elsewhere. He has also served his brethren as a prior.

Richard Finn OP, of the English Province, is regent of studies of his province, and sub-prior at Blackfriars, Oxford. He is a member of the theology faculty of Oxford University where he lectures in Augustine and in Church history.

Donald J. Goergen OP, of the St Albert Province, is a preacher, teacher, lecturer, author, and theologian who has taught Christology and spirituality for many years. He has been the prior provincial of the Dominican friars of the Central Province in the United States. His books include *The Jesus of Christian*

History and *Jesus, Son of God, Son of Mary, Immanuel* (both Liturgical Press), *The Theology of Priesthood* (also Liturgical Press), and *Letters to My Brothers and Sisters* (Dominican Publications). He is currently in residence at the Friends of God Dominican Ashram in Kenosha, Wisconsin.

Cathleen Going OP (Sister Mary of the Savior) is a member of the cloistered Dominican community of the Monastery of the Blessed Sacrament in Farmington Hills, Michigan. She received her doctorate from St Mary's School of Theology, Notre Dame, Indiana, in 1956. She is known as the co-editor and co-interviewer for *Caring about Meaning: Patterns in the Life of Bernard Lonergan*, Lonergan's intellectual autobiography by interview, published by The Thomas More Institute, Montreal, in 1982. Before entering the the monastery, she also served for about fifteen years as an assessor for grants to be awarded by the Humanities Research Council of the Canadian Government.

Barbara Green OP, a member of the Sisters of St Dominic, Congregation of the Most Holy Name, San Rafael, California, is professor of biblical studies at the Dominican School of Philosophy and Theology, Berkeley, California. Her most recent book is *Jonah's Journeys* (Liturgical Press, 2005).

Mary Catherine Hilkert OP is professor of theology at Notre Dame University, Indiana. President of the of the Catholic Theological Society of America (2005-2006), she specializes in contemporary systematic theology with particular interest in theological anthropology and feminist theology and spirituality. She is the author of *Naming Grace: Preaching and the Sacramental Imagination* (1997), *Speaking with Authority: Catherine of Siena and the Voices of Women Today* (2001), *The Praxis of the Reign of God: An Introduction to the Theology of Edward Schillebeeckx* (co-editor, 2002), and numerous articles on theology, preaching, and spirituality.

Edward J. van Merrienboer OP, of the St Albert province, is academic dean of St John Vianney College Seminary, Miami, Florida. He served on the General Council of the Order during the years when Damian Byrne was Master.

John Orme Mills OP, of the English Province, who lives at Black-friars, Cambridge, served for many years as editor of *New Black-friars* and also as editor of *The Eckhart Review*.

Michael Monshau OP, a member of the St Albert Province, is professor of homiletics at the Dominican School of Philosophy and Theology at the graduate Theological Union in Berkeley, California. His articles have appeared in *Living Pulpit*, *Listening: Journal of Religion and Culture*, *Scripture in Church*, and *The Priest*. Sincer 2003 he has served as prior at St Albert's Priory, Oakland.

Paul Murray OP, of the Irish Province, lectures on the literature of the mystical tradition at the University of St Thomas, Rome. Author of four books of poetry, he has also published *T.S.Eliot and Mysticism: the Secret History of 'Four Quartets'* (Macmillan).

Albert Nolan OP, of the General Vicariate of South Africa, has ministered in university chaplaincy, in theology, and in witnessing for justice. During his second term as vicar general of South Africa, he was a member of the General Chapter which met in Rome in September 1983. Despite his protests he was elected Master of the Order. But, on being persuaded of the Gospel value and special impact of his opposition to apartheid (conditions in South Africa were particularly troubled in the early 1980s), the Chapter allowed him to decline the office, and proceeded to elect

Damian Byrne as Master.

Mark O'Brien OP, of the Australian province, is lecturer in Old Testament at Catholic Institute, Sydney. He served as prior provincial from 1993 to 2000. His publications include contributions to *The International Bible Commentary*, to *Concilium*, and to *Priests and People*.

Thomas F. O'Meara OP is professor of theology at Notre Dame University, Indiana. His publications include *Thomas Aquina, Theologian* and *Church and Culture: German Catholic Theology 1860–1914* (both University of Notre Dame Press), as well as *Theology of Ministry* (Paulist, 1983, revised edition 1999). In addition, he contributes to many journals, both scholarly and pastoral.

Timothy Radcliffe OP, of the English Province, taught theology at Blackfriars, Oxford, and served as prior there and as provincial before being elected to succeed Damian Byrne as Master of the Order, in 1992. Since then, he has been principally engaged as a lecturer, preacher and writer.

Barbara E. Reid OP, professor of New Testament studies at the Catholic Theological Union, Chicago, has a keen interest in relating the studying of the Scriptures with the ministry of preaching. She is the author of *Choosing the Better Part? Women in the Gospel of Luke* and *Parables for Preachers*.